Wakefield Press

AMONG THE PIGEONS

John Read is an ecologist and author, passionate about informed and pragmatic approaches to environmental and animal welfare issues. His ecological research has featured in over 120 scientific articles and he sits on a range of scientific advisory groups. He has also published three acclaimed books on topics as diverse as desert ecology, saving an indigenously owned tropical rainforest and cross-cultural attitudes to war. John lives on South Australia's, largest privately managed nature reserve with his wife, children and endangered malleefowl and marsupials.

www.johnlread.com

Also by John Read

Red Sand Green Heart:
Ecological Adventures in the Outback

The Last Wild Island: Saving Tetepare

Dear Grandpa, Why?:
Reflections from Kokoda to Hiroshima

AMONG THE PIGEONS

Why our cats belong
indoors

John L. Read

Wakefield
Press

Wakefield Press
16 Rose Street
Mile End
South Australia 5031
www.wakefieldpress.com.au

First published 2019

Cover designed by Liz Nicholson, Wakefield Press
Edited by Julia Beaven, Wakefield Press
Typeset by Michael Deves, Wakefield Press

ISBN 978 1 74305 614 1

NATIONAL
LIBRARY
OF AUSTRALIA
A catalogue record for this
book is available from the
National Library of Australia

CORIOLE
McLAREN VALE

Wakefield Press thanks
Coriole Vineyards for
continued support

Set the cat among the pigeons – to cause trouble

CONTENTS

PREFACE

No other animal in the history of man has experienced such vagaries of fortune as the cat. Eugenia Natoli

Connection with nature grants us automatic inclusion into a worldwide fraternity of diverse yet kindred spirits. The pitiful round eyes of orphaned orangutans in a clear-felled rainforest inspire universal empathy. Paradoxically, many an ornithologist entered their vocation through collecting rare bird eggs, while expert hunters often become the most astute and dedicated wardens.

But our views on cats often represent a striking aberration. More so than any other animal on the planet (with the possible exception of snakes and sharks) cats divide opinions. Any group of compassionate animal lovers is likely to harbour diametrically opposite views on the rights or impacts of free-ranging domestic cats. Let me demonstrate.

Outside, right now, an unknown cat meows at your door. What do you do? Offer it a bowl of milk or hurl your boot at it?

Presumably the extremists, anyone either predisposed to torture the cat or unconditionally invite it inside, would not have read this far into the book. But for the rest of us, this desperate cat represents a conundrum. Could it be the ultimate companion animal, both vulnerable and affectionate? It's not the cat's fault it is hungry and unloved. This cat, or its mother or grandmother, was probably allowed to roam by an irresponsible owner.

Cats, particularly kittens, exemplify characteristics that endear vulnerable animals to caring humans. Their large eyes, baby-like crying and inherent vulnerability tug at our heartstrings. Kittens inspire many of us to take pity or show affection in ways a beady-eyed rodent or impassionate reptile do not. Anthropologist Peter McAllister has categorised the ability of cats to trigger parenting responses in humans as a form of 'brood parasitism', analogous to cuckoo chicks deceiving their hosts to feed them. Like it or not, we are instinctively programmed, and sometimes even hormonally hardwired, to care for cats.

But hang on. Back to that cat outside the door. Maybe it's the infuriating culprit that uses your sandpit as a toilet, exposing your kids to insidious diseases that may come back to haunt them decades later. Or the raider of the bird nest your family had been carefully watching for a month until an empty nest and tatty feathers dashed your hopes. Or the stray tom that beat up your adored pet cat.

Some of us sympathise with the outspoken proponents of Trap-Neuter-Release (TNR), those who vehemently oppose euthanasia of any unowned cats. Others side with the more discreet, self-confessed practitioners of SSS; or Shoot, Shovel and Shut-up.

Intriguing and divisive, alluring yet despised, cats fire our emotions and can distort our perceptions. How cats have managed to walk this tightrope of human affection and disdain for so long remains a perplexing question for animal lovers and social commentators.

The most common and widespread pets in the world, domestic cats are among the first animals seen by infants and the primary pet of choice for many elderly. Cats are welcomed into our homes and farms and typically tolerated in our villages and cities. The number of pet cats continues to increase in all corners of the globe, exceeding dog ownership in many countries including the United States, United Kingdom and China. In concert with bourgeoning human populations, the number of pet cats sped past the 200 million mark in 2005 and shows little sign of abating. Pet cat numbers in the USA have tripled since 1970, with 15 million additional cats added each decade. From Manhattan high-rise apartments to remote villages in Papua New Guinea, more cats are invited into our lives than ever before. Cats are truly ubiquitous and remarkable, adaptable and fascinating. And their besotted owners surely rank among the most tolerant and obsessed of pet keepers.

The domestic cat has been living in close association with humans for at least 3500 years and maybe twice as long, since their 'domestication' from the African wildcat. Ironically, despite their somewhat misleading common name, domestic cats have only ever been partially domesticated. The plethora of specialised dog breeds, from Great Danes to lapdogs, is testament to the ability of dog owners and breeders to segregate and determine the mating options of their pets. By contrast, the vast majority of pet cats belong to a homogenous cosmopolitan gene pool. Litters are typically sired by multiple toms, sought out by oestrous females, not their 'owners'. Even when deliberately kept indoors and typically reluctant to venture outside, a queen cat on heat becomes single-minded and elusive. Their determined reluctance to acquiesce to the desires of their would-be masters epitomises the characteristics that make cats both intriguing and frustrating.

The Egyptians, who first domesticated cats from their wild

Georges Cuvier was the pioneering biologist who first recognised that extinction occurred and hence paved the way for the Theory of Evolution. Ironically, Cuvier flatly refused to believe species could change through time. His evidence was that cats had been intransigent; there was no significant difference between fossils of several thousand years ago and recent cat skeletons. Marion C. Garretty summed up Cuvier's belief when she observed: 'Humans remade dogs to suit their own ends. Cats are exactly the same as they were 10,000 years ago.'

northern African ancestors, held them in such high esteem their deaths were mourned like beloved family members, complete with embalming and burial in mass cemeteries. In what must surely rank as the most bizarre mineral deposits ever commercially mined, a staggering 19 tons of mummified cat bones, calculated to have originated from 80,000 pet cats, was shipped from Beni Hasan on the banks of the Nile to England in the late 19th century to make fertiliser. However, despite their obvious abundance and widespread appeal, domestic cats were very rarely seen in Europe until 300 AD. But once there the cat was, quite literally, out of the bag. The medieval king of Wales, Hywel Dda (the Good), was so enamoured by cats he passed the first animal welfare law in the world by making it illegal to harm a cat. To this day, cats are afforded more free licence than any other pet. Australia's peak animal welfare organisation, the RSPCA, acknowledge that 'Cats are some 30 years behind dogs in terms of legislation and some 300 years behind in terms of pedigree breeding'.

However, the rise of the domestic cat from a partially domesticated pet in Egypt to its current cosmopolitan number-one pet ranking has not been a smooth transition. After the Europeans

Domestic cats have lived with and near people since before the Acropolis was built in about 1400 BCE. (Photo: J. Read)

initial love affair with pet cats, the tides turned. Cats were almost universally associated with the devil in the Middle Ages and were persecuted as sly accomplices of witches. Cats, particularly black cats, were routinely killed to drive away the devil. Perhaps it is no coincidence the words 'catastrophe' and 'cataclysm' invoke a feline etymology. It is indeed testament to their adaptability and durability that domestic cats survived this prolonged period of targeted persecution.

Although public perceptions of cats subsequently improved, remnants of this loathing persist to this day. The number of self-proclaimed 'cat haters' in America is reported to be seven times greater than the number of 'dog haters'. Most individuals prepared to adopt this parochial and confronting title are not concerned about the cat's connections with witchcraft or the devil. Rather, incidents of cats hunting wildlife, traumatising pets, caterwauling and transmitting debilitating diseases have galvanised the ire of the contemporary anti-cat lobby. Estimates of billions of birds, reptiles and mammals killed by domestic cats each year have confirmed what wildlife enthusiasts have known for generations: outdoor cats are disastrous for many native animals.

A cat snoozing indoors by the fire or playfully chasing a toy down the corridor is a delightful, ideal pet. Cats inspire and entertain, teach and learn from us. More importantly they impart and receive affection. When they snuggle up for a cuddle on the couch or stretch out when being rubbed behind their ears, it is difficult to conceive of their potential danger. But that all changes once they dart outside. The typical backyard fence confining dogs and children provides, by contrast, an elevated catwalk for felines. It's these outdoor cats, not the cute indoor 'fur-babies', that polarise society's opinions.

Since my first memories I have been enthralled by animals and have spent my professional career searching for, researching and protecting wildlife. For the past three decades my research has repeatedly led me back to the vexed and complex challenge of outdoor cat management. Unlike most other issues an ecologist deals with, the most effective, ethical and affordable techniques to deal with unowned cats are often overlooked; instead demonstrably ineffective strategies are selected.

In the following series of adventures and anecdotes, I explore attributes of domestic cats and their management that should diffuse the typically emotive conflict between all but the most irrational felinophobes and cat devotees. Three decades ago, chapters on compassionate euthanasia or innovative cat control techniques would not have been countenanced in a book written for responsible cat owners. Any mention of the problems or challenges created by cats was typically met with incredulity, even hostility, by cat devotees. But times are changing. In many cases led by responsible cat breeders and owners, our societies are increasingly differentiating between the desirability of indoor pet cats, the disease threat of dense clowders of unowned outdoor cats, and the incompatibility of free-ranging cats in areas with vulnerable wildlife. We will never, and arguably should never, breed out the unique, inert feline characteristic of aloofness and spunk. But society now has the opportunity to redefine cats to enhance their companionship values and decrease their predatory and disease-spreading tendencies. The challenge our generation now faces is how to embrace cat's virtues while limiting their iniquities. My hope is this book may help us find common ground to achieve both objectives.

Chapter 1

A TALE OF TWO CATS

Time spent with cats is never wasted. Sigmund Freud

Tigger was an awesome cat. True, his name was not imaginative for a ginger tabby, but neither Tigger nor the children who named him knew that. And with a mother named Snowball – yes, she was pure white – unoriginal names ran in the family. Snowball was a gift to Grant Sizemore's six-year-old sister from their grandfather, who had noted ten-year-old Grant's and his sister's affection for his cat whenever they visited.

Soon after moving into their home in West Chester, Ohio, Snowball was taken to the veterinarian for a standard check-up and to be spayed. That's where Grant's family learned their latest addition to the household was pregnant. A few weeks later, tucked away in a back corner of a closet, the Sizemore family discovered a litter of four tiny kittens. Although she was white, Snowball's kittens came in a range of colours including white, black, and one striped orange kitten. That ginger kitten was the most energetic of the little furballs and the first to look up at the adoring Sizemore children when he opened his eyes a week later. Once the kittens were weaned, they were given away, continuing the pyramid-style gift process that saw Snowball arrive at Grant's house. But the ginger kitten, Tigger, remained.

Grant and Tigger grew up together in a typical American

Midwestern neighbourhood of cul-de-sacs, expansive blocks and unfenced front lawns that had recently sprung up on former farms. Paddocks and small forested patches remained just a short walk down the road. Grant doted on the kitten. He patted and brushed Tigger and fed him cheese, his favourite treat. But just as Grant also enjoyed visiting the nearby Kings Island Amusement Park with his friends, Tigger also gained his independence, wandering further from the house, exploring and developing his predatory skills. He started small, with insects and spiders; curiosity followed by a tentative pounce. Tigger wasn't hungry, he made no attempt to eat the insects. Rather he was experimenting and learning.

As Tigger honed his stalking and pouncing skills, his prey became larger. Mice, then fledgling birds and even a den of rabbit kittens and their mother were added to Tigger's haul. Throughout it all Grant watched on, imagining – as children sometimes do – he was observing some great lion stalking wildebeest in the African plains. For young Grant, Tigger's behaviour provided insight into the wondrous world of nature that was instrumental in shaping his later vocation.

One memory from Grant's childhood stands out. On a clear spring day, a noisy northern cardinal that had taken up residence in a neighbour's hemlock tree caught Grant's attention. This brilliant crimson bird was one of a handful Grant could identify. But Grant was not the only one who had spied the cardinal. He watched, transfixed, as Tigger inched closer and closer to the tree. The agitated cardinal was clearly watching the cat and calling in panic. Tigger paid little attention.

Grant watched as Tigger shimmied up the tree trunk then crouched motionless in the nook of the main branch. Pressed down hard against the bough, the cat inched his way out from the trunk, maintaining a fixed stare. The red bird continued to chatter frantically while flitting just out of Tigger's reach.

Unfolding before Grant was an unscripted, 4D, wide-screen, natural history documentary, without a narrative. Grant was unsure why Tigger seemed to ignore the brilliant, fluttering red bird. Finally, he noticed the focus of Tigger's attention. Concealed in the foliage was a rounded bowl of fine sticks, with a drab bird perched inside: the female cardinal. In a flash of motion and loud protests, Tigger leapt forward and snatched the bird. To Grant, this was a triumph of predatory skill and a natural part of the circle of life.

The nesting cardinal was but one of many birds and other animals Tigger subsequently caught. Sometimes he would bring the dead animals home. Other times, he would just catch them and 'play' with them until bored. No matter the outcome, these interactions were fascinating to a young boy, and entirely natural. However, some of the hyperactive cat's other exploits did worry him. One day Tigger stalked too far onto a small branch and fell out of a tree, miraculously avoiding fatal injuries. Not everyone was so enamoured with the cat's adventurous spirit. There were protests from neighbours about the spraying, cat fights and wildlife hunting. But limiting Tigger's exploits were as impossible as confining the birds that moved around the neighbourhood. Cats belonged and needed to live outdoors. Grant's grandfather and parents and friends kept their cats outdoors, no questions, no options. This collateral damage was the compromise they accepted in order to learn from, and love, a cat.

Eventually Tigger's wandering exploits became terminal. One evening, Tigger was struck by a car. In agony, he wandered off to die alone in brush behind Grant's house. Grant, and Tigger, had learned the cost of being an outdoor cat.

It was not until years later, when at college studying ecology, that Grant Sizemore realised domestic cats do not have to live outdoors as he had assumed and believed. It crystallised in one subject. Ornithology educated him about the diversity of bird species and their particular habitats and behaviours. No longer was his understanding limited to the few common species of birds that had visited his backyard. A world of incredible diversity opened up around him, and he now recognised dark-eyed juncos, white-breasted nuthatches, chipping sparrows and red-bellied woodpeckers.

What had previously appeared to him to be an inexhaustible procession of birds moving through his garden was now a discrete selection of birds facing a multitude of threats. One of those threats was cats.

Sizemore went on to study wildlife ecology and conservation at the University of Florida, where he specialised in ornithology. He studied great egrets and little blue herons in South Florida for his master's thesis. He discovered how even small changes, like the introduction of just one species, can disrupt entire ecosystems. Exotic Burmese pythons, for example, represented a key threat to the Everglades' wading birds he was studying. In many other cases, cats were the main threat to the wildlife he valued. In the US alone, billions of birds were killed each year by cats. Ironically, Grant conceded his interest in nature, then wildlife and ultimately conservation, was sparked by his boyhood obsession with this most pervasive of all introduced carnivores, the domestic cat.

Like Sizemore, many other naturalists and conservationists can trace their passion for wildlife to childhood experiences with

David Attenborough was so enamoured with his intriguing childhood pet, a fire salamander, he decided to reciprocate his father's gift on his son's eighth birthday. Attenborough, who through six decades of observing wildlife is an unparalleled authority, considers: 'People are not going to care about conservation unless they think animals are worthwhile.' There is possibly no better way of nurturing this empathy for animals than through raising and caring for pets ... even salamanders. Jane Goodall also attributes much of her understanding of animal behaviour to her inspirational childhood experiences with her adopted dog, Rusty. Rusty taught Goodall that dogs have feelings and can think and solve problems. These formative lessons inspired much of Goodall's innovative and ground-breaking research on wild chimpanzees, and ultimately led to her joining David Attenborough as one of the world's most influential conservation advocates.

their pets. Caring for pet cats can teach children about wildlife behaviour, while also teaching responsibility and compassion. A child helping their kitten through the toilet training process may hone their own patience and skills at grasping challenging tasks. Training cats to perform tricks or obey simple commands can teach kids valuable lessons about goal setting and persistence. And pet cats can expose children to a variety of emotions they can't actuate in a computer game; not only love, compassion and care but also awe and wonder, which seem to be diminishing rapidly in our increasingly cloistered world. And as Tigger's unfortunate demise proved for Grant Sizemore, children inevitably learn to deal with anguish and loss when there are pets in the house.

But although Sizemore is acutely aware of the devastating impacts of cats on wildlife and the ecosystems in which they live, he has retained affection for his childhood pets. Unlike reformed smokers, born-again Christians or others whose mid-life epiphany has caused them to stridently denounce their former ways, Sizemore has always loved and kept cats. His current pet, named Amelia Bedelia in a moment of inspiration, was adopted from a shelter as a feral kitten. Desexed and vaccinated, she is an affectionate and interesting pet.

Amelia Bedelia on Grant Sizemore's lap, inside of course. Grant learnt the hard way about the perils of outdoor cats when his boyhood pet Tigger was killed on the road. He now leads the American Bird Conservancy's 'Cats Indoors' program. (Photo: G. Sizemore)

Accustomed to justifying his dual life as a cat owner and wildlife advocate, Sizemore clarified. 'Amelia Bedelia is strictly an indoor cat. That makes all the difference.' Instead of hunting like Tigger had done, Amelia Bedelia plays with laser pointers and feather toys and enjoys sunning herself in her fully enclosed outdoor tent, watching birds fly by.

Sizemore is not alone in straddling the worlds of passionate conservationist and proud and committed cat owner. Many of his co-workers at American Bird Conservancy and throughout the conservation community have pet cats.

Cats, like other behaviourally complex pets, have sparked understanding, enthusiasm and compassion for wildlife among many environmental champions. Rather than solely being considered environmental villains, pet cats should be part of the solution to improving our empathy for wildlife. Just how this can happen is explored in later chapters. But first we will explore other issues that arise when we allow our cats out among the pigeons.

Chapter 2

SURVIVAL OF THE FITTEST OR SUBLIMINAL GENOCIDE?

No matter how much cats fight, there always seem to be plenty of kittens. Abraham Lincoln

Silent and apparently weightless, the red squirrel scampered lightly over the pine needles. Its movements defied gravity, as if controlled by a puppeteer high above in the Scott pine canopy. Seemingly held aloft by a tight string, its red fluffy tail floated along behind. The squirrel stopped and turned, showing off its tufted ears. I was captivated. The squirrel was paler than I had anticipated but definitely orange, not grey. Suddenly my little friend raced up the closest pine. Half an instant later a steel-blue and white flash swooped to the ground where the squirrel had been. I couldn't be sure the jay was attacking the squirrel but the little orange bundle hadn't taken any chances and had disappeared into the safety of the canopy.

Despite being spellbound by the evasive squirrel, my evening walk in the Queen Elizabeth Forest Park near Aberfoyle in central Scotland had not yielded my main quest. I had hoped to observe an animal most Scots have never seen, although nearly all can spin a yarn or two about them. And I was under no allusion that finding my quarry would be easy. By all accounts the Scottish wildcat is as elusive as Rob Roy MacGregor, the infamous stock thief who once roamed these parts. The following morning at the Park headquarters I sought guidance. The ranger's eyebrows quickly rose in response to my queries before he fixed me with a knowing frown. 'Yes, they are here, but you can't expect to just go out and see them,' he said.

Scottish wildcats resemble a boldly striped cat with a broad face, pushed-back ears, prominent white whiskers and a short, banded tail terminating in a black tuft. Once widespread throughout Europe and Britain, the wildcat, *Felis silvestris*, now only cling to a precarious existence in isolated areas such as the Scottish Highlands. As its specific name *silvestris* or 'of the woods' attests, the Scottish wildcat is largely restricted to forests. Conservationists have been concerned the wildcat will join the wolf, beaver, brown bear and wild pig on the depressing inventory of British endemic mammals exterminated by man. At the turn of the 19th century the 'cat of the woods' probably reached its lowest levels in Britain, after being forced out of the southern areas by forest clearing and merciless persecution by gamekeepers who were concerned it was reducing stocks of pheasant and other game birds.

The night after my encounter with the squirrel I was again patrolling the forest at dusk, this time with my recent bride and fellow wildlife enthusiast Katherine. The air was crisp and cold enough to taste the pine-scented cleanliness and I shivered at the thought we were visiting at the warmest time of the year. Checking the soft mud at the side of the track for prints, scats or other signs of cats, I knew our search was a long shot. Anne and John, the long-time proprietors of the local B&B, had seen their first-ever wildcat at their bird feeder at the edge of the forest a few months earlier. This exciting news had helped me stoically swallow the black pudding I had been offered for breakfast, thinking in order to deserve a wildcat sighting I should fully immerse myself in the local culture. Now, with the dark glug still sitting heavily in my stomach after almost a full day in the forest, the lengthening shadows heralded the optimum time to find a cat.

All of a sudden a rabbit burst from the bracken by the side of a track traversing a football-field-sized forest clearing that had been harvested a year or so earlier. The fallen timber had been colonised by dense swathes of grass, gorse and bracken. Although initially disappointed, I knew the rabbit was a good sign. Like most of their close relatives, Scottish wildcats prey heavily upon rabbits, particularly young ones. The juxtaposition of dense forest and rabbit habitat provided ideal conditions for the cats.

Although the park ranger had been reluctant to talk about wildcats, I met a man who held no such inhibitions. Sir William Alan Macpherson of Cluny and Blairgowrie was the chief of the proud Macpherson clan. Along with the Mackintoshs and other central Scottish tribes, the Macphersons had adopted the wildcat as their badge. I asked William whether their motto, 'Touch not the cat bot a glove', was a warning for his clan that the wildcat was a ferocious species that should be handled with care. Oh my goodness! His response suggested I had accused the wild and rugged Macphersons of being soft.

On William's official crest, the clan's insignia had been modified to 'Touch not the cat but a glove'. In his own words, this translated to: 'If you are going to mess with a Macpherson you had better be damned careful!' Following the demise of the bear and the wolf, the wildcat is now the most formidable natural predator throughout much of Scotland. William confessed he had never actually encountered a wildcat, but was adamant they would be feisty, resist domestication and should not be persecuted.

I was interested in William's opinion on whether domestic cats represented a threat to wildcats through disease or hybridisation. Some biologists feel wildcats are at risk of extinction, even in the forests deliberately reserved for them. Although gamekeepers may still wage a clandestine battle with wildcats, hybridisation possibly represents a more insidious threat. Like the displacement of the red squirrel by its imported grey cousin, Scottish wildcats were increasingly under threat from domestic cats that arrived in Great Britain thousands of centuries after them. Although, like the squirrels, direct competition for food between the cats was a concern, a greater risk for the wildcat was hybridisation with its recently arrived cousin.

Wildcats, like truly feral domestic cats, are for the most part loners. A solitary life offers the best outcomes for a predator of small animals that are most efficiently captured alone. Unlike lions or wolves, small cats don't hunt cooperatively to subdue larger prey. Indeed other cats in the vicinity are more likely to compromise their expert stalking ability. Although maintaining distinct territories confers advantages for hunting efficiency, a solitary lifestyle presents challenges for reproducing. A wildcat's strategy for finding a mate renders them susceptible to crossbreeding with free-roaming domestic cats in the vicinity.

Scottish wildcats usually come into oestrus in late winter and give birth in spring. Female free-living wildcats have little opportunity to assess or choose optimum sexual partners; mate selection in cats is highly dependent upon being at the right place at the right time. So they can fulfil their breeding urges when in oestrus, female wildcats are intrinsically promiscuous, advertising their imminent receptiveness by leaving alluring scents and emitting seductive yowls to notify males. Free-ranging domestic cats, like their wild cousins, are polyandrous, meaning litters are often fathered by several different toms.

There are two very good reasons why females, either wildcats or their domestic cousins, need to attract as many males as quickly as possible. Firstly, and most obviously, it's a better strategy for females to bear kittens sired by one or more sub-optimal toms, than to miss out on the chance of breeding if their oestrus passes without conception. Because the female in oestrus only has limited opportunity to appraise the virility or fitness of potential suitors, they increase the chance of bearing some healthy kittens by multiple fathering. But there is an even more compelling driver for their promiscuousness.

So unlikely and unpredictable are the chances of carnal encounters in the life of the loner wildcat that they have developed a canny strategy to optimise their periodic oestrus. The timing of ovulation, or the release of the egg from the ovary, is beyond the control of the female of most mammals. Ovulation in cats is triggered by intercourse. Both queens in oestrus and toms are ever alert to the opportunity for copulation, which inadvertently increases the chance of interbreeding with domestic cats that are invading the shrinking territory of wildcats. As more hybrids are produced, the wildcat genes become diluted.

William Macpherson and the nonplussed Queen Elizabeth Forest Park ranger both suggested if I wanted to see or learn more about wildcats I should head further north. To find out more about this elusive beast I tracked down Dick Balharry, MBE, the pre-eminent authority on Scottish wildlife and in particular the enigmatic wildcat. Balharry was at the Royal Society for the Protection of Birds (RSPB) reserve at the Insh Marshes. Together with a team of students and volunteers, which now included Katherine and me for a few days, Balharry was attempting to

Despite her hormones screaming, queen cats can delay ovulation by up to two weeks until the physical stimulation of intercourse triggers release of her eggs. Research has shown a female cat that manages a fleeting encounter has only an even chance of falling pregnant. But following at least four copulations, a litter of multi-sired kittens will inevitably follow. Unsurprisingly, male cats are willing to oblige but, surprisingly, research shows they do not stop other males mating with 'their' queens. This ambivalence toward their rivals thwarts attempts to manage feral cats by neutering. Female domestic cats reach sexual maturity at about six months of age and can have two or three litters a year. *The Guinness Book of Records* lauds one cat that allegedly produced 420 kittens in her lifetime.

protect rare goldeneye duck nests from pine martens. The RSPB had designed cone-shaped zinc baffles to protect strategically placed nest boxes for the tree-nesting ducks on isolated boughs. Pine martens were incredibly agile and persistent predators, even more so than feral cats, which were considered a less serious threat to the rare ducks. Like tiny furred Houdinis, they had breached earlier nest-box designs and purpose-built guards and robbed the duck nests. Every day we monitored the nest boxes, hoping for safe eggs and chicks but sometimes recording the telltale signs of predation.

After we had finished the morning rounds, Balharry challenged my assertion we had not yet managed to find a wildcat. 'How would you know if you had seen one or not?' he questioned. Bemused by his enquiry I explained we had been looking for a large, short-tailed, broad-faced, stripy cat in the forest, without success.

Looks can be deceiving. Balharry told me of a court case where it was established that there is no definite way of distinguishing a pet cat from a Scottish wildcat. The popular notion, and the image

I had fixed on, was of a broad-faced snarling cat with its ears pinned back. But Balharry pointed out this could also describe a threatened domestic cat. Balharry then told me of a form of wildcat that was even rarer than the widely recognised tabby form. The 'Dallas' cat was a black cat with white, longer guard hairs, a colouration he had never seen in a domestic cat. Had we observed a frosted black cat, or even a stripy moggy, we may indeed have been looking at a wildcat, or at least a feline with wildcat genes.

Balharry recommended our best chance to see a genuine wildcat was to visit the Highland Wildlife Park where two certified wildcats resided. He would arrange for the director, Jeremy Usher Smith, to show us the cats – but with one caveat. First we were to visit the pine marten enclosure and question Usher Smith on exactly what specifications were required to keep these escape artists in their cage. Balharry figured similar specifications would be required to make his nest boxes truly marten-free.

Typically I steer clear of small-town zoos and wildlife parks, but the Highland Wildlife Park was exceptionally well set up. Usher Smith was an energetic and helpful man, with a confidence bolstered by his imposing intelligence. He purposefully marched us towards the wildcat enclosure, pausing briefly to examine the cause of a raucous disturbance in the pine marten pen. Two russet-coloured arrows were streaking around the spacious enclosure, effortlessly scampering up and leaping off trees and the mesh sides of their pen. We asked the knowledgeable Usher Smith about the design of the pen, explaining the reason. Through trials of different enclosure designs, Usher Smith had learned despite being nearly as long as a cat, the agile pine marten could squeeze through holes only five centimetres square. Protective baffles must be set snuggly against tree boughs otherwise the martens would squeeze through. I scribbled notes for Dick Balharry as we were ushered towards the wildcats.

In stark contrast to the marten enclosure, where a dominance hierarchy was being decided with vigour, the Scottish wildcat enclosure was an anticlimax. Lying like a tabby on a sunroom lounge was a passive, indistinctive-looking cat in a mesh runway, which passed over our heads and linked with a large, well-vegetated aviary. A few metres away, propped in the fork of a tree, was its mate. If not for the signage and Usher Smith's insistence, we could have mistaken them for a couple of pet park cats sleeping off their meal. I was reminded of how underwhelmed I had been at my first sighting of the rare Iriomote cat in Japan, which also looked, to the unfamiliar eye, just like a domestic tabby. I took a closer look.

Sure enough, the tail was ringed and shortish, just reaching the ground when the cat eventually left the tree. However, there was no noticeable thickening like a club at the end of the tail, as I had expected. Like Balharry had conceded, distinguishing a wildcat from a domestic cat without the aid of genetic confirmation was fraught. Usher Smith then threw another spanner into the works. The widespread belief Scottish wildcats are considerably larger than domestic moggies is another misconception. Apparently, one of the early museum curators made it widely known he was after 'large specimens' of the enigmatic Scottish wildcat. The legend of super-sized wildcats was born.

Within hours of studying the wildcats in the Highland Wildlife Park I was looking at a near carbon copy. Unlike the Park cats, this feline had a name, Renny. Despite her Aussie-sounding name, Renny's owner Sheila Street spoke with such a broad Scottish accent that all my powers of concentration were required to understand her. Like many other Highland residents I spoke to, the pale-skinned, blonde-haired local Cats Protection officer claimed to have never seen a wildcat. When I remarked Renny looked just like the wildcats I had just seen, Sheila fixed me with a bewildered stare. 'No,' she exclaimed indignantly, 'just look at him!'

Noting the irony in the RSPB bird logo displayed near her door, I learned that Renny was a great mouser and like the other half-dozen semi-tame, or part-feral, cats Sheila 'keeps', Renny also brings in voles, moles, rabbits and some birds. Yet her cats were desexed and vaccinated, Sheila declared proudly, pointing out that encouraging cat owners to desex their pets was one of Cats Protection's most important roles.

I wondered how many other animal lovers in Scotland let their cats roam and, especially if not desexed like Sheila's, what their impacts might be. With hybridisation of wildcats clearly presenting a serious threat to their survival, I visited David Macdonald's laboratory at Oxford University to get the lowdown from one of the world authorities on small-cat conservation.

Oxford is the oldest university in the English-speaking world and regularly makes the list of top-ten academic institutions in the world. Perhaps that is why, unlike other universities I have visited, maps of the extensive grounds came at a price. Refusing to buy a map I sketched directions in my notebook and headed off on foot around the town that encompassed the university, or vice versa. Although a number of stately buildings met my expectations of grand historic architecture, the tacky concrete Wildlife Conservation Research Unit of the Department of Zoology definitely did not.

The eminent Oxford cat researcher David Macdonald was away

on a field trip but one of his protégés, Carlos Driscoll, was happy to fill me in on the genetic status of the Scottish wildcat. Driscoll was a slight, goateed American who was researching the origins of cat domestication and genetics at Macdonald's lab.

'In a word, the Scottish wildcat is stuffed.' This was Driscoll's blunt appraisal when asked about the fate of Scotland's apex predator. Reinforcing Balharry's opinions, Driscoll described evidence of extensive hybridisation with domestic cats. A camera-based study of Scottish wildcats in Cairngorms National Park by Macdonald and other co-workers found only four of the 13 wild-living cats they detected could be confidently considered to be wildcats; the rest were hybrids with domestic cats. Hybridisation with free-ranging pets or feral domestic cats is also eroding populations of black-footed cats in southern Africa. Known as 'anthill tigers', local legend claims these strikingly spotted little cats are able to bring down giraffes. However, their feistiness is not sufficient to keep their randy domestic cousins at bay.

Scottish and other wildcat species typically have one litter of three or four kittens a year. This has served them well through evolution by keeping their population numbers in balance with their prey. But domestic cats can be prolific breeders, due to more reliable access to protein and having thrown away the evolutionary shackles of coexistence with prey species. With life expectancies of around 10 years and litter sizes averaging three to five kittens, a single female can conceivably produce well in excess of a hundred kittens in her lifetime. Even if all other aspects of their biology were equal, this phenomenal and ecologically unsustainable breeding rate totally swamps the fewer than 20 kittens their wild cousins generally produce.

Ironically, but hardly surprisingly, *Felis silvestris lybica*, the origin of the domestic cat, is also now threatened through hybridisation with the domestic cat. In contrast to their wild Scottish cousins, African wildcats are noted for their longer, skinnier tails and fainter markings than most domestic cats. Driscoll's mention of the African wildcat reminded me of my first experience with this unexpected animal on the African plains.

Before we married, Katherine lived the dream of an intrepid graduate ecologist by hitchhiking her way around southern Africa, volunteering on various conservation projects for a year. She had followed elephants in Zimbabwe to monitor their diets, trapped mole rats in Namibia and counted whales in Mozambique before I flew over to visit. Within the first few weeks of my arrival we left the well-worn tourist trail in Tanzania and made our way by train, bus, truck, and hitchhiking in the back of a van to Kasungu National Park in Malawi.

Slightly taken aback but sympathetic to the two dishevelled backpackers who had been unexpectedly deposited at his classy Lifupa Lodge, the helpful and infectiously happy manager Louie found a place for us to pitch our tent and whispered we could join the night tour for a fraction of the fare paid by the lodge guests. Louie informed us there was a chance we would see a leopard so we keenly accepted his offer. In such an out-of-the-way place, and after immediately spotting both rare puku and chameleons close to camp, I was hoping to tick off some really unusual creatures with the aid of a spotlight and a knowledgeable guide.

The first animal we spied from the roofless converted Land Rover was a spotted dickop, which closely resembled the bush thick-knee birds we were familiar with back home. Next we saw a Mozambique nightjar, with its bright-orange eyeshine and white spots in the wing – again, similar to nightjars or goatsuckers around the world. But when the spotlight eventually stopped on a mammal, I was excited.

All cats reflect the most piercing bright eyeshine from their specially adapted reflective eye layer, the tapetum lucidum. To improve their nocturnal vision, the cat's pupil enlarges allowing more light to reflect off this mirror-like film. The last time I had seen a distinctive cat's eye reflection was when I spotted the widely separated twin beacons of a lioness's eyeshine at our camp a week earlier. My heart started racing again as I remembered the fear those mighty eyes struck in me at close range when I was armed with only a head torch and BBQ tongs. But this time we had little to fear, being perched in the back of an elevated stretch Land Rover. Katherine and I had quietly joked that the patrons resplendent in their finest safari clothes on the comfy seats down the front were far more accessible and tastier morsels than we two dirty backpackers. I grabbed my binoculars, hoping to identify an elusive leopard.

Inexplicably, the main spotlight operated by the tour guide had already moved on. But Katherine had trained our smaller light on the eyeshine and staring at me, a lot closer and a lot smaller than I had hoped, was a cat, just like the feral domestic cats back home. Katherine, who had seen these cats before I joined her in Africa, pointed out its slightly longer legs and auburn patch behind the ears that only became apparent when the cat became tired of staring into the light and turned to walk off. Without this last-second glimpse I would have sworn we were watching a domestic moggie that had strayed from the lodge. Yet, just as the nightjar was slightly different to the species back home, this cat was a unique species: the African wildcat, or *Felis lybica*.

The confidence both the tour guide and Katherine had in the

The domestic tabby, due to its association with the most dominant animal on the planet, is now the world's pre-eminent medium-sized predator. By clearing forests and providing warm refuges in the snow, humans have modified once harsh habitats to favour the domestic cat over its wild cousins. Most importantly, by feeding free-ranging domestic cats, we are allowing them to breed faster, raise more kittens and genetically swamp their wild compatriots.

identification of the small feline at Kasungu could well have been misplaced. As Driscoll pointed out in his Oxford laboratory, there was a reasonable chance the cat was a hybrid with the all-pervading domestic cat. Indeed that promptly identified wildcat, if it really was one, may soon be more threatened than many of its high-profile big cat cousins and may rank higher on the wishlist of future African mammal twitchers than the leopard I still failed to tick off my list.

Inadvertently humans have contributed to what invasive species ecologist Tim Low refers to as the 'McDonaldisation' of the environment. Aficionados of the particular species of burgers created at the Golden Arches likely welcome the spread of their staple food across the globe, even though they sometimes replace regional specialties and arguably set in train unfortunate secondary effects in communities where they establish. By the same token, some blinkered cat lovers welcome the spread of their increasingly ubiquitous domestic breed to all corners of the globe, unaware or unconcerned we are engineering the extinction of distinctive specialist cats. And it's not as simple as replacing distinctive wildcats with a more advanced model, like an accelerated natural selection experiment. Without the benefit of having their reproductive rates governed over the eons by the capacity of their prey populations, the new cat has already driven prey species with low reproductive rates to extinction.

My quest for the Scottish wildcat took me to some of the remotest and most iconic forest reserves in this cold and rugged but strikingly beautiful country. But unlike my serendipitous glimpse of an African wildcat, my pursuit of its Scottish cousin proved fruitless. Like most Scots and wildlife enthusiasts from around the globe, I will need to be content with meeting the native cat in a wildlife park. For most contemporary wildcat enthusiasts, our time has come too late. Indeed hybridisation with the domestic moggie may have already effectively consigned the Scottish wildcat to the perilous and unenviable status described by conservation biologists as 'functional extinction', a vortex from which recovery is virtually impossible.

Chapter 3

FEEDING CATS BIRDSEED

Cats: Public enemy No. 1 British *Birdwatching* magazine

Like many South Australian boys of the 1960s, Dave Paton revelled in the freedom of exploring the old mines and bush of the Adelaide foothills, a short bike ride from where he grew up in the leafy suburban outskirts of Beaumont. Sometimes Dave accompanied his father tending beehives for honey. In blackberry season the entrepreneurial lad made tidy pocket money by selling wild-picked blackberries to his neighbours. But even from an early age, Dave's escapades amounted to more than idle wanderings or odd jobs.

Much of the area explored by young Dave Paton was the bushland immediately to the west of what was to become the iconic Cleland Conservation Park, named after his famous grandfather, an acclaimed pathologist. J.B. Cleland's successful medical career was only one of his many accomplishments. Paton's grandfather, known by his family as 'JBC', was an inspirational overachiever who somehow found time to preside over both the Royal Society of South Australia and the Royal Australian Ornithological Union. JBC was also a skilled and prolific naturalist and his collections and observations on rare plants, fungi and wildlife remain as valuable today as they were during his pioneering collection expeditions. One of his less publicised but most important contributions was to the health of Aboriginals who had just abandoned their traditional hunter-gatherer lifestyle. Struck by the high mortality rates of these once tough and proud people at the Hermannsburg Mission in Central Australia, JBC recognised their new diet, dominated by flour and beef rather than their traditional lizards and wild plants, had made them vulnerable to scurvy. Once diagnosed, the health of the survivors was quickly restored, saving several tribes from annihilation.

Like John Muir had achieved in California, J.B. Cleland is most fondly remembered for his advocacy for national parks, for which he received an Australian Natural History medallion. His daughter Joan followed in her father's footsteps, continuing the family's ornithological tradition and meticulous study of the birds and other wildlife of Adelaide and surrounding national parks. Surprisingly though, given his rich ornithological pedigree and penchant for outdoor exploration, Paton traces his formative introduction to the systematic study of birds to the week he was incarcerated indoors, recuperating from a serious bout of influenza. The impressionable young naturalist was spellbound by a television documentary featuring Jack Hood, an enthusiastic bander of birds. Paton was inspired by Hood's ability to catch wild birds in fine mist nets and then follow their movements and survival by recapturing and reading numbered bands he had placed on their legs.

Paton caught birds by stringing up nearly invisible mist nets in his backyard. When his mother or grandfather were not nearby Paton would consult the pioneering Gregory Matthews tome *Birds of Australia*, bequeathed to J.B. Cleland in appreciation for the specimens he had donated. The budding naturalist learned to expertly extract the birds from his nets, identify and then clip on the correct-sized band, first with special pliers and then deftly with his teeth. Tiny wrens and silvereyes were fitted with the smallest, size-one, bands. His favourite New Holland honeyeaters, caught near the flowering Western Australian eucalypts his famous grandfather had planted, were given size-three bands. Before long, Paton became proficient at banding larger parrots and even hawks that pierced his fingers with their sharp beaks and claws. On weekends and holidays, Paton would be out in the garden before sunrise, when his shaded nets were nearly invisible to the hungry birds on their early morning foraging sorties. Unlike some of his mates who collected stamps or chased girls, Paton accumulated an inventory of birds he had banded and released.

The budding ornithologist confidently announced to the curator of birds at the South Australian Museum that he had sighted a leaden flycatcher in his garden. But despite his detailed description and the confidence placed in him by his respected ornithological family, curator Herb Condon was not convinced. Leaden flycatchers had not been recorded in the State before. Not to be deterred, Paton headed home and set a mist net before the rare flycatcher departed. Within hours he was on his way back to the museum, carefully nursing his prize. Impressed, surprised and a little put out, the curator informed Paton he would have to donate the bird to the museum. The plucky young ornithologist refused and raced the bird back home to be released, banded of course, before the museum could add his flycatcher to their collection. Fifty years later, when I interviewed him for this book, Paton could remember the date and the tree he first sighted his prize find, which was described in detail in his first scientific publication at the tender age of 12. A couple of years later he celebrated another ornithological milestone with the first confirmed sighting of a rose robin for the State, also banded in his backyard.

The biggest thrill for bird banders is not when they record a new species or recapture one of their own birds but when someone else records 'their' bird. Paton started catching birds in his yard that others had banded elsewhere. And not only birds caught in his nets yielded interesting results. To this day Paton cannot ride or walk past a road-killed bird without rolling it over with his foot to check for bands. In the days before emails and tweets, Paton learned the details of band recoveries through little cards mailed to him by the national body managing the Australian bird-banding scheme. The most amazing record he received was from the second boobook owl he ever banded. The same band, attached to a still feathered leg, was handed in to the South Australian Museum 49 years later!

Paton's bird-banding expertise was, predictably, passed down to his children, the fourth generation catching and recording birds in the Adelaide suburbs. By the time he, as university lecturer, was instructing me in the art of setting nets and extracting tangled birds, his young daughters were already experts. Paton's wife Penny, an avid and respected ornithologist in her own right, also assisted in the compilation of the multigenerational dataset on the local birds. But young Lydia and Fiona Paton were not catching the same birds as their grandparents.

Paton's mother Joan had recorded the boldly marked black-chinned honeyeaters in her garden. Spectators at the Adelaide Oval in the heart of the city used to remark on hearing their distinctive calls from the nearby eucalypts. But by the time Paton started banding birds, black-chinned honeyeaters were rare on the Adelaide Plains and he concedes it is unlikely his daughters will ever see them, or the once common yellow-faced, crescent or white-naped honeyeaters, in Adelaide.

Paton watched the last banded brown treecreepers disappear from Belair National Park, the site of the annual J.B. Cleland walk, which emulates his pioneering conservationist grandfather's yearly walk around the perimeter of the park. Nine bird species have become locally extinct since JBC conducted his annual surveys, and the Patons are confident a further 18 species are destined for the same depressing fate, due mainly to widespread vegetation clearance.

However, nearly a century after local ornithologist S.A. White warned of the impact of cats on birds, Paton's growing inventory of band recoveries attributed to cats raised the alarm again. From the porches and front yards of neighbours' houses, and even as far away as the other side of the city, pet cats were catching his birds. Trained to collect evidence, Paton set out to measure cat predation rates more directly. Through his ornithological contacts, who he trusted to provide accurate identifications of killed birds, Paton sent out questionnaires to households around Adelaide, asking how many cats they owned and how many birds they killed.

Of the 700 cats monitored, well over 400 brought home birds. But the really alarming statistic was, even including those not known to hunt, the average pet cat killed 32 animals a year. Paton's figure almost exactly mirrored the average kill rate recorded by pioneering cat predation scientist George Field in Massachusetts nearly a century earlier. In Paton's case, confirmed cat kills amounted to an average of 64 prey per hectare, or 80% of the annual productivity of several bird species. He then reached the alarming conclusion that in both Adelaide and Melbourne, pet cat predation rates alone were capable of incrementally extinguishing bird species with slow breeding rates such as robins, flycatchers

In a small English village, vets Churcher and Lawton documented the prey brought home by pet cats. Their most productive cat brought home roughly two prey per week, whereas six cats came back empty-pawed the whole year. Their tally revealed cats were a significant cause of sparrow mortality in an environment where native sparrows were in decline. Throughout the United Kingdom, tree sparrows, along with yellowhammer, reed bunting and bullfinch populations, are declining, despite these species all making increasing use of food supplies in gardens. Destruction of their natural habitats and increased predation by cats in their adopted gardens and parks present a double whammy for these birds.

and thrushes. Even the occasional, seemingly trivial, cat attack could decimate these birds.

Before long vets and ornithologists were repeating these findings around the world.

Scientists from the University of Otago recorded a conservative average kill rate of one animal per month from the 200 pet cats observed by their owners in Dunedin, New Zealand. Due to in excess of 200 cats per square kilometre, the Dunedin study supported what Paton had found in Adelaide: cat predation rates on fantails and the iconic bellbirds exceeded their reproduction rates.

These cities, with birds attracted or forced into gardens in search of food were, in ecological parlance, 'population sinks'. The chorister New Zealand bellbirds were innately attracted to the rich food supplies in the gardens, despite the high predation rates by pet cats that actually reduced the birds' survival and reproductive rates. These bellbirds and fantails were only being maintained in cities by nesting elsewhere, where cat densities were lower. Those that moved into the city to delight residents with the twinkling dawn chorus were going down the metaphorical gurgler of the population sink.

On continental United States the situation was no better. Chris Lepczyk and colleagues set out to survey the 1700 or so private landholders along three breeding bird survey routes in southeast Michigan, an area experiencing rapid landscape change. One quarter of respondents owned outdoor cats that on average killed just over one bird per week. Locally rare eastern bluebirds and ruby-throated hummingbirds featured among the tens of thousands of birds killed by pet cats during the breeding season. Like his peers in other countries, Lepczyk did his sums. A predation rate by pet cats that initially seemed insignificant to most of his respondents amounted to a rate of more than a bird a day per kilometre. Again, especially vulnerable species were the slow breeders that moved through the territories of dozens of pet cats.

Each of the studies on house cat kill rates used deceased prey left visible for the owners or researchers as a basis for their sums. It is acknowledged this underestimates the problem. Kerrie Anne Loyd and collaborators from the University of Georgia set out to determine the scale of this underestimate; that is, what percentage of animals killed by pet cats were actually brought back to their homes. Loyd placed video cameras on 55 cats and filmed their daily and nightly activity. She found on average 23% of cat prey was returned to households, half was left at the site of capture, and the remainder, just over a quarter, was consumed.

Studies in the Australian northern savannah found that even totally wild cats also failed to consume many of their captures. Energetic ecologist Hugh McGregor used muzzled dogs to chase 16 cats up trees so he could sedate and then fit them with mini video recorders. From over a hundred recorded hunting events, only about one third were successful. What surprised McGregor was despite the effort the cats had expended to find and then catch their prey, and knowing they had no bowl of cat food at home as backup, his feral cats made no attempt to eat 28% of their kills. This information derived from voyeuristic cat researchers enables them to determine the fatality rate of wildlife from cats is likely to be three or four times that recorded on the porches and back lawns by observant owners. When this correction factor is included, the devastating impact on birds in urban and agricultural landscapes around the world is three times as serious as conservatively estimated by Paton and others.

If Loyd's video information wasn't shocking enough, the true toll pet cats have on wildlife is even greater, as UK veterinarian Peter Budd can attest. Budd managed a private practice for 24 years before joining the RSPCA's West Hatch Wildlife Centre in Somerset, England. A vet devoted to animals goes without saying, and in Budd's case he was almost obsessed by caring for cats. Before he started working for the RSPCA, Budd and his wife always kept at least seven cats. But after his experiences at West Hatch he has vowed not to get any more.

As a wildlife vet Budd sees hundreds of injured wildlife a year and a fair proportion of them are recorded as 'catted' on his files. These findings from Britain mirror those from other wildlife rescue centres where over a fifth of the patients had been caught by cats. Becoming frustrated at the failure rate for treating wildlife from the catted file, Budd trialled a range of antibiotic and other treatments to improve the recovery rate. Despite all his efforts, Budd was alarmed that nearly three quarters of all 'catted' birds died within 24 hours. Cat attack mortality is consistently higher

In her survey of over 8000 cat-attack victims taken to 82 wildlife rescue centres in the US, Kerri Anne Loyd found that 78% received medical attention (typically for more than six days) before they were eventually euthanased or succumbed to their injuries. In Victoria, Australia, it was 70% of the cat attack victims brought in to animal shelters and veterinary practices that died. In probably the largest study of outcomes of veterinary treatment of more than 20,000 wildlife presented to the Wildlife Center of Virginia, over 80% of birds admitted from cat attack died rapidly despite treatment, a higher mortality rate than any other cause of admission. Cat attack was the second greatest cause of small-mammal admissions and second greatest cause of avian mortality.

than any other cause of admissions, even vehicle collisions, at West Hatch and other animal hospitals. In addition to physical injuries, this high death rate was also attributed to systemic infection from cat-bite wounds associated with *Pasteurella multocida*, a highly pathogenic bacterium typically found in cat's oral flora.

Recognition that the majority of wildlife injured by cats soon dies exacerbates the findings of the other studies that only considered carcasses found with cats. The actual wildlife effects were far higher when the 'rescued' and released victims that crawled or flapped away to succumb to stress or infection are included.

Groundbreaking domestic cat predation studies spurred further surveys and even countrywide appraisals of the predation impact of pet cats. The results were staggering. A study published in *British Wildlife* magazine estimated 60 million birds were killed by cats in the UK every year. Before you read on to even more alarming statistics, consider for a while the enormity of this figure and the ensuing outrage had air rifles, oil spills or wind turbines been responsible for 60 million bird deaths.

Scott Loss from the Smithsonian Conservation Biology Institute and his co-workers estimated free-ranging domestic cats kill somewhere between 1.3 and 4 billion birds and upwards of 6 billion mammals each year in mainland United States alone. Un-owned cats, as opposed to owned pets, were responsible for the majority of this mortality. These numbers are nearly impossible to comprehend, but we need to try. Just imagine the size of a pile of two billion birds and six billion squirrels. You can do your own sums based on the average size, or volume of the animals your own cat catches but my calculations put this figure at over 40 Olympic-sized swimming pools filled to the brim with carcasses. Every year. Then remember many of these animals have been forced into towns and gardens, where the majority of cats reside, by changes in their native habitats. The Sminthsonian authors concluded: free-ranging cats are likely the single greatest source of anthropogenic mortality for American birds and mammals.

These northern American cat kill statistics are particularly surprising considering the value so many residents place on birds. Upwards of 27 million Americans consider themselves to be 'active birders'. Some of these birders attend birding festivals or group excursions; others embark on or assist with detailed studies of migration patterns or species ecology. Many simply enjoy identifying or observing birds closer to home. Collectively, in 1996 alone, 63 million Americans spent US$31 billion on watching and observing wildlife. In the UK, the RSPB, which owns several bird conservation reserves including the Insh Marshes where I met wildcat authority Dick Balharry, now has over a million financial members. Despite living in an increasingly urbanised world, more

Typical 20-hectare patches of semi-cleared forest adjacent to houses in southern California support 35 free-ranging cats compared to only one or two native predators of similar size. Pioneering trophic cascade (or food chain) ecologists Kevin Crooks and Michael Soulé attributed these high densities of cats to removal of coyotes that had either killed cats or influenced cat owners to keep their cats indoors. Crooks and Soulé attribute the predation by domestic cats of over 500 birds annually in those small forest fragments to have contributed to the local extinction of at least 75 bird species. Similarly, Peter Blancher calculated that the 9.9–12.7 million cats in Canada exceed combined densities of all native carnivores, and kill up to 350 million birds per year in Canada. As a result, Canadian Breeding Bird Census database suggests 31 bird species are vulnerable to cat predation, particularly because of their high use of bird feeders in winter and habitat or nesting choices that bring them into contact with human-dominated landscapes where cats abound.

and more of us value the opportunity to observe and interact with nature, especially wild birds.

An amazing array of different bird feeders using grain, nuts, sugar water, specially baked biscuits, grape jelly or suet are used to feed birds in backyards. In 2011, Americans spent over US$4 billion on birdseed alone, in an increasing global trend. Feeding wild birds makes them easy to observe and often fulfils an innate desire in many of us to help animals. Backyard feeding can also assist birds that suffered from having their customary food supplies removed by our all-pervasive impacts on their habitats. Blackcaps traditionally migrated from northern Europe to the Mediterranean and Africa in winter, in what was thought to be an escape from harsh winter conditions. But taking advantage of the increased offerings from planted berry bushes and bird feeders in Britain, some blackcaps have abandoned their long-distance migrations and now only fly across the English Channel.

Animal lovers who keep pet cats but also attract birds or other wildlife to their gardens are caught in a paradox. Can wildlife be enjoyed, even assisted, while we allow our pet cats to roam? As Paton described in suburban South Australia, certain bird species and the pollination or seed dispersal services they provide to remote bushland remnants are now dependent on seasonal food supplies found in domestic gardens. Yet these are the same environments where free-ranging domestic cat densities far exceed natural predator levels.

Can we have the best of both worlds? Can we continue to encourage birds in our gardens but protect them from our cats? That is the subject of the next chapter.

Chapter 4

BELLS AND WHISTLES

'Bell the cat' is a medieval expression referring to any task that is difficult or impossible to achieve.

Hindsight often provides a skewed appraisal of the importance and brilliance of major scientific discoveries. Wallace and Darwin's theory of evolution seems blatantly obvious to contemporary biologists and even most students. Rather than celebrating the inspiring intellect of these esteemed biologists, we are more inclined to wonder why it took scientists so long to figure it out. How many of us would have pieced together the theory of natural selection by observing barnacles, butterflies or finches?

Probably the most ubiquitous law of nature is gravity. Our urges to stand, jump or fly are resisted by an all-pervading force. But until 1687, the word 'gravity' and indeed the understanding of how we keep our feet on the ground eluded humankind's brightest minds. Enter Isaac Newton, argued by some to have been endowed with the greatest intellect the world has ever known. That falling apple was no fluke. He also demonstrated how rainbows are formed by splitting white light through a glass prism.

One of Newton's least noteworthy but most controversial inventions was the cat flap. In retrospect it's difficult to comprehend why it took a genius to work out that a cat, but not a burglar, could be allowed free access into and out of a house through a door big enough for cats but too small for bipedal interlopers. Perhaps the great physicist was aware cats are one of the few four-legged animals to not have rigid collarbones, which enables them to slink through openings far smaller than even babies of a similar size. Legend has it Newton drilled a hole in his wall and covered it with a light felt blind, to stop him from being annoyed by a complaining cat while he concentrated on understanding the world around him.

Newton's simple invention provided a convenient solution to a trivial annoyance. But the smartest mind in the world was clearly focused on physics rather than the wellbeing of his cat. Any vet or cat owner knows the safest and best place for a cat is indoors, away from the fights, disease and car accidents that typically shorten an outdoor cat's life. Many cat owners are also concerned about what their cat may be up to after departing through the cat flap.

A modern equivalent of Sir Isaac Newton's cat flap with contemporary warning of the perils to cat welfare and human health of allowing cats outdoors, unless as in this case, the flap leads to an enclosed 'catio'.
(Photo: Damon Oliver)

As we learnt in the previous chapter, the hunting escapades of pet cats can lead to localised or even total extinctions of vulnerable species. Ever since the significance of predation by pet cats became apparent, concerned cat owners have strived to reduce this impact. The tactics and inventions designed to minimise the effect of outdoor pet cats, would no doubt both intrigue and trouble the great physicist.

Cats Protection in the UK has collated a range of initiatives to limit the predatory actions of pet cats or to reduce predation by uninvited cats. Scattering old tea bags and broken eggshells is purported to discourage cats from hunting. More work is involved in placing laminated cat faces cut from pet food boxes at strategic locations around the garden. These faces, presumably called 'scarecats', supposedly intimidate transgressors in much the same way as a broomstick with a face and hat is supposed to scare birds from crops. In a clearly parochial statement that makes no mention of either the lure of a cat on heat or the proven effect of several dog breeds at chasing cats, the 'ultimate deterrent for unwanted cats in your garden' promoted by Cats Protection is to 'have a cat of your own'.

Probably the most widespread tactic employed by responsible cat owners is to restrict the time their pet is allowed outside. Cat owners with a bird feeder nearby can lessen predation rates on day-feeding birds by keeping their cat inside while the birds are active or being fed. Feeders can be strategically placed to reduce the success of cat attack at the feeder but it is rarely possible to limit a cat's hunting opportunities throughout the whole garden. Where most concern is for nocturnal mammals, cats are kept in at night. But you don't need Newton's intellect to find flaws in this approach. A hunting cat, even if only allowed a few hours outside,

Experimental psychologist Robert Adamec determined that all six cats in his feeding trial preferred tinned salmon to commercial cat food and, least of all, warm rats. However, even when feeding on their favourite salmon, when he placed a live rat into their cage Adamec's cats would leave the bowl, kill the rat and return to their preferred salmon diet. He concluded 'their response to predatory stimuli takes precedence over gustatory stimuli motivations'. In layman's terms, Adamec's study reinforces the popular notion that cats, irrespective of their hunger, are hardwired to hunt.

will find plenty of opportunity to fulfil its instincts. Temporary curfews may limit the types of prey but not solve the problem.

Many cat owners ensure their cat is well fed before being allowed outside under the belief that a cat with a full belly is less inclined to hunt. Picture the sated rotund-bellied cat napping in the sun. A study from southern Chile found well-fed pet cats indeed caught less wildlife than hungry cats. However, as many devoted cat owners who are presented with trophy kills next to a cat food bowl can attest, feeding rarely dampens the hunting instincts of most cats. Rather than pinning their hopes on a strategy that has so often proved ineffective, cat owners typically opt for another logical option.

David Attenborough, the undisputed master of interpreting animal behaviour and conservation issues, has publicly encouraged cat owners to buy bells for their cats to protect the 'huge number of birds in gardens'. Cat bells make sense. Newton, but possibly not Darwin, would have been impressed by Attenborough's plea. A typical hunting foray by a domestic cat culminates with a lightning-fast pounce before being noticed by its unsuspecting prey. However, having been alerted to an approaching cat by a

During a school talk on responsible pet ownership I explained to the class that when cats learn to hunt with bells on their collars it might resemble the skills of those amazing African and Pacific Islander women who expertly balance enormous, unstable loads on their heads. I flippantly suggested the class could master this skill by walking with bells in their earrings or headbands, instead of risking injury or damage by practising with heavy loads. After the talk a 10-year-old girl approached me and asked, 'Why don't you put bells on the cat's legs so they can't learn to hunt quietly?'

tell-tale bell, the little bird visiting the flowering shrub or the lizard basking in the backyard sun will have greater time to escape. A tinkling bell should shift the odds towards the prey and reduce the piles of feathers accumulating on the back porch.

Unfortunately for caring cat owners, many cats learn to hunt perfectly well with a bell. Domestic cats have not reached the zenith of the world's adaptable, widespread and successful predators by chance. Their stalking technique, perfected and selected over eons, serves to nullify the potential value of bells. Like their big cat cousins on the African plains, a stalking domestic cat is a natural marvel of concentration, anatomy and prowess. Cats approach by pressing low to the ground and patiently inching forward without sudden movements alerting their prey. Then, like a coiled spring, the killer pounce is unleashed so fast and from such close range that the unsuspecting prey has no time to react.

The general consensus from several studies across the globe into the value of fitting bells to cat collars is that they reduce hunting success, at least initially, by somewhere between a third and a half. However, in time, even this partial curtailing of hunting prowess declines as the cats learn to perfect their stalking techniques by

Despite wearing multiple bells, and attempts by his owner Emma Coates to first contain him then train him to stop hunting, Chopper the Russian blue continued to catch birds like this New Holland honeyeater. Bells and other alarms typically only reduce cat predation rates by less than 50%, or until cats improve their stalking prowess. (Photo: E. Coates)

eliminating sudden movements. Paradoxically and tragically, this self-training by bell-wearing cats may actually assist dedicated hunters and make them more effective.

To circumvent cats learning to stalk prey without ringing their bells, the British Trust for Ornithology developed a collar-fitted device in the 1990s that produced a simple tone repeated every seven seconds. Their theory was no matter how stealthy the hunting cat, potential prey would be alerted to their presence, because it typically requires far more than seven seconds to approach within pouncing range. In theory, the CatAlert collars should overcome the major flaw of conventional movement-activated bells. Even Darwin might have been impressed by this invention!

I met Nigel Clark, the archetypical bearded biological doctorate student, in 2000 when as the head of projects at the British Trust for Ornithology he had tested these prototype CatAlert collars, after finding bells ineffective. Although Clark's initial trials showed some success and a slight reduction in hunting efficiency, the results were mixed. Some birds and many reptiles apparently did not equate the periodic beep with danger. Clark found these persistently beeping collars reduced hunting success by about a half, which was becoming the apparent success ceiling for anti-hunting devices. Mooted modifications, such as a motion sensor that activated when the cat jumps, would likely suffer the same limitations as bells. The beep would either be delivered too late, when the cat was mid pounce, or the cats would simply get used to stalking without activating the beep. Although sceptical of the success of pounce-activated beeps, Clark was a fan of installing a switch that turned off the sound once a cat had re-entered the house. The persistent beep was more effective at annoying him than it was at alerting prey.

Another innovative strategy is to shield the cat from their prey. Ultrasonic cat scarers emit high frequency sounds, inaudible to humans and most wildlife but annoying to cats. Mounted outside the house in an area where cats are not welcome, the units are activated by a motion sensor when a cat appears. These cat scarers, if aligned strategically and operating effectively, could deter cats from hunting around fishponds or bird feeders, even a whole backyard if enough units are installed. They are the only devices tested and recommended by the RSPB and the deterrent of choice for many non-cat owners seeking to keep the neighbours' cats away. But, inevitably, like the bells and whistles, ultrasonic cat scarers have their drawbacks. White cats and blue-eyed Persians are often deaf and hence untroubled by the ultrasonic warnings. But the most serious limitation is these devices do not stop a pet cat from hunting, they merely discourage cats from hunting in small 'protected' areas. Keen hunters simply operate further afield, which may be out of sight of their concerned owners but has the same result for wildlife.

Necessity is the mother of invention. Human nature decrees cat owners with a compassion for wildlife will continue to devise solutions to reduce the concerning piles of feathers. The next innovation to reduce pet cat predation was the most intrusive technique yet. If cats tease each other like schoolboys I would hate to be a cat fitted with a 'cat bib', a hybrid neoprene necktie-cum-plastic napkin, tucked into the collar of a sheepish-looking cat. The theory is the bib will interfere with the cat using its front paws to seize, snatch or press down on its prey.

Although designed in the United States, one notable trial of CatBib® took place in Perth, Western Australia, over a six-week period. A prerequisite for qualifying for the trial was that all cats were known hunters. Most of the 56 cat owners in the trial participated in the trial due to concern about their cats' impact on wildlife. The majority had already unsuccessfully tried at least one method of reducing predation. Confinement, bells, scolding or splashing with water had failed to produce the desired results and they were willing to give the new device a go.

Professor Michael Calver from Murdoch University and his PhD student Sandra Thomas closely monitored their subjects wearing a bib for three weeks and three weeks without. One particularly savvy cat, less than impressed with its clumsy fashion accessory, managed to lose its bib six times during the three-week trial but for the most part the bibs stayed on. Owners recorded the number of animals they found that had been killed by their cats during the period their cat was, and was not, wearing the bib.

When the results came in, cats caught a third as many birds, half as many mammals and nearly the same number of lizards and frogs when they were wearing the bibs compared to their time without. Calver felt he had sufficient evidence to suggest the bibs were partially successful but left the final say to the cat owners who were desperate to find a solution to their cats' hunting ways.

Perhaps fittingly, given the established trend for predation reduction being effective for about half of all trial cats, 25 of the owners thought the bib had worked and exactly the same number considered the bibs a failure. The remaining six cat owners were either less attentive or possibly more honest. They were undecided whether the bibs had worked or not.

In 2007, the year after Calver's equivocal results on the cat bib came in, scientists were trialling another collar-mounted device to reduce pet cats' kill rate. Ridiculous-looking apparel resembling a clown's collar crossed with the brightest Hawaiian shirt was fitted over a standard quick-release cat collar. These Birdsbesafe® cat collars were trialled on New York cats with apparently impressive results. Extrapolating from the observed kill rate in their study, the scientists from St Lawrence University concluded the average cat wearing a five-centimetre-wide psychedelic collar brought home 1.4 birds a year, compared to those without the collar bringing home an average of 8.4 birds a year. At long last, a success rate that exceeded a 50% reduction. However, scientists did concede mammal predation rates were not significantly reduced. Furthermore, hopes were dampened by recognition that a quarter of their trial cats were either distressed or point blank refused to wear the gaudy devices.

Brightly coloured Birdsbesafe® collars appear to reduce bird
(but not mammal) predation success of some outdoor cats

Without doubt there are hundreds, perhaps thousands, of annoyed or embarrassed pet cats cowering around the globe fitted with the next generation of hunting-aversion devices. Those cat owners who care about wildlife will continue to search for the silver bullet that enables pets the liberty of a free-ranging lifestyle without the problems caused by their hunting. Some cat owners, especially those who also feed birds in their yards, will inevitably wake up in the wee-small hours, possibly after hearing the tinkle of a bell outside the window, with a novel solution to this age-old problem. Their invention may annoy some cats and save some wildlife. It may even net the inventor a tidy income. But before we get too carried away with notions of a profitable panacea from cat-hunting deterrents, there are several compelling reasons, discussed in the next two chapters, why cat flaps should be boarded over and banished to the museum of outdated inventions.

Chapter 5

STEALTH AND SUBTERFUGE

The last thing I would accuse a cat of is innocence. Edward Paley

Deep in the rainforests of Central America live an extraordinary group of spectacular iridescent green-and-blue animals. Highly specialised and incredibly beautiful, their striking appearance is only overshadowed by their astonishing adaptations.

'Poison dart frogs?' I hear you guess, those tiny frogs in a bewildering range of colours known by their predators to be too poisonous to eat. Poison dart frogs are a textbook example of how poisonous animals advertise their danger by bright colouration. But no, this story is about even smaller, brighter and more bizarre beasts than the dendrobatid frogs, and is the first of four examples of amazing natural relationships that help explain why cat flaps are dangerous for cat owners.

Just as the dawn chorus of one of the world's most diverse bird communities reaches its crescendo, shining green bees swirl around a tree trunk, their colour exploding in the spotlights created where the morning sun penetrates the canopy. Gradually the excited bees hone in on a yellow butterfly unfurling its new wings in the sunlight. But closer inspection reveals the 'butterfly' is a bizarre leaf-like appendage, dangling from the drooping stem of an epiphytic orchid. Semi-concealed behind the 'butterfly', and obviously of more interest to the buzzing emeralds, lies a tiny fairy's boot.

This 'butterfly and boot' is the flower of a *Coryanthes*, or bucket orchid. The top of the boot actually resembles a bucket, hence the common name of the orchid. Bees are seduced to the bucket by a heavy sweet scent, released strategically at dawn when the emerald insects become active. The scent permeates from aromatic oils bound in a waxy substance lining the inside of the bucket. The only way the bees can reach the alluring wax is to land on the bucket rim and frantically scrape with their brush-like front feet. Like crows descending on a carcass, more bees arrive and clamber for the wax. So frenzied is the activity that the bees bump into each other and eventually one is knocked down the slippery walls and splashes into the bucket. But despite all the rain there isn't water in the bottom of the bucket, rather a fluid containing a wetting agent that reduces the surface tension and dunks the bee. Wet and slippery, the bee struggles valiantly to climb the waxy walls.

When early naturalists first watched the bees being trapped they assumed they were witnessing one of the carnivorous pitcher plants that trap and digest hapless insects. But what transpired next in the orchid flower was even more extraordinary. Hauling itself out of the mire, the bee clambers out along a spout that promises freedom. Forcing its way to the daylight ahead, the waterlogged bee looks set to escape when the spout constricts and holds the bee again. A projection strategically pushes pollen packages precisely into the gap between the bee's thorax and abdomen. Eventually, after a harrowing near-death experience often lasting over half an hour, the bee is released with its precious payload.

But delivering the pollen is only half the story. Somehow the laden bee has to deliver the pollen to another flower. Fortunately, like a clucky mother who has put aside the ordeal of earlier childbirth, the bee forgets its harrowing experience and is once again lured by the irresistible aroma to another siren-like flower. Perhaps exhausted and maybe still a bit wet and slippery, the bee may again fall into the mire and splash around until it finds the lifeline back up the spout. Again the hapless bee struggles against the constricting spout. This time, instead of triggering the deposition of more pollen sacks, a purpose-made hook on the ceiling of the spout plucks the pollinia from the bee's back as it forces its way past. The pollen, collected from another flower and couriered by a duped and exhausted bee, is now perfectly placed to pollinate the second flower.

This cross pollination, or mixing of genes from one plant to another, provides the very mechanism for these truly bizarre relationships between plants and animals to evolve.

Charles Darwin, the forefather of research into these relationships, devoted considerable attention to the pollination of bucket orchids by orchid bees in his verbosely titled work, 'The Various Contrivances by which Orchids are Fertilized by Insects'. Although underplayed by his non-emotional title, Darwin must have been dazzled by the deception of orchid bees by the bucket orchids. He likely considered their relationship to be near the pinnacle of his seminal theory. What intermediate stages, what subconscious rolling of evolutionary dices, could have accounted for such a complicated and intricate relationship?

It is not only the bucket orchid flower that gains from the relationship. Most orchid bees never fall in the bucket but simply reap the sweet waxy rewards on offer from the flower. The relationship between flower and insect is one of mutual benefit. The food plants we eat, from rice to apples, did not evolve to fuel our voracious society, but to reward animal dispersers for mixing and spreading the plant's gene pool. Other plants provide energy-rich nectaries for ants that fight off herbivorous insects from their generous hosts. Since Darwin's description of the pollination of the bucket orchids, scientists have uncovered a myriad of mind-blowing symbioses between plants and plants, plants and animals, and even animals and animals.

But not all relationships between different life forms provide a win-win for all players. Sometimes, these complex webs include a loser, like the honey bee, whose hive is revealed by the honeyguide bird. These small birds expertly lead humans to beehives. The honeyguide, as its name suggests, has a penchant for eating bees' wax but lacks the firepower to confront an angry hive alone. After the hive has been overwhelmed and drained of much of its honey by appreciative humans, the honeyguide is left to mop up the spoils including remaining larvae and wax. Any surviving bees with the potential to plot an evolutionary course to outwit or outgun the raiding humans or the betraying bird are eaten too.

Some of the most ingenious cases of one animal using another for its own benefit involve the use of subterfuge rather than brawn, teeth or claws. *Camponotus leonardi*, or 'zombie' ants, are so named because they have been deceived by an insidious fungus to sacrifice themselves for the 'lower' life form. Yeast stages of the *Ophiocordyceps unilateralis* fungus penetrate the ant's brain and change their host's behaviour. These changes are designed precisely for the benefit of the fungus, not the ant. Infected ants suffer from convulsions causing them to fall out of the tree canopy, then climb to a predetermined height. When the fungus is ready to reproduce after a week or so, its fruiting bodies grow from the dead ant's head like tiny umbrellas and rupture, releasing the spores at the optimum height for sporulation. The zombie ants have unwittingly created the perfect conditions to maximise the success of their debilitating pest.

Another example of fatal mind-altering subterfuge by a microscopic organism on a far larger quarry is performed by perhaps the world's most dangerous creature. Without immediate treatment, exposure to this killer is almost inevitably fatal. And rather than being a potent, yet shy, snake or scorpion that typically avoids confrontation, this little killer does everything in its power to maximise its exposure. At only about 180 nanometres, the tiny rabies virus would seem unlikely to be one of the world's most lethal organisms; but like the zombie ant fungus, its weapon is deception. The rabies virus is transmitted from the saliva of an infected predator to the animal it bites. In order to maximise the likelihood of being transmitted as widely as possible, rabies infection literally turns hosts into crazed and aggressive biters. Indeed the term 'rabies' is a direct derivation of the Latin for 'madness'. Rabies has evolved to maximise its chance of reproducing and it achieves this by inducing its victims to bite as many other animals as possible.

Once entrenched in the central nervous system several days after infection, rabies is typically fatal for humans. But despite the enormous risks and costs of rabies treatment, another microscopic creature, even more closely associated with cats than the rabies virus, represents a greater – but more subtle – threat.

Given the benefits of colluding with or deceiving other beasts, it is perhaps surprising more predators have not formed allegiances with mind-altering allies. Imagine the benefit to a wolf if it could entice eagles or ravens to muster deer in exchange for leftover carrion. Even more bizarre would be if Tom the cat could

Although rabies is typically associated with dogs, at least twice as many cases of rabid cats have been recently reported in the United States. With thousands of people requiring treatment due to exposure to rabid cats every year, at a cost of $3000 each, the social and medical costs are staggering. The treatment costs for one extreme case in New Hampshire, caused by mass exposure to a single rabid kitten, amounted to well in excess of a million dollars.

somehow deceive Jerry the mouse that he is a friend not a foe. This may sound like the outlandish plot of a cartoon series, but scientists have now observed this bizarre scenario in real life and proclaim it as the most important reason for keeping cats indoors.

Rats have not become one of the most ubiquitous and evasive pests on the planet without exceptional adaptiveness and cunning. Despite cohabiting with cats in most cities of the world, rats have not declined to extinction like many other small mammals less adept at avoiding cat predation. Indeed they fall in the critical weight range of mammals considered most vulnerable to small feline extirpation. Rats are alert and wary, attuned to detecting cats and expert at avoiding encounters. But some rats, inexplicably, have lost this fear of cats with predictably disastrous consequences. This aberrant behaviour confers the rat no evolutionary advantage because its genes lay wasted in the next cat dropping. Instead this suicidal behaviour appears to be the result of a meticulously scripted multispecies deception, a double cross where the rat's death is programmed for the mutual benefit of two very different and unlikely allies. Working with the cat – indeed orchestrating the deception – is *Toxoplasma gondii*, a single-celled organism measured in micrometres, the sharp end of a pin.

Robert Sapolsky, neuroscientist at Stanford University, has documented the transformation of a rat's innate cat aversion into an attraction following infection by the parasite. The parasite interferes with the rat's brain via a bizarre neurobiological process, in particular with the area controlling such basic emotions as fear, anxiety and sexual arousal. Rats infected by toxoplasmosis spend more time in areas reeking of cat urine, whereas their uninfected brothers and sisters show the predictable aversion to the smell of cats. Lacking fear, the rats become easy meat and the parasite increases its chance of being transmitted through the cat population. If you are reading this and, like me, questioned the validity of Sapolsky's findings, we are not alone. Studies in at least three other laboratories that set out to disprove these results found supportive evidence.

Toxoplasma's deception is more complicated than just doping the fear receptors of their rat hosts. Infected rats still avoid bright lights and open spaces just like their uninfected siblings, just not cat urine. What's even more impressive is *Toxoplasma* parasites have conned the rats by mimicking the mammalian gene that stimulates attraction and fear. Amanda Worth and co-authors from Murdoch University question whether the behavioural changes exhibited by infected hosts result from deliberate adaptive manipulation by the *Toxoplasma* parasite, or rather might represent inadvertent but fortuitous outcomes of infection. Irrespective of whether the responses are deliberate or not, this amazing ruse has the excitable Sapolsky both scratching his head and pondering the opportunities. If a microscopic parasite can tap into the mammalian genome to change cognitive processes, what potential options exist for his fellow neuroscientists to treat mental disorders?

Cats are the only definitive hosts for *Toxoplasma gondii*, which means the parasite can only reproduce sexually in the intestinal tracts of cats. Although some cases of transmission between other hosts have been recorded, without cats the parasite would probably become extinct within years. Presumably also carefully orchestrated by the parasite, cats typically show no symptoms from toxoplasmosis. When cats ingest infected prey the parasite multiplies in the wall of the small intestine and produces oocysts, or microscopic seed-like eggs. So perfect is the cat intestine for the reproduction of *Toxoplasma* that many millions, yes millions, of oocysts are typically produced within a few days of infection.

Unlike the relatively simple lifecycle of the rabies virus, *Toxoplasma gondii* employs at least two other animals in its subterfuge. Infective sporulated *Toxoplasma* oocysts measure only about 30 micrometres and can survive in soil for years. At densities of tens to hundreds of thousands of oocysts per gram of soil adjacent to cat scats, those little parasitic cluster bombs literally swarm in sandpits and gardens used by cats. Health professionals have calculated our fingernails typically trap up to a hundred toxoplasmosis cysts after we have been digging in contaminated soil. And we don't need to be playing around cat toilets to become infected. Oocysts are spread to grass or roots or other places where they may be inadvertently consumed by earthworms, ants and other soil invertebrates. Microscopic oocysts are even small enough to be inhaled in dust originating from litter trays and sandpits, and from soil brought into houses on dirty shoes. Any animal accidentally ingesting or inhaling these tiny oocysts is likely to become infected, resulting in the formation of tissue cysts that remain for life. These tissue cysts are then infectious to cats, people and other intermediate hosts like

Domestic cats were calculated to deposit up to 106.4 tons of faeces per year around three small towns near the California coast where endangered sea otters are infected with toxoplasmosis. Indeed an estimated 1.2 million metric tonnes of cat faeces are deposited annually in the US accounting for between 32 and 4672 *Toxoplasma* oocysts per square metre of soil. Scientists in Costa Rica and Kansas followed the fate of chemically marked *Toxoplasma* oocysts after they simulated the shallow burial by cats. The parasite persisted far longer in buried cat faeces (at least 12 months) than unburied faeces, leading the authors to conclude 'These data support the concept that *Toxoplasma* infectivity in nature may be increased logarithmically by cats'.

otters, seals and dolphins, if the cyst-containing tissue is eaten.

As anyone with a sandpit and/or an outdoor cat can attest, cats are fastidious about burying their business. Careful flicking with a boot typically reveals a buried deposit in the mounded centre of the distinctive rosette shaped scratching in the sand. But scientists who actively search for cat scats (yes, those people do exist) have noted such modesty is typically reserved for cats when nature calls close to home. When venturing afar cats more often leave their deposits unburied on the surface. When I was tracking wildcats in Andalucía, acclaimed master tracker José Galán showed me that feral domestic cats typically bury their scats whereas wildcats leave them on the surface.

Several explanations are possible for this dichotomy in toileting habitats. Burying scats close to denning sites may simply fulfil a cat's hygienic instincts, which may be less attuned when they are travelling. Another scientific camp suggests the burial of cat faeces in core areas of their home range may help conceal their position from predators. Cats living with coyotes or dingoes avoid confrontation with these larger predators by being active when they are not around. But habitual use of toilet sandpits in dog-free yards suggests hiding from predators is not the only motivation for cats to bury their faeces.

An infected rat can typically infect only one cat, whereas an infected cat can potentially infect thousands of animals with the *Toxoplasma* parasite. Although difficult to prove, maybe the cats are in on the toxoplasmosis ruse. The only way for cats to optimise their role in the lifecycle of their beneficial parasite is to ensure *Toxoplasma* oocysts are as accessible as possible to rats and other prey.

Fortunately for the parasite, hungry rats are partial to high protein cat scats; the main limitation is the parasite's oocysts cannot survive in hot and dry conditions for more than a few weeks. Remembering cats evolved in deserts, along with their parasitic allies, buried scats will help insulate the oocysts and enable them to be more readily taken up by soil invertebrates and rodents. A cat that has inherited a beneficial evolutionary trait should deposit and curate their oocyst delivery packages with the best interests of their parasite collaborator in mind.

One of my favourite annual activities is a 15-kilometre loop walk into the Great Sandy Desert, one of Australia's – and indeed the world's – most isolated locations. I search the furnace-hot red sand for the distinctive diggings and burrows of the bizarre greater bilby, an unlikely combination of kangaroo and rabbit, but a close relation of neither. Prior to European colonisation bilbies were widespread and common throughout most of Australia but now the Great Sandy Desert provides one of their last tenuous refuges. Scanning the sandy margins of ephemeral claypans for any sign of bilby, I often encounter the unmistakable starfish-shaped scrapings made by a cat meticulously burying its scat. With the toe of my boot I roll out three or four nuggets, which are then bagged to determine the native creatures eaten by the abundant cats. Careful inspection of cat scats can often reveal the presence of bilbies and other rare mammals overlooked by my traps or other searches.

Before I bag my first cat deposit of the day I soak in the honey-popcorn smells of the flowering desert grevilleas and the sweet aromas of carpets of native daisies and peas. But no matter how tightly I seal the collection bags, the stench of fresh cat deposits exposed from careful burial overwhelms me for the remainder of my walk. I can still smell the moist cat scats days after the bags have been removed from my backpack. But on days when I only find scats desiccated by the baking desert sun I barely notice their aroma. Anyone trying to account for the cats' habit of shallowly burying their scats to hide their smell are kidding themselves. Dogs and foxes, with far better attuned sense of smell than me, would be able to detect a shallow-buried moist cat deposit for miles. If the cats wanted to conceal their dens or home ranges from dogs they would walk a few hundred metres away and complete their toileting with less effort than it takes to dig a hole and meticulously cover with sand close to home. Within days their baked deposit will barely smell and probably will no longer host live *Toxoplasma* oocysts either, whereas a buried scat nearby will remain an odorous parasite-laden bomb for months.

Unfortunately for humans and other animals, the chemical cues used by *Toxoplasma* to render rats more susceptible to cats can cause severe brain damage, epilepsy, blindness and even still births in infected human foetuses. *Toxoplasma gondii* is an intracellular parasite that invades cells in the brain and retina, where it replicates slowly as a chronic, lifelong infection. Along with excluding soft cheeses and oysters from my wife's diet due to risk of listeria when we excitedly embarked upon our first pregnancy, Katherine was also advised to stay clear of cat-litter trays, sandpits and raw or rare meat. These are believed to be the main pathways of toxoplasmosis to expectant mothers. Judging by the fact more than half of the human population and half of the free-ranging cats in many countries have been infected by toxoplasmosis, the risk of transmission from cats to humans is high. Indoor cats cannot be infected by toxoplasmosis if they do not hunt or scavenge for their prey and are not fed infected meat. This reduces the threat of this ghastly disease for foetuses and newborns and is one of the driving motivations for keeping pet cats indoors, as we will revisit in Chapter 22.

Evidence from China suggests, not surprisingly, toxoplasmosis infections are increasing with increasing cat populations. Pet keeping only started to become prevalent in China after the death of Mao Zedong in 1976, and did not become common until recently. Infection rates have more than doubled from around 5% prior to 1992 to over 12% after 2006.

Unfortunately, victims and their doctors remain largely in the dark about infection rates. Researchers from New England Regional Newborn Screening Program found only two of 52 infected infants were recognised to have congenital toxoplasmosis before their screening results for toxoplasmosis were known. Follow-up examinations, however, revealed symptoms including abnormal cerebrospinal fluid examinations, hydrocephalus and retinal lesions in 40% of the other infected infants, which had previously gone undetected. Another example, this time from an outbreak of acute toxoplasmosis originating from contaminated drinking water in Canada, is even more alarming. Even without direct contact with either free-ranging cats or their faeces, the insidious *Toxoplasma* parasite can infect unsuspecting people. The Humpback reservoir in Greater Victoria province was the likely source of a toxoplasmosis outbreak affecting thousands of Canadians in March 1995. Yet despite a screening program in pregnancy, a high level of media attention, and intensive education campaigns and awareness among physicians, only 3% of the infections in this outbreak were diagnosed.

Given this high rate of human exposure to the *Toxoplasma* parasite, we are fortunate that the risks of birth defects only occur when mothers are infected immediately prior to, or during, pregnancy. On average, only 40% of such infections will pass to the unborn baby and only rarely are these fatal. Approximately 750 deaths a year are attributed to congenital toxoplasmosis in the United States. However, the more subtle effects of toxoplasmosis are more difficult to detect and far more prevalent.

The dreaded cat-borne disease is also a major threat to patients with weakened immunity. In the early days of the AIDS epidemic, before effective antiretroviral drugs were developed, toxoplasmosis was blamed for the dementia afflicting many patients at the disease's end stage. It's not only pregnant women or those with compromised immunity who are affected by toxoplasmosis. Adult immuno-competent patients with toxoplasmosis at the University of Auckland suffered from higher than expected rates of fatigue and headaches and a decrease in overall physical and mental health during the first two months of their illness. Fortunately such symptoms are usually resolved within a few months.

But – and this one is a mighty big but – evidence now suggests that even when it is not active, past exposure to the *Toxoplasma* parasite can translate to profound and measurable effects on humans. Czech evolutionary biologist Jaroslav Flegr from Charles University in Prague resembles the archetypal mad professor, with his Bozo-like red fuzz of hair framing a gaunt pale face. He too wondered if he was going slightly mad. For years Flegr's considerable scientific and psychological nous suggested that something beyond his control often caused him to behave in strange, often self-destructive ways. In what must have been a bizarre self-revelation, Flegr recounted occasions when he allowed himself to be swindled by unscrupulous contractors or incorrect change given by shopkeepers. At the time, despite being blatantly duped, he felt an inexplicable and troubling sense of superiority and victory, although his rational side screamed he was a loser. Flegr self-diagnosed the likely cause of his troubling behaviour after confirming the presence of toxoplasmosis antibodies, indicating his exposure to toxoplasmosis. Reading accounts of Flegr's symptoms suggests the biology-cum-psychology lecturer may have been a little paranoid. However, Flegr assures me he was only joking when writing that he suspected Freddy, one of his six cats, was actually sabotaging his studies on the psychological effects of toxoplasmosis by lying on his computer keyboard!

Despite Freddy's foiling tactics, Flegr set out to determine whether exposure to toxoplasmosis had subtly manipulated his own personality and was also affecting others who had contracted the disease. About a third of the Czech population tested positive for toxoplasmosis, so Flegr had a readily available experimental cohort. The results were both astounding and confounding. Compared with uninfected men, males testing positive to toxoplasmosis were more introverted and oblivious to other people's opinions of them. Infected women were the opposite; they

After self-confessed 'slightly mad' Professor Jaroslav Flegr, pictured here with Macik, one of his pet cats, linked his irrational behaviour to toxoplasmosis, dozens of studies from around the world have found this cat-borne disease influences rates of schizophrenia, suicide, obsessive-compulsive disorder and Alzheimer's, among other mental health issues.
(Photo: Monika Flegrova)

presented as more outgoing and image-conscious than uninfected women. Admit it, right now are you wondering whether you, your partner or your nemesis is a candidate? Did you always wash your hands after playing in the sandpit?

From his psychological training, Flegr recognised that although their behaviour differed, men and women might both be responding to chronic stress. Stressed women typically seek solace through nurturing and social bonding; men often become antisocial or even hostile. Flegr believes the supposedly latent *Toxoplasma* parasite is making millions of people around the world more fearful. If this does not worry you, consider the following research. The increased risk of traffic accidents for drivers infected by toxoplasmosis has been confirmed by studies in Czech Republic, Turkey, Mexico, Poland and Russia, as a result of more risk-taking behaviour or because infected drivers exhibited slower reaction times. Even more insidiously, rates of suicide appear to be increased by exposure to the cat disease.

Since these subtle but alarming effects of toxoplasmosis were first described in the mid 1990s, doctors have linked this devious cat parasite with an increasing range of human health disorders. A recent French study suggested links between toxoplasmosis and brain cancer, while a Brazilian study found students exposed to toxoplasmosis performed more poorly in mathematics tests. Higher incidence of obsessive-compulsive disorder, Alzheimer's, autism, memory loss, epilepsy and even rheumatoid arthritis have recently been reported in patients testing positive for toxo-plasmosis. Due to the reluctance of both doctors and patients to increase health risks by deliberate infection allowing comparison

One 2018 soccer World Cup tipster reasoned that increased testosterone or dissent of authority, both symptoms of toxoplasmosis infection, could explain why nations with a higher incidence of toxoplasmosis tend to win more World Cups. A scientific appraisal of 38 studies from around the world found that toxoplasmosis represented the same risk as cannabis and a far greater risk than traumatic brain injury and prenatal stress in the development of schizophrenia. If you are concerned about your own health you may be interested that one potential hint of latent toxoplasmosis infection comes from a study reporting infected men (but not women) rate highly diluted cat urine as pleasant while non-infected men do not. (*Author's note – I therefore consider I am, at present, safe!*)

of subsequent behavioural or health changes with the uninfected, these studies can only point to a correlation with toxoplasmosis, rather than attributing the symptoms to the disease. One indirect way to assess the effect of latent toxoplasmosis is to study the effect of psychiatric medications on the parasite itself. Haloperidol and valproic acid, prescribed to patients with bipolar symptoms, have also proven effective in inhibiting reproduction of *Toxoplasma* parasites. Toxoplasmosis researchers also found antipsychotics administered to infected mice and rats reversed their perverse attraction to cat urine.

The psychiatrist E. Fuller Torrey provides a historical context for this seemingly improbable relationship between cats and psychological disorders. In the latter half of the 18th century a 'cat craze' was instigated by the avant-garde in Paris and London. As the keeping of cats as pets spread rapidly, so did the incidence of schizophrenia, Torrey's primary research interest. Schizophrenia had been a rarely reported complaint before the explosion in pet cat ownership in the late 1700s. Looking more closely to determine whether there was any causality in this correlation, Torrey and his neurovirologist colleague Robert Yolken found exposure to toxoplasmosis correlated with a reduction in brain grey matter. Furthermore, mental illness was two to three times more prevalent in people with the parasite than others from the same region who had not been infected. Equally as alarming, a 2011 study found that the national suicide rate among women from 20 European countries increased in direct proportion to the latent toxoplasmosis infection rate of women in each country. None of this information proves toxoplasmosis is a major driver of mental illness, but the growing weight of medical research raises concerns. As a result of his extensive research Torrey advocates for prohibiting contact between children and outdoor cats due to their increased risk of schizophrenia in adulthood.

Rather than being an inadvertent biological aberration, the psychological changes in humans infected by toxoplasmosis may reflect our relatively recent evolutionary history when big cats preyed on humans. Clémence Poirotte led a team in Gabon using wildlife surrogates. Her team found infected chimpanzees did not display the same aversion to leopard urine exhibited by non-infected chimps. Although this correlation doesn't necessarily imply that the toxoplasmosis caused the chimps to lose their fear, Poirotte suggested that *Toxoplasma*-induced behavioural changes in modern humans could be an ancestral legacy from the time when our forebears were important prey for big cats.

Charles Darwin would have been mesmerised by the complexity of this biological deception, perhaps even more than his astonishment of *The Various Contrivances by which Orchids are Fertilized by Insects*. Ironically, with toxoplasmosis likely to be affecting our state of mind, our ability to rationally respond to these newly discovered threats might be compromised by the parasite itself. *Toxoplasma* may be hoodwinking humans into tolerating and even deliberately creating high densities of free-ranging cats and thus the optimal environments for its own persistence, but with alarming consequences for ours.

Chapter 6

MORE THAN MEETS THE EYE

*Keeping your cat inside will reduce his chances of getting sick,
making the most of his nine lives.* Dr Denise Petryk

Again I found myself studying a small native cat in a zoo, but this feline was stunningly different to the tabby-like Scottish wildcat. Its most distinctive feature, evident when it was curled up on the ground looking away from me, was the snow-white patches behind the ears. The cat's strongly blotched pelage was almost reminiscent of a young leopard. When the cat eventually awoke from its slumber and stood up, I could clearly see the distinctive four longitudinal dark-brown bands running up its forehead. The Tsushima leopard cat at the Kyoto zoo was also more elongated and leggy than a domestic cat. More the build of a sprinter than a fighter, its head was proportionately far smaller than many tom cats.

Because they occur higher on the food chain, carnivores require larger tracts of habitat than herbivores and are also often persecuted by humans because they may represent a threat to people, pets or livestock. It's little wonder predators are over represented in threatened species classifications. Despite this already elevated threatened status, native cats feature twice as often as other carnivorous mammal families in the International Union for the Conservation of Nature list of threatened species. I visited Japan, home to two of the world's most endangered small

Most Japanese and visiting wildlife enthusiasts acquiesce to viewing Tsushima cats in zoos, like Kyoto, because the endangered cats, threatened by road accidents and FelineAIDs transmitted from domestic cats, are now seldom seen in the wild. (Photo: Masako Izawa)

felines, to better understand the disproportionately high threats faced by native cats.

I hadn't planned to observe another rare native cat in yet another zoo. The Tsushima leopard cat and Iriomote cat are two of only four Japanese mammals designated as National Endangered Species of Wild Fauna. My guide, Japan's pre-eminent native cat researcher Masako Izawa, had discouraged me from visiting Tsushima Island, midway between Korea and Japan, or the more southern Iriomote Island to search for these rare cats. 'In recent years Tsushima cats have disappeared from the most populated and accessible Shimojima Island,' Izawa told me, before explaining that even when she visits for several weeks she usually doesn't see a live wildcat. Nearly all her information comes from photos on camera traps or road-killed specimens. Iriomote is even harder to visit and with even less chance of seeing an Iriomote cat.

Reluctantly I took Izawa's advice and visited the Fukuoka and Kyoto zoos instead. But I also accepted her offer of spending a week with her while she researched the effects of feral domestic cats on other Japanese islands. While we were driving to remote field sites I quizzed the quietly spoken but composed biologist about the threats to Japan's two iconic but disturbingly rare native cats.

After learning of the effects of hybridisation with domestic cats that threatened the Scottish and African wildcats, I assumed crossbreeding with introduced cats may also be a key threat in Japan. Izawa was unsure and noncommittal. Although she had never encountered obvious hybrids, she reiterated how difficult these elusive wildcats were to study and conceded no one really knew about the risk. Izawa did remind me that the attractive and vaunted 'Bengal' breed was a hybrid between domestic cats and the Asian leopard cat, which was closely related to these rare Japanese species.

The main risks she had identified for her rare native cats were road kill and competition for food with the more abundant and fecund domestic cat. To emphasise the point she pointed to the 'Stop Roadkill' sticker with a stylised Iriomote cat on her car and later handed me a bundle of magnets, which adorn my fridge to this day. Disease transmission from feral cats is another of her gravest fears. These fears were heightened in 1997 when feline immunodeficiency virus, transmitted from domestic cats, was found in a Tsushima leopard cat. Another debilitating virus, feline leukemia, has also been found in feral cats in Tsushima and could readily jump to their wild cousins, made more susceptible because wildcats have no antibodies to cat viruses. With less than a hundred Iriomote cats in existence, risk of disease and hybridisation could have dramatic consequences.

Across the other side of the world in the Lorraine region of eastern France, wildlife biologists are concerned the small and isolated populations of European wildcats sampled are at risk of 'complete extirpation' due to the high incidence of feline leukemia and other viruses recorded. The French researchers concluded domestic cats are likely to be a source of these viruses.

Just south of France in the Andalusia region of Spain, is Doñana Nature Reserve and El Acebuche Iberian Lynx Breeding Centre. Doñana is a global drawcard for ecotourists and scientists visiting the unique wetlands that provide vital habitat for migrating birds. But as the largest nature reserve in Europe, Doñana also provides one of the last refuges for other wildlife, especially predators driven to extinction from their former habitats, now consumed by agriculture and urban sprawl. The king of these predators and the world's most endangered cat species is the Iberian lynx, a German shepherd-sized cat with tufted ears.

Antonio Rivas, the good-natured manager of the El Acebuche Breeding Centre at Doñana, offered to demonstrate the internationally significant efforts made to conserve these mighty cats. Before observing a pair of these bob-tailed cats at close range, Rivas produced pull-on disposable white slippers for us both to wear. At first I assumed the lynx recovery team were endeavouring to reduce the likelihood of their captive animals becoming accustomed to human smells, and reducing their chances of successful wild integration. Rivas explained his motivations while I hopped unceremoniously into my boot coverings and walked through a tray of disinfectant.

A decade before my visit, in December 2006, 12 lynxes living in the northern part of Doñana were found to be infected with feline leukemia virus. Four of them died in the wild less than six months

Antonio Rivas, manager of the El Acebuche breeding centre in Doñana Nature Reserve, Spain, sterilises his boots to reduce the risk of transmitting domestic cat diseases before visiting his critically endangered Iberian lynx. (Photo: K. Moseby)

after the first infected animal had been discovered; three captured for treatment died shortly afterwards. The remaining viremic lynxes were quarantined to stop the spread of the infection the biologists feared could extirpate the entire population, which at the time numbered fewer than 200 individuals. Ascribing the outbreak to cross infection from domestic cats 'which are increasingly frequent in Doñana', Rivas stressed the urgency for domestic cat control to protect his lynxes.

When seven of less than 200 Iberian lynxes died from feline leukemia in 2006, survivors like this male were brought into quarantine by the Lynx Recovery Team who then rapidly removed 74 feral cats, the source of the outbreak, from Doñana Nature Reserve, Spain. (Photo: J. Read)

Around-the-clock veterinarian staff have identified several other cat-borne diseases in their wild populations of lynx, including infection by our mind-altering nemesis *Toxoplasma gondii*. In addition to vaccinating lynxes against these diseases and observing strict quarantine procedures, such as our white slippers, the Iberian lynx recovery team have concluded 'it is crucial to decrease the infectious pressure domestic cats exert over Iberian lynx populations by preventing domestic cats from entering lynx habitats and vaccinating them too against feline leukemia'. But like Izawa and other threatened species ecologists around the world, the lynx team are facing a continuous tide of feral cats. Between May 2007 and September 2008 alone, 74 domestic cats

Cougars in California and Florida have also contracted feline leukemia virus from infected domestic cats. Even when cat leukemia is not fatal, immunosuppression caused by this virus leaves infected cougars with greater susceptibility to other diseases. Bobcats, which have also died from feline leukemia, also exhibit greater incidence of another cat-borne disease, feline calicivirus, when they live near urban areas with high densities of wandering cats.

were trapped in lynx habitat in the Doñana National Park, seven of which were infected by feline leukemia.

Cytauxzoon felis is another fatal protozoan receiving growing attention as an emerging threat to native felids, as its name suggests. The increasing trend of supporting high-density aggregations of unowned cats at feeding sites in the US over the past three decades may be related to growing rates of infections of *C. felis* on the east coast. Alarmingly, this cat-specific parasite has also been recorded from the Iberian lynxes at Doñana.

The pattern confirmed at Doñana and repeated in Africa, America, Europe and Asia is consistent: interaction with domestic cats typically spells danger for native cats. If it's not competition for food or genes, feline-specific viruses transmitted by domestic cats could prove the death knell for many rare felids. Endangering the survival of rare cats is of course a significant concern, especially for people like Izawa and Rivas and their cultures that value wildcats. But cat-borne diseases affect far more wildlife than wildcats. The main culprit we know of is that most intriguing of all feline protozoans, *Toxoplasma gondii*.

Rats, chimps and humans are not the only species to fall victim to toxoplasmosis. Eastern barred bandicoots are the Australian ecological equivalent of a shrew. These rat-sized marsupial omnivores are perfect cat prey size, and cat predation has long been blamed for their demise. However recent studies have confirmed the prevalence of toxoplasmosis in populations of these rare bandicoots in both Tasmania and mainland Australia. In an eerie refrain to Flegr's research in humans, scientists studying this threatened small mammal consider it 'highly probable' toxoplasmosis infection causes bandicoots to become disoriented and atypically active during the day, thus predisposing them to predation and to being killed on the road. The cat disease has likely contributed directly to the decline of the species. It seems Australian feral cats, descended from domestic cats sometime over the past three centuries, are now benefiting from the parasitic advantage concocted by their African ancestors. And small marsupials are now falling victim to the ruse designed to render rodents more susceptible to cat predation.

Alarmingly, it is not only cat prey falling victim to *Toxoplasma gondii*. Leading mammologist Chris Dickman has surmised the disappearance of eastern quolls, ('marsupial cats') from eastern Australia may be linked to toxoplasmosis. Large cats can, and do, tackle quolls but these feisty marsupial predators put up much more of a fight than little bandicoots. The insidious repercussions of toxoplasmosis infection are considered more likely to be a major role in the quoll's demise. Some ecologists also attribute the sudden demise in the early 1900s of Tasmania's even larger marsupial predators, the tenacious Tasmanian devil and quoll, to disease outbreak. Furthermore, Australia's equivalent of the dodo, the enigmatic and ill-fated thylacine, may also have succumbed as much to disease as the more oft-cited persecution. Yet because Tasmania's 'tiger' is now extinct, we will never know the role toxoplasmosis may have played, nor are we able to remedy its impact.

On other continents the debilitating effects of toxoplasmosis are playing out on a wide range of wildlife. Over half the white-tailed deer in Cleveland Metroparks in northeastern Ohio tested positive for *Toxoplasma*. Veterinary student Gregory Ballash attributed these high rates of infection to extreme densities of stray cats from a trap, neuter, release program in the Greater Cleveland area, where over half the cats also tested positive. Ballash raised the obvious concern that not only did high levels of infection affect the deer, it also posed a considerable threat to humans consuming the infected venison.

And it is not only mammals that are susceptible to toxo-plasmosis. Researchers in Hawaii, one of the global epicentres of feral domestic cats (as we will discover later), have recorded fatal toxoplasmosis in the endangered nene or Hawaiian goose, the critically endangered Hawaiian crow and the red-footed booby. With such a diverse range of birds confirmed as victims in Hawaii alone, it is likely many other wild birds that cohabit with free-ranging domestic cats are also affected in other countries.

Marine mammals share neither habitats nor food webs with cats, yet are highly susceptible to toxoplasmosis. Resulting brain inflammation, which renders otters more susceptible to predation, has been implicated in the death of southern sea otters in California. These deaths have stalled the recovery of this federally listed threatened species, now numbering fewer than 3000. Biologists were alerted to the problem when they noticed otters in the vicinity of urban centres were three times more likely to be affected than otters in more remote areas. The source of the infection was traced to faeces from dense populations of pet cats and the plethora of unowned cats concentrated in major cities. Otters are exposed to *Toxoplasma* when cat faeces are washed out to sea, or maybe after kitty litter is flushed down toilets. So great is the threat of toxoplasmosis to sea otters, where up to 70% may be infected, that California has passed a law instructing cat owners not to flush cat faeces down the toilet or dispose of them in gutters or storm drains.

Not only otters in US waters are affected by the cat parasite. In a survey of European otters in England and Wales, nearly 40% were infected by *Toxoplasma*. Now that biologists have been alerted to the threat of toxoplasmosis killing marine species, a host of other victims have come to light. *Toxoplasma gondii* has been detected in sea lions, dolphins and even whales. The Save the Whales movement has been one of the most successful international conservation collaborations of all time. How ironic if these mighty leviathans, spared from the whaler's harpoon, fall victim instead to one of the world's tiniest killers, a killer supported by many of those same passionate animal lovers who campaigned tirelessly for a cessation in whaling.

Of all the marine creatures to be affected by toxoplasmosis, the critically endangered Hawaiian monk seal has drawn most attention. As in other animals, monk seals exposed to *Toxoplasma* may not always develop disease symptoms. But for those seals that are infected, it can be deadly. Toxoplasmosis was first observed in Hawaiian monk seals in 2004, but it is likely the disease has been taking a toll on these appealing seals ever since cat populations exploded on the Hawaiian Islands. Infections in seals can cause death by inflammation and dysfunction in multiple organs, including the heart and liver. But it is the inflammation of the brain and the compromised immune system associated with infection that presents the most serious risk. In an eerie reprise to the effects of latent *Toxoplasma* exposure recently discovered in humans, seals that survive initial infection may suffer from a compromised immune system or brain function, threatening their survival.

Just as concern is now mounting about the widespread and dangerous – yet under-diagnosed – impact of *Toxoplasma* exposure in humans, the same insidious psychological effects could be playing out in wildlife from the deserts to the sea. How would we know if the rare bandicoot that falls prey to a cat or fox, or simply stumbles in front of a car, had been rendered more vulnerable due to a previous infection? Could the mind-altering parasite be affecting the navigation of the world's great migrants, from birds to whales? Maybe the sudden demise of the Tasmanian tiger and extinction of other wildlife was caused, or at least accelerated, by the unseen actions of *Toxoplasma*. One thing for sure is I for one, will never view a cat scat as simply a toxic-smelling parcel again.

Health professionals, like wildlife biologists, have investigated human cases where cat diseases have been implicated. When I began researching domestic cats I had no idea of the reach or the range of human maladies that cats were associated with.

Bartonella henselae is the bacterium that causes 'cat-scratch fever' (or cat-scratch disease, CSD). It is especially prevalent in cats living in high densities, with the increased likelihood of transmission by scratching or biting. Historically considered a relatively mild illness, doctors now recognise CSD can cause chronic infection and have serious repercussions for patients with suppressed immune systems. In 1994, five Florida children were hospitalised with encephalitis associated with CSD. Patients may suffer relapses because *Bartonella* periodically cycles through the blood system, a bit like malaria. Like toxoplasmosis, bartonellosis is now recognised as sometimes triggering psychiatric symptoms and memory loss. Patients with bartonelliosis are more likely to have visited a neurologist than members of the general population. It's little wonder Chinese researchers have argued for better control of unowned cats after about a third of the cats surveyed in Beijing tested positive for *Bartonella*.

Other cat-related ailments include typhus-like diseases, Rocky Mountain spotted fever, and the debilitating Q fever – all transmitted by the cat flea. Giardia and related Cryptosporidium parasites, the dreaded tummy bugs that have destroyed many an exotic holiday, can also be linked to cats. One study found 28% of cats in London were infected by roundworm. *Toxocara cati* is another insidious parasite associated with cats. Cats may also be implicated in spreading other diseases not historically associated with felines, including H5N1 avian influenza. Even more disturbing, cases of human plague are traced to cat exposure almost annually in the western United States, with several of these being fatal.

I'm guessing that you, like me, might now be reacting to this inventory of cat-borne sicknesses. But we need to be rational so this barrage of vilifying evidence is not viewed as being misrepresentative of the real risks to cat carers. Most indoor cats and the vast majority of responsible cat owners will never contract any of these diseases. However, dense congregations (known as clowders) of outdoor cats represent significant health risks to humans and wildlife, unimaginable only a generation ago.

Chapter 7

I WAS CRUEL ONCE TOO

You kill my dog, you better hide your cat. Muhammad Ali

I did not grow up with strong feelings towards cats. Largely by chance, we were a dog family and never owned a cat. Cats were like swimming pools, orange trees or outside incinerators. Some houses had them, others did not, and it didn't really concern me either way.

The first time I harboured strong feelings towards cats was at our family farm in the South East, in South Australia. To a trained ecologist the farm was an ecological desert of black clay, the sorry remnants of a once-thriving swamp 'reclaimed' for agriculture by a series of drains. But despite its lack of wild habitats and animals, to a young kid the farm was an exciting new world.

As an eight-year-old it was not the colour of the soil, the hay carting, fence building or shearing that really captivated my imagination, but rather what happened underneath the shearing shed. We had purchased the hobby farm in a dilapidated state and decades of sheep manure had piled up under the slatted floor of the shed to the point where the sheep waiting to be shorn were slipping around in their accumulated faeces. It was my job, along with older sister Meredith and younger brother Pete, to dig out under the slats to enable the sultana-sized pellets to fall through. As a reward, we bagged the manure, which Dad then drove back to the city where we sold it to neighbouring gardeners. The pocket money was secondary to the hours of fun we had exploring under the shed in tunnels we had 'mined' with rakes and shovels.

We came across 'prehistoric' duck eggs, mummified rabbits, faded eartags and all sorts of broken tools and other treasures. On one occasion, after a couple of months away, a cat shot out of the hatch where we had just started digging. Soon afterwards we heard the plaintive meow of kittens nestled at the terminus of our tunnel. Through the slats we could make out several with barely opened eyes, by far the most exciting find we had made under the shed. Our discovery of course caused great excitement and by chance the visiting neighbour's sons were outside and came running to see what was going on. What followed was the country boys giving us city kids a shock introduction to farm life.

The boys, a few years older than us, quickly took charge of the situation. Rather than seeing the kittens as amazing treasures, we were told they were 'stinkin' spittin' little shits' as the boys attacked them with sticks and wire through the slats. When they had finished they stood up proudly and excitedly pronounced what they would do to the mother if they got their hands on her.

Along with my terrified siblings, I was shocked, stunned and speechless. I had never witnessed such bloodthirsty cruelty, and couldn't stop thinking how the poor mother would feel when she returned to find her impaled kittens. When the boys' father deftly cut the throat of the sheep he was butchering it was at least quick and had a purpose, but his boys were just cruel.

I had been cruel too. My earliest memories are from a pivotal experience in my life that occurred at the ripe old age of three. I was playing under the steps of our house while Mum was doing the washing in the laundry next door. 'Doing the washing' back then took most of the morning, loading clothes and my baby brother's nappies into the old blue tub to wash, squeezing them through the corroded ringer on top, transferring them to the sink for rinsing, then loading them in the spin drier as cascades of water covered the concrete floor. Mum would then hang that load out on the line and start on the next, maybe Dad's business shirts and her tennis dress.

Mum's laundry labours were not what entertained me as a young lad, exploring under the stairs was far more captivating. One morning I picked up a daddy-long-legs spider and held it fearlessly while pulling off one of its improbably long legs. I was surprised the spider did not make a noise and no blood came out. I did it again and again, eight times in all, until I had reduced the hapless spider into a limbless ball, rolling haplessly in my palm. Just then Mum emerged from the laundry. She dropped her basket of wet washing with a crash and fixed me with one of those looks that meant trouble; a look I still remember many decades later. 'What do you think you are doing to that poor daddy-long-legs?' she said. 'I can't believe you could be such a cruel, nasty little boy! How would you like it if someone pulled off all of your legs?'

Remorse and shame are not in the vocabulary of three-year-olds but these two emotions swamped me. I silently vowed I would make it up to Mr Daddy-long-legs' friends and spent much of the next week out in the garden catching bugs and throwing them into the spiderwebs under the stairs.

My role of provider then spread to other spiders, which I fattened in my bug catcher, and to the snails I rescued from winter nights on our front lawn. Mum still relates the story of how she was horrified one morning to find me asleep, covered in green slimy mucous from a handful of snails I had tucked into my pyjama pocket. I had felt sorry for them out in the cold.

When I started school I took this newfound compassion for small animals with me. On hearing the school was planning to spray spiders under the eaves I hatched a plan. At recess and lunchtime I snuck around outside the classrooms searching for spiders. Black house spiders were not a favourite. They were too sneaky and didn't interact once I had fooled them into dashing out of their silken tunnel by jiggling their web. The much-maligned redbacks, however, were cool. They showed no fear, particularly the large ones with the vivid red slash down their bulbous black bodies. I used to delight in feeding them grasshoppers or flies and watch them bind their prey so they could inflict their deadly bite.

Despite protestations from classmates, the spiders seemed quite unfazed, walking over my hands as I collected them up in my lunchbox and snuck them to safety under the lift-up lid of my school desk. I never found out who dobbed on me, but after school on the second day of my collection Miss Hatzi asked me to stay behind.

'What have you got under your desk?' my mild-mannered and patient teacher asked, suspicious rather than cross.

'I'm saving spiders from the pest exterminators,' I explained, neglecting to tell her they were the potentially deadly redbacks.

Miss Hatzi gave me a look, part 'you can't keep spiders in my classroom', but also 'I understand you are trying to help'. Was I going to be sent to the headmaster's or would my mum be called in? Sensing my building panic Miss Hatzi calmly stated, 'You're not going to get into trouble as long as you take them all out right now.' I learnt more from that interaction than from most of the rest of my schooling. I learnt it's OK, even honourable, to break rules if you have a good reason.

My fascination with animals continued into university where I studied biology, and geology. Although geology parties and field trips were more memorable and jobs easier to come by in the more respected profession, I followed my heart into the developing and fascinating world of animal ecology. One of my first research interests was studying three species of rare firetail finches, largely restricted to small remnants of scrub spared from clearing – the same patches of scrub where David Paton had been documenting the incremental decline of native birds. The exquisite diamond firetail headed his list of species likely to become extinct in the near future.

One such patch of scrub was a belt of mallee eucalypts and heath on a railway reserve adjacent to an Adelaide Hills vineyard. I had strung a series of mist nets in flyways to catch the rare finches moving along the corridor. My favourite bird at this locality, which even eclipsed the boldly patterned and crimson-rumped diamond firetail, was the golden whistler.

The golden whistler is blessed with both brilliant yellow plumage and a melodic call. I was still learning how to distinguish birds by their calls and was particularly challenged by the different whistlers, all of which possessed striking calls. The rufous whistler generally inserted a whip-crack-like 'ee-chow' and I had learnt the Gilbert's whistler's repetitive 'jew wee-jew wee-jew wee-jew'. But the golden whistler's repertoire was not governed by such conventions. Perched on a prominent branch, I watched and listened to them in awe as they sang the most unbridled and imaginative whistles heard in the Australian scrub. A certain spectacular male had thrilled me with his penetrating whistle from a high branch. I wondered whether he was the same bird I had banded several weeks earlier. A couple of hours later I was to find out.

Dangling unceremoniously from the centre of my net, I spotted the unmistakable hue of a golden whistler in his prime. I was concerned he wasn't struggling and sending the fine net into spasms, as recently netted birds typically do. I was alarmed when I spied a black-and-white cat slinking away from the side of the net. Rather than finding the black-edged white throat above his glowing yellow breast I was met with a bloodied mess.

Instinctively I raced after the cat, screaming obscenities and searching for rocks. Hurdling a rusty barbwire fence, I followed the fleeing cat along rows of vines until it disappeared in the direction of the winery's house. Now I was fearful that other cats might be on the prowl. A few days earlier I had seen a tabby cat nearby chewing on a juvenile red-bellied black snake. Although I felt sorry for the beautiful reptile my feelings were nowhere near as strong as my current remorse since I had contributed to the cat-inflicted death of the whistler. For once I was relieved the other nets were empty and I quickly furled them to prevent further losses. The whistler's stiff body displayed the silver metal band I had placed there weeks ago and a pathetic scatter of black, white and yellow feathers littered the net and moss-covered sand below.

Not since my daddy-long-legs incident 16 years earlier had I felt such remorse. But this time I had a scapegoat: a sleek house cat from a rural winery. Just as a university course had alerted Grant Sizemore to the damage to wildlife inflicted by his pet cat, this epiphany in the scrub had shone a spotlight on an emerging issue. Weeks earlier, my honours zoology supervisor, David Paton, had informed his class about the tally of cat-killed birds he had started compiling from his ground-breaking survey of Adelaide cat owners. At the time, Paton had yet to place the cat-killed bird deaths in the context of their regional population declines. Now I assisted Paton review his survey data, and contributed information from my own survey into household cat predation on the threatened pygmy copperhead snake I was also studying. These little snakes clinging to a tiny distribution in the Adelaide Hills were, like Paton's honeyeaters and finches, falling victim to pet cats as houses encroached upon their dwindling habitats.

Around this time, another South Australian was making a public and provocative stance against irresponsible cat owners. Dr John Wamsley had turned a degraded farm in the Adelaide Hills into a bourgeoning wildlife sanctuary by erecting one of the world's first cat-proof fences.

The former mathematics lecturer was to go on and win accolades, such as the Prime Minister's Environmentalist of the Year Award in 2003. His conservation organisation was to be listed on the stock exchange by placing a dollar value on the threatened wildlife he was reintroducing and breeding in spectacular numbers. But back in the late 1980s, when I was coincidently studying other rare finches in his first Warrawong sanctuary, Wamsley's message was simple. We need to make a choice between free-ranging cats and wildlife. There was no middle ground. Famously, when his opinion on desexing and releasing unowned cats was sought, Wamsley replied, 'They are eating our animals, not having sex with them!'

While I researched the effect of cats, Wamsley waged war. Ever ready to promote his mission, the outspoken and controversial environmentalist guaranteed his public appearances would grab headlines by wearing a hat fashioned from a feral cat pelt. He attacked legislators and opponents head on, alienating many bureaucrats and animal liberation advocates but nevertheless helping to change laws, enabling him to shoot cats, collared or otherwise, that strayed onto his sanctuaries. Wamsley went to great pains to deliberately embarrass the authorities by claiming, with some validity, that his conservation efforts were far more successful and better value for money than the National Parks were achieving by 'pussy-footing' around the feral cat issue.

Wamsley's no-frills but patently successful approach informed and mobilised thousands of passionate supporters, who volunteered their time and savings to his ambitious conservation exploits. Wamsley also revelled in challenging and antagonising his opponents. I remember overhearing the outspoken wildlife advocate engaging in a serious debate with a local cat owner, while I was nearby, peering through my binoculars at colour-banded finches. The increasingly indignant cat owner was adamant that no neighbour, even if they managed a wildlife sanctuary, had the right to kill his cat if it was hunting on his neighbour's land.

'Its just nature,' the cat owner reasoned, hoping the argumentative nature-lover would see the error of his ways. Wamsley's response was gold. He took a breath, calmed down, and told a story.

An elderly couple had been astounded at the industriousness of their young neighbour. For most of the day they had been watching young Johnny doggedly digging a deep hole in his backyard. Eventually their curiosity got the better of them and they leaned over the fence and enquired why he was digging a hole.

'I'm burying my goldfish,' came the response.

'That's a very big hole for a goldfish,' the neighbour said, still intrigued by the solemn demeanour of the normally bright young kid.

The boy looked up at last, with tears in his eyes. 'That's because it's inside your bloody cat!'

For the first time, the public thrilled at the profusion of bandi-coots and bettongs they could view as a result of simply excluding cats and foxes. While Wamsley drew the ire of those who believed pet cats should be allowed to roam and hunt as they pleased, I continued to accumulate evidence on the impact of cats and how best to address it.

Through nearly three decades of research I came to understand the extent of the damage caused by uncontained cats in environments around the world. At the same time, I came to appreciate how cats captivated people in powerful and apparently contradictory ways. Striving for the elusive nexus between appropriate management of free-ranging cats and sympathy for the deep-felt emotions of cat fanciers became an obsession, and the motivation for writing this book. And in spite of consulting and interviewing hundreds of stakeholders from dozens of countries, perhaps the most enlightening perspectives came from within my own home. Katherine, my headstrong and intelligent wife, negotiated this impasse more confidently than most.

Chapter 8

CATASTROPHIC CATS

Cats can be dangerous too; it depends where they are.
Marilyn Monroe

Today I was her field assistant. The task sounded simple and the distances between adjacent cameras seemed insignificant on the compressed display of my GPS. But the task was anything but straightforward. The Flinders Ranges are the most rugged mountains in South Australia and Katherine's study site occupied the most challenging terrain in the park.

With a backpack bulging with remote-activated cameras I was following my GPS to predetermined locations about a kilometre apart. Loose shale slipped under my boots as I scrambled up 60-degree slopes, often sending me sliding back down, losing metres of elevation and skin in the process. Dense stands of pine trees, which had grown en masse 50 years ago when an introduced rabbit virus temporarily protected them from intensive browsing, blocked my path. Gaps between the trees were booby trapped by golden orb spiderwebs so strong that they pulled off my hat as I pushed through. A straight line linking successive camera sites on my handheld navigation device belied the fact that I had to walk at least twice that distance dodging cliffs and impenetrable pine groves. When I reached the destination preselected by Katherine on her aerial photograph, I was to search for the best site to install a camera to detect feral cats and also quolls, or marsupial cats.

Both were more likely in clearings in wooded areas, maybe dry creek beds or around rabbit warrens that provided them with shelter and prey. I looked for a sturdy pine or eucalypt to strap the camera at the eye height of my targets.

Although my planned pick-up was in three hours, it soon became obvious I would need far longer to complete the job. Each time I summitted a hill I would try to contact Katherine on my radio, but she too was setting cameras along another transect out of range. All day while I sweated up and down those hills, thighs burning like a King of the Mountain cyclist, I thought about Katherine's quoll project and the technical and moral challenges that it presented her. That evening, when we had both finally finished setting the cameras, Katherine described again the day a year earlier when these challenges were best exemplified.

She was only a five-minute walk from the Wilpena Pound Resort and campground, used as a base for thousands of local and international tourists exploring the geological masterpiece of the Flinders Ranges National Park. With two cage traps strapped to her back, Katherine periodically swung her radio-tracker aerial from side to side, confirming the strongest beeps were in the direction she was walking. Three paces behind and also hauling cage traps was Katherine's intern Charlotte, who had confirmed Kojo the collared quoll's location that morning from the air. Flying a grid pattern in a light aircraft typically used for scenic flights over the peaks of Wilpena Pound, Charlotte had detected Kojo's location.

Once integral components of the regional ecology, these plucky marsupial predators would tackle any small mammal, bird or reptile their size or smaller. Quolls, or *idnya* in the Adnyamathanha language, were also integral to the local Aboriginal Dreamtime stories. According to this legend, their distinctive white spots on their pelt originated from spear wounds after the ancestral unspotted quoll secretly eloped with a goanna and was followed and attacked by the Adnyamathanha Elders in retribution. But until 2014, no white-spotted marsupials had been seen in the Wilpena area since the 1880s, having been wiped out by cats and foxes soon after European settlement.

Katherine thrived on this exciting and applied work. Kojo was one of the 21 female and 20 male western quolls that her team had reintroduced to Wilpena. Today was to be even more exciting than confirming the survival of these pioneering marsupial carnivores, which had captured the attention of the local Aboriginal and conservation communities. It was late June and Katherine suspected that Kojo might have pouch young. The first local quoll pouch young had been confirmed, with great excitement, just a few weeks earlier.

Mostly Katherine was relieved that the radio receiver was not sounding the dreaded slow beep that indicated the collar had entered a stationary, or mortality, mode. In the three months since they had been flown 2000 kilometres from their last stronghold in the forests of south-western Western Australia, nearly a third of the reintroduced quolls had been found killed.

With the exception of one clumsy quoll that apparently fell to its death off a cliff, all other losses had been predated by cats that Katherine and her team were almost powerless to prevent. Breeding female quolls suggested that the habitat and food available in the release area were suitable but, more importantly, they were the only solution to the ongoing cat carnage. The trail-blazing quolls needed to breed faster than they were predated. Kojo was one of the pioneers that Katherine hoped would enable this reintroduction to succeed.

None of the reintroduced quoll mortalities in the Flinders Ranges of South Australia were attributed to foxes. This attested to the success of the regional Bounceback baiting program, which distributed thousands of poison fox baits over 5500 sq km each year for two-and-a-half decades. Foxes were the most serious predator of the threatened yellow-footed rock wallaby which, like the quolls, have benefited greatly from regional baiting.

Radio tracking 41 quolls over three months had enabled Katherine to predict their daytime refuges, usually under rock ledges or in rabbit warrens, occasionally in the hollows or fallen logs of a eucalypt tree. As the radio-transmitter beeps became louder, indicating the quoll was nearby, Katherine felt a strange sense of unease. She was approaching the foot slopes of the Heysen Range with no known logs or warrens for refuge. Katherine did not expect to find Kojo among the low brush in daylight. A healthy mother quoll should be safely tucked away in her shelter.

Then she saw a cat. Still scanning for Kojo's signal, Katherine noticed a large grey tabby slinking away from the direction of the transmitter beeps. Her heart sank. Even though the transmitter signal suggested Kojo was still alive Katherine feared the worst. Eight days earlier, the bloody carcass of Narelle, another pioneering female quoll, had been found a kilometre away; Zamia had been killed by a cat in the same region. Katherine feared the tabby was a serial killer. Despite sending in expert cat shooters, laying special cat baits, and setting dozens of baited cage traps, the quoll killer had not been caught. The previous month a spate of three quoll kills in the same area within a week was only arrested after a five-kilogram male cat was shot.

Sure enough, within a couple of minutes the radio tracker led Katherine to a white-spotted carcass, semi-concealed under a small bush. Her heart sank as she bent down to the bloodied quoll and counted two-and-a-half jelly-beaned sized juveniles in her half-eaten pouch. Engorged nipples indicated that there would have been six of these juveniles only minutes earlier. So fresh was the kill that Kojo was still warm, her soft under parts, including part of the pouch, already eaten. Distressingly, the two remaining young were still grasping tenaciously to the teats of their lifeless mother.

After a second or two of horror and near despondency, Katherine clicked into conservation scientist mode. By now she had perfected the routine. Charlotte was dispatched back to the field base to collect a large cage trap and fresh rabbit-meat bait. The cages she carried on her back were too small to trap the large cat. The accomplished quoll killer would also turn its nose up at the semi-rotten meat she carried as prized bait for the scavenging quolls. Katherine photographed Kojo and swabbed her collar and fur for DNA. Subsequent analysis could indicate whether saliva left on the carcass at the kill site (usually on the neck or collar) originated from the same cat as other quoll kills, or captured cats.

Charlotte returned puffing after lugging the large wire cage up the hill from her car, and the trap with fresh bait was placed carefully under the bush where Kojo had been found. Katherine suspected the cat, which seemed to have developed a taste for her rapidly diminishing cohort of pioneering quolls, would return. The reintroduction was now on a knife edge, with nine of the quolls, including five precious females, killed by feral cats in the first three months.

Three hours later, just before dark, Katherine and Charlotte followed their GPS back to the kill site. Climbing up the hill they noticed that the door of the trap was closed. Katherine held her breath. As soon as she peeled back the hessian bag cover Katherine knew she had her quarry. Crouched in the back of the trap, the large grey tabby spat at the biologists. Katherine recollects the bittersweet emotions at the time.

'It was an incredible relief to have captured the cat that killed Kojo, and we later confirmed Zamia,' she recounted. 'It was also rewarding to have used my experience as a field biologist to outsmart the cat, because feral cats, especially old and experienced hunters like this one, can be incredibly difficult to catch.'

Zamia (pictured), one of at least 20 quolls (idnya) reintroduced to the Ikara Flinders Ranges National Park that were killed by 'catastrophic' feral cats. (Photo: Mel Jensen)

But Katherine also felt empathy for her captive. She considered its spitting and hissing as signs of distress and fear, rather than aggression. Killing cats was the aspect of her work she found most confronting. Katherine had always kept cats as a child and loved them unconditionally. They had intrigued and inspired her, even more so than her pet dog, guinea pigs, rabbits, cockies, mice or rats.

'They are not like other pets,' Katherine explained to me once, when I questioned her on her special affinity to cats. 'Dogs are loyal, attentive and forgiving. They are easy to understand and love but maybe a little two-dimensional. Cats are more aloof and self-reliant. You need to earn their love. Because a cat chooses whether to show you affection, rather than being hardwired to do so like a dog, winning over the affection of a cat is a challenge.' To this day, whenever she encounters an unfamiliar pet cat at someone's home Katherine strives to befriend it, to break through its inherent aloofness.

'It probably sounds weird,' Katherine conceded, 'but I really like cats. They are amazingly adaptable and interesting to study. But that doesn't mean I accept them as wildlife. I don't think we should sit back and let our native species become extinct because we brought cats to Australia. We have a moral obligation to protect our unique wildlife.'

She quickly covered the cage with hessian to calm the terrified creature and carried it back to the park rangers' quarters. Arthur, the on-duty ranger, was eating dinner when Katherine returned but he responded promptly to her request for him to shoot the cat immediately to lessen its distress.

While Arthur returned to his dinner, Katherine pulled the lifeless cat from the cage. First she weighed and measured it, including the distance between its two top canines for comparison with the puncture wounds or marks on collars of killed quolls. Next an ear biopsy was taken and preserved in alcohol. If this sample matched the DNA swab taken from Kojo's fur and collar it would confirm that she had caught her quoll killer. Then Katherine cut through the belly fur of her 4.1 kg cat to expose its stomach. Sure enough, she retrieved freshly chewed dark pink meat tinged with the unmistakable rufous orange hair with white spots of a quoll.

As she later described finding quoll remains in the stomach of the dead cat I felt empathy, and an unexpected tang of jealousy. For many years I had been dissecting the stomachs of feral cats that hunters had shot in Australian deserts. The numbers of animals that a cat could eat in a single night blew me away. My record was a black cat shot more than 40 kilometres from the nearest town with a staggering 32 freshly killed lizards plus a zebra finch and a

This 3.8 kg female feral cat, dissected by the author in the Australian desert, contained the undigested remains of three central bearded dragon, two earless dragons, three striped skinks, a mouse, zebra finch and a whopping 24 painted dragons. Until a cat was dissected in New Zealand with 49 skinks in its stomach this 'black devil' held the record for the greatest number of vertebrates known to be killed by a cat in a single day. (Photo: J. Read)

mouse in its stomach. This haul represented the hunting success of the cat over just the previous day and night, because none of the animals were digested.

> Feral cat numbers in Australia probably vary from 2.1 million cats after droughts or rabbit disease, to 6.3 million after wet years. Based on these figures, scientists now estimate in an average year that cats kill 650 million reptiles and 377 million birds in Australia.

This cat, nicknamed the 'black devil' for its catastrophic carnage, was an exception. Most cats I dissected had less than eight prey items in their stomach; many were empty-bellied and hungry when they had been shot, trapped or inadvertently run over. Every time I encountered a road kill or a shot cat I recorded the number and type of prey in their stomachs and eventually amassed an inventory from thousands of feral cats. Hugh McGregor, who worked with me in the desert before conducting his doctorate on feral cat ecology in the northern savannahs of Western Australia, used a more high-tech method to calculate cats' impact. By fitting small video cameras on their radio-collars, McGregor was able to observe and calculate their hunting prowess. The 13 feral cats he monitored killed on average seven prey a day, but only ate five of these. Tallying McGregor's findings, my stomach samples and cats seen by spotlight, I calculated that each year feral cats killed approximately 700 reptiles, 150 birds and 50 mammals in every square kilometre of the desert.

Although most of the prey items were common species, very occasionally I would find unexpected prey, like a cockatoo, duck or python in a cat's stomach, or the chewed remains of a lizard or native mouse species not even known in the region. A mate had recently rediscovered a presumed extinct lizard in the stomach of a road-killed snake he encountered. One day I too hoped that I would discover a hitherto undescribed or presumed extinct animal in the belly of a feral cat and I seldom let the opportunity to dissect a dead cat pass, no matter how smelly it was. Now Katherine, who doesn't typically share my passion for dissecting dead cats, had recorded a prey item that I had not even considered feasible only months earlier.

Later DNA analyses matched this cat with the deaths of both Kojo and Zamia. Although the DNA was inconclusive, Katherine strongly suspects the same cat also killed Narelle, because of the proximity of the kills. This tabby grey male became known as Cat 3, the third in the sequence of multiple quoll killers that earned the infamous title of 'Catastrophic Cats'. Close monitoring of the Wilpena quoll kills provided unequivocal evidence that individual cats can be responsible for disproportionately large numbers of kills of threatened species. These results support previous anecdotes of catastrophic predation events. Entire colonies of delicate rufous-hare wallabies in Central Australia were exterminated by a single large cat that learnt to hunt them. Such catastrophic predation by individual cats has also been recorded by researchers studying the demise of kākāpō parrots in New Zealand, rock wallabies in Queensland, and large seabirds in Japan.

Many small mammal and bird reintroductions fail, especially those at sites around the globe not protected inside predator-proof fences, like those John Wamsley pioneered. Katherine had experienced this firsthand during her doctoral studies on reintroducing threatened mammals, when attempt after attempt with increasingly sophisticated techniques were thwarted by

One individual cat on Dassen Island off the coast of South Africa was believed to kill more than 50 terns in only three months. Not surprisingly, researchers found that removing just a single cat from another sooty tern nesting colony in the Mozambique Channel, where 400 terns were killed by 10 cats each week during nesting season, lowered short-term predation 10-fold. Evidence like this supported Katherine's obsession in removing the culprit catastrophic cats that were slaughtering her quolls.

feral cat predation. Yet she embraced the extra challenge of the unfenced quoll reintroduction at Wilpena. Katherine respected the Adnyamathanha spiritual ties to *idnya* and appreciated that quolls provided the most likely control option for feral rabbits that threatened vegetation in the park, especially after baiting had eradicated foxes. Former Wilpena ranger turned pest-management scientist and quoll enthusiast Dave Peacock, who had instigated the quoll reintroduction, had cited sustainable rabbit control as one of the key motivations to leverage support for bringing his favourite feisty marsupials to the Ranges.

But Katherine had other motivations, citing her appreciation for nature and her joy at helping recreate natural environments to explain her desire to embrace the quoll reintroduction and the control of cats. Despite a determination to remove the killer cats to safeguard her pioneering quolls, Katherine was keen to implement non-lethal control methods wherever possible.

Although she laments that cats are sometimes blamed unnecessarily for wildlife decline, Katherine concedes that cats are more efficient hunters of our threatened native species in areas where the land has been extensively overgrazed, cleared or burnt. Such land degradation also prevents many of our wildlife from breeding at high enough rates to offset predation. Katherine advocates improving vegetation cover and productivity – and better control of rabbits that sustain high feral cat populations.

But her quolls couldn't wait for farmers to place a greater emphasis on the condition of their country or for the politically expedient managers of national parks to stop displaying plagues of kangaroos for the benefit of international tourists and restore a more natural balance for all species. For the time being, her little spotty quolls were totally dependent upon painstaking and persistent control of feral cats.

Chapter 9

SOMEONE ELSE NEEDS TO SOLVE MY PROBLEM

Dogs live with you, cats board with you. Pam Brown

With a flurry of urgent yet inefficient wing beats, the small bird erupted, quail-like, from the path in front of me. Veering off toward the sun, it was impossible to make out colours or distinguishing markings. Just as I leapt into a clearing for a better view, the panicked bird dropped like a stone into the undergrowth. A barred hawk was gliding past but too high to present an immediate threat to the small bird. At last a bird I recognised! I made a mental note to add Pacific baza to my Simbo Island bird inventory. I looked back to Katherine who at least had time to raise her binoculars to her eyes but had no better luck identifying the small bird. For over a month now in the South Pacific Solomon Islands we had experienced the challenge and frustration of being in a country with no field guide for birds, or other critters for that matter. Before long we needed neither a field guide to identify the ungainly bird, nor to determine whether the bazas or ospreys flying overhead represented its major threat.

We were walking near the tail of a procession of over a hundred locals carrying plastic buckets of every hue. Our colourful parade snaked away from a small natural harbour cluttered with dugout wooden canoes and a collection of multi-coloured fibreglass canoes. Together with the rest of the convoy we had dragged our canoe, uniquely emblazoned with a stencilled panda, along the edge of a blue lagoon. Steam rose from one section of the water and the stench of sulphur wafted on warm gusts.

This procession was no Sunday school picnic. We had been invited, as feral cat researchers, to the opening of the megapode-egg harvesting season on Simbo Island. Ascending the Ove hill, the vegetation became sparser and the air thicker with the stench of volcanic sulphur. Gradually the locals with their bright buckets peeled off the line and headed to their private leaf shelters. The low inclined roofs of sago palm were not tall enough for even large kids but apparently they make perfect nesting sites for the Melanesian incubator bird, or megapode, as it was widely known.

Like other incubator birds, megapodes rely on environmental temperature rather than their own body heat to incubate their eggs. Known as lape, pronounced *larpay* by the locals, the megapodes on Simbo, a series of active and inactive volcanic vents emerging from the Pacific Ocean, enjoyed arguably the perfect incubation conditions. Black sand, warmed by volcanic gasses percolating up through the active Ove volcano, provided ideal temperatures, and the low shelters, somewhat extravagantly called 'lape houses', shielded the nesting birds from aerial predators while they dug their egg-laying chamber. The price the small chicken-like birds had to pay for such optimal conditions was that their large off-white eggs had been harvested by generations of Simbo residents. Like the ultimate free-range chickens that required neither feeding nor husbandry, megapodes laid eggs with a size and richness that embarrassed domestic chooks.

In 1844, the trader Captain Cheyne visited Simbo to collect turtle shell and *bêche-de-mer*, or sea cucumbers. Just days before he arrived, natives returning from a headhunting sortie yielding 93 heads had proudly displayed them to the visiting captain. Along with their apparent headhunting skills, Cheyne and other traders commented on the megapode eggs, reliably harvested by Simbo residents from palm-roofed shelters. An easy and reliable industry was established.

However, for several decades the lape egg harvest had been declining, to the detriment of the local diet and economy. The family of our guide Posala had approached World Wildlife Fund (WWF), as they were still known at the time, to help them manage the dwindling numbers of lape. The coordinated harvest that we were now witnessing was one of the outcomes of the international conservation organisation's intervention. Ornithologist Ross Sinclair studied the Simbo megapode population for WWF, and identified what Posala and his fellow villagers probably already knew. So many eggs were being harvested that not enough chicks were hatching to maintain megapode populations.

The evening before the official season opening, we had joined the community in the Nusa Simbo village to pay homage to their most important bird and provider. With the cadence and tone of a Sunday school choir, four generations of Nusa Simbo residents harmonised a heartfelt song in their distinctive language. Only when local WWF employee Lorima Tuke translated the song did its full relevance and irony become apparent, especially the stanza:

> *Even though we don't help you, we say sorry.*
> *We should help provide your food*
> *Please forgive us because you are still our friend,*
> *Even though you fly away upset when we come.*

This song elegantly encapsulates the shallowness of the symbiosis between Nusa Simbo locals and their main source of income. Residents understood the value of the lape to their livelihoods and culture and acknowledged their responsibilities to the bird. Yet apart from singing sorry at the commencement of their egg-raiding season, the locals were not moved to help the birds.

Within minutes of arriving at the lape house owned by Posala's family, I had been handed a kicking slimy chick. 'Tunilagi,' Posala announced proudly. 'Picanniny blong lape.' The hatchling megapode, extracted fully formed from a harvested egg, exhibited the outsized feet from which their common name is derived.

With a hint of reluctance, Posala agreed that I could release the chick into a small patch of regrowth forest near his lape house. Despite its feet having never touched the ground, the quail-sized bird scrabbled off into the undergrowth, and I recognised the species we had flushed when scrambling up the hill half an hour earlier. Within minutes I realised why Posala had been reluctant for me to release the chick. His young niece was eagerly devouring a freshly extracted slimy chick, vigorously sucking off the meat and feathers while gripping the mighty feet. Even fully formed, pre-hatched *tunilagi* were a delicacy for the Simbo locals and this girl would not have tasted her favourite food for at least two months.

Along with the unsustainable harvest, ornithologist Sinclair suggested that the residents of Nusa Simbo dramatically reduce their cat population to limit predation on the rare chicks that did hatch. For reasons that were soon to become apparent, cat control had not been implemented during previous closed seasons but the village organisers and local WWF staff were eager that we should assist. We had been stumbling for several months through coral reef and logging assessments as volunteers for WWF, feeling a bit out of our league. The Simbo project piqued my interest because I felt I could contribute to this applied cat management problem. Katherine, as you now understand, was more confounded. Although relishing the travel and experiences she was not keen on confronting the emotional challenge of killing cats on her honeymoon.

After the excitement of the harvest day we assumed the villagers would be queuing up to help us help them control their cat numbers and guarantee their future harvests. Not so. The village was a scene of tranquil South Seas idleness. Lads wearing faded Bob Marley T-shirts listened to incessantly repeated lollypop music in the shade of coconut palms. Adults, many of whom we had met at the harvest, seemed either too shy to engage us in conversation or were reluctant to discuss their cat issue. With more spare time than I am accustomed to and no one willing to engage with us, Katherine and I found ourselves sitting on the verandah of Posala's family house, watching the sleepy village life.

Pawpaw trees were a feature of most gardens and a welcome diversion from the staple potatoes, taro and rice that formed the mainstay of our diet. The mature pawpaw fruits resemble pendulous breasts, which presumably was the inspiration for one of their early names, 'mummy-apples'. My attention was caught by a barely weaned naked infant staring up at a pawpaw tree with particularly large fruit. He tottered over to the trunk, embraced it and began to shimmy up the tree. To my surprise, the child ignored the fruit, reaching instead to hack off a pawpaw leaf with a knife he had been carrying in his teeth. Sliding back down the trunk, the boy pursed his lips and blew into the hollow leaf stalk. Reminiscent of the vuvuzela played by South African spectators at the 2010 FIFA World Cup, the lad tottered around the village blowing his leaf bugle like a little town crier.

When Posala returned I suggested that we use the boy to drum up attention or support for the cat project. But our guide had other ideas. Despite overtures from their chiefs to deal with the cat predation, Posala was well aware that most residents considered the management of cats to be someone else's problem. He encouraged us to visit the hub of the village social and administrative scene to drum up support.

After the second blow of the conch shell I donned my best field clothes and we joined other barefoot villagers making their way to church in their Sunday best. I was to sit on the floor on the right side of the church while Katherine sat with the women on the left. After a couple of hours of fire and brimstone sermons punctuated by harmonious unaccompanied singing, I was unsure what our attendance had achieved. But Posala assured me the congregation were now informed and supportive of our visit.

Posala encouraged us to visit every hut in the village, asking residents to bring us stray cats lurking near their houses or 'surplus' pet cats that we could painlessly put down with an injection. Before we had departed the provincial capital of Gizo, Posala had sourced euthatal, a euthanasia drug widely used by vets. I asked Posala why the informed and concerned residents wouldn't simply bring him the surplus cats that they could not look after. It was better if we explained the situation to his people ourselves, Posala said. 'They will believe and trust you, not me.'

From hut to hut, we went, explaining that wandering cats were limiting the lape numbers and affecting their egg harvests. We reminded them that village elders had asked that they assist in reducing cat numbers by bringing us surplus cats for a quick and painless injection. Some householders confidently stated that they had two or three cats but others would admit, '*Me no savvy,*' when asked how many cats they owned. They did not mind if their cats were trapped at the lape houses but they did not want to be directly implicated in their deaths by assisting with more humane control methods. I noted at one household a dishevelled island pigeon sitting on a rail, a leg and wing poking out awkwardly. 'What happened to this poor bird?', I enquired naively. 'Nothing is wrong, we break its wing to stop it flying away.'

None of the Simbo locals we met could be described as devoted pet owners. They seemed to like having dogs or cats, even deliberately maimed wild birds around, but showed little concern for their welfare. This insouciance was compromising our ability to reduce their cat numbers.

In a day of canvassing the village with Posala, his assistant Si and other members of the local Lape Management team, only a handful of cats had been handed over for euthanasia. Echoing sentiments heard in our own society, one of the most common reasons provided for not surrendering cats was: 'My cat does not eat *tunilagi.*' When Posala explained, yet again, that the multitude of cats was threatening the egg harvest he was invariably informed that it must be someone else's cat causing the problem. Had the chorus of the lape song been composed following Sinclair's work the Simbo megapode egg harvesters could well have included the lines, 'We should stop our cats from killing all of your young, but really we will do nothing about it but say sorry again next year'.

Due to the reluctance of their community to cooperate, Posala and Si tracked down cat traps left after Sinclair's study and set them near the lape houses. The following morning, Katherine and I carried all the euthanased cats to a wave-cut coastal platform

Self-denial of the impacts of their own cats is not restricted to Solomon Islanders. Only 9% of respondents to Nils Peterson's US-wide survey of clowder feeders believed feral cats harmed bird populations. Likewise, a University of Exeter study in a village in Cornwall and one in Scotland found most cat owners failed to perceive the magnitude of their cats impact on wildlife, and were not influenced by ecological information.

just outside the village. Among a throng of spellbound children I dissected the cats. Each time I opened a stomach I spread the contents in my hand and showed the apprehensive, yet captivated, kids. '*Tunilagi!*' they exclaimed in unison as they made out the distinctive chicken-like feet and grey-brown feathers of hatchling megapodes.

As I cut into the next cat, Katherine stressed to the crowd in Pijin, '*Pussycat algetta garem tunilagi blong belly,*' – all the cats had been eating baby megapodes. '*Dispella pussycat very bad lo tunilagi,*' the kids acknowledged. Off they raced, telling their older siblings stories about the cats that had all eaten *tunilagi*. After that, in addition to trapped cats, the inspired kids volunteered several more semi-tame cats for euthanasia.

The penultimate day of our four-day session was my last spent dissecting. Again the results were damning. Every cat, whether brought to us from houses or trapped near the lape houses, contained *tunilagi*. Posala, Si and other locals acknowledged the damage inflicted by the cats as Katherine recorded the disastrous toll. The proud cat retrievers were photographed with their quarry before I turfed the carcasses into the angry Solomon Sea. There was no other land in sight and I felt sure the sharks, revered in Simbo custom, would welcome these sacrificial gifts.

Next morning, feeling sceptical of the long-term impact of our assistance, we prepared to leave Nusa Simbo. Just as we carefully placed our bags in the unstable canoe, a commotion erupted on the outskirts of the village. Three waterlogged cat carcasses were floating into the sheltered village waterfront, uneaten by sharks, crocodiles, or ripped apart by giant tuna. It seemed that even the predators and scavengers around this island needed to be coerced into action. We boarded the small canoe, dodging the carcasses, and another we encountered out to sea.

> Nusa Simbo was not the only place where cats cause economic losses to 'poultry'. On a farm two kilometres east of Corralillo in Cuba, Carlos Ortiz Ruiz documented a single feral cat killing 46 of his 52 chickens in four nights in July 2014 before the cat was killed on the fifth night.

Our Nusa Simbo cat management experience had been informative and enlightening, but thoroughly unrewarding. Even as we left we spotted several unloved cats slinking along the shore; there must have been dozens, maybe even hundreds, left to prey on megapode chicks. Two years later, we learned that the megapode egg harvest had declined further but no one was addressing the number of cats.

The Nusa Simbo community had more access to biological researchers and resource management planning than most villages in developing countries. Historically these traders have had a greater familiarity with the value of money and resources than their neighbouring islanders. Cats were not revered spiritually or cherished as companion animals. Even though cats threatened the very existence of their economy they were tolerated; demonstrating the damage inflicted and providing the means to control them, made no difference to the villagers; they were unable to motivate themselves to manage the problem. So what hope is there for other communities less educated and with less to gain from managing cats? My ecological travels in the tropics provided plenty of opportunities to find out.

One of the most exciting projects I have been involved with was the compilation of a wildlife inventory for a recently proclaimed wildlife reserve on traditionally owned lands in the New Guinea rainforest. By walking the scarcely discernible jungle paths of the Kau Wildlife Area near Madang at night with my local guide, I caught the mighty Amethystine, Papuan and D'Albertis pythons on consecutive nights. Within a couple of weeks we had found bizarre red-eyed crocodile skinks, spectacular green tree pythons, and a host of brilliant birds and butterflies that my host tribe hoped would attract fee-paying wildlife enthusiasts to their reserve. I also got to know my guide Aisaya and learn about his life in the jungle though many hilarious Pijin conversations, including an explanation of how bachelors and fathers calculated bride price, paid in pigs. Bride price aside, one of our most informative discussions centred on cats.

Aisaya's grandfather had never seen a cat but by the time of my visit they were commonplace in villages, and often seen in the forest too. Sometimes pig hunters caught wildcats with their dogs and occasionally ate them, but mostly they are tolerated, even welcomed, to keep rat numbers down. The village cats also catch many cuscus and bandicoots; flying foxes are one of their favourite foods. Aisaya conceded that there were few cuscus and bandicoots around the villages now, he had to venture deep into the forest when hunting them.

When I suggested to Aisaya that these cats represented a threat to both his health and his wildlife-viewing tourism income, I was viewed as crazy (as I had been when I had caught the locally feared and highly venomous 'white snake', which turned out to be a very chilled snake). Not only were the recently introduced cats exposing naïve animals to unnatural predation, they were also exposing the villagers to hitherto unknown cat-borne diseases like toxoplasmosis and ringworm.

Twenty years earlier, when cats were being introduced to many New Guinea villages, less than 2% of village residents exhibited antibodies to toxoplasma. However, Gordon Wallace and co-authors reported increasing cat-borne disease risk in New Guinea villages in the *American Journal of Tropical Medicine*. They detected the mind-altering *Toxoplasma* antibody in up to a third of New Guineans living in areas where cats were more numerous. The impacts on these communities, with limited access to medical and psychiatric support, was concerning. Wallace cited a troubling scenario whereby half the Nonama Indians, living a similar lifestyle to Aisaya and his family but in the jungles of Colombia, had been infected by toxoplasmosis.

Several hundred kilometres south-east of Aisaya, I worked with Enoch, a man I briefly adopted as a grandfather, given he was the same age as my grandfather, killed in World War II. Enoch had assisted in the war when he alerted American outposts to the advance of Japanese troops along jungle trails in the far north-west of the Solomon Islands, between Simbo and New Guinea. I met Enoch on his home island of Choiseul. Three times the size of Manhattan Island but with fewer than 25,000 inhabitants, Choiseul was one of the most scarcely populated tropical islands in the world. The proud independent people had their own Lauru

Land Council laws to protect their unique culture and customs. Enoch proudly showed me the island's flag, a multi-coloured striped pattern with an unusual bird motif circled in the centre.

The bird silhouette resembled a stylised stocky cassowary with a prominent backward-pointing knob on its head. I was intrigued. What type of bird was it and why did it have this rear-facing horn, unlike the forward and upward-pointing casque of the cassowary. The bird was a kukuvojo, Enoch said, and indicated with his hand the size of a goose. He also corrected me. The prominent protrusion was not hard like a horn but soft, and he patted his tightly coiled hair for effect.

It turned out that kukuvojo, a bird that Enoch had either seen as a child or heard about from his parents, was the Solomon Islands equivalent of the dodo. Albert Meek, a pioneering British ornithologist, had collected six kukuvojo and one egg in 1904. He named the large ground-dwelling grey-orange bird with striking red legs the Choiseul crested pigeon. Both the peculiar black-and-orange facial skin and the prominent paddle-shaped crest that stuck out behind the kukuvojo's head were distinctive. Meek described them nesting on the ground or low branches on the margins of lowland swamps. Although kukuvojo had coexisted with pigs and dogs for millennia, the introduction of rats and cats coincided with their dramatic demise. In 1927, an expedition to Choiseul by the American Museum of Natural History failed to locate the enigmatic species, although they did encounter several locals who knew of the distinctive pigeon. Since then several other searches, including by the famous ornithologist and author Jared Diamond, failed to locate kukuvojo. The consensus from ornithologists who have studied the bird is that predation by cats was largely responsible for its extinction.

Conservation organisations have been slow to recognise or act on the threats of cats in Melanesia, which is partly excusable given that the over-riding regional environmental issues are destructive and unsustainable logging and fisheries. One lauded and promoted strategy for preserving these spectacular and productive environments has been to encourage small-scale ecotourism as an alternative source of income for villagers lured by the opportunities of quick and easy logging money. WWF, who had coordinated the cat control to protect megapodes on Simbo Island, had assisted another Solomon's village to establish a lodge in lieu of logging their land.

Michi village occupied one of the most spectacular landscapes on Earth. Michi's backdrop is, or at least was, the magnificently forested recently extinct Vangunu volcano, which thrust up into storm clouds most afternoons. A cluster of traditional sago-palm-thatched huts lined the beach and looked out onto Marovo lagoon. Marovo is the largest double-barrier lagoon in the world, a geographic and aesthetic masterpiece, teeming with tropical fish and coral. The Michi community decided to oppose logging and to establish the WWF-supported Vanua Rapita Ecolodge, on an idyllic palm-clad island a 10-minute canoe paddle from the village.

Katherine and I were spellbound. We had the island completely to ourselves, apart from daily visits by local staff who brought fresh smorgasbords of fruit and vegetables from their gardens and fish they had caught from the lagoon. Guided walks through the forest or local gardens on the adjacent larger island were offered but we spent our time snorkelling in the amazing coral and seagrass lagoon and attempting to master the unstable dugout canoe that had been thoughtfully left for us. But there were two downsides to this otherwise sublime ecolodge.

Katherine is not a big fan of cockroaches. Not scurrying across her plate as she is eating, probing their heads into her toothbrush, or darting across her face when she is reading a book. Although she had become accustomed to a few roaches when staying in other villages, the sheer numbers and persistence of the Vanua Rapita beasts really soured the experience for her. Likewise, I'm not a big fan of cats with sores and weeping eyes rubbing against me and whining for food while I eat. Vanua Rapita hosted a scrawny ginger tomcat, our constant companion on the tiny atoll. Even Katherine was not impressed. Like just about every other village cat in Melanesia, our constant companion was on the point of starvation and resorted to scabbing for food whenever the opportunity arose. After a couple of challenging days it dawned on us that our nemeses were linked.

There were very few lizards on the Vanua Rapita atoll and none of the large pale geckoes that lived in most huts we had stayed in throughout the Solomons. We had amused ourselves watching these chunky *Gehyra* geckoes stalking and messily chomping on a range of bugs and spiders. But not on Vanua Rapita, and the prey, especially cockroaches, were out of control. My ginger companion was the most likely reason for the lack of geckoes or skinks and hence the plagues of cockroaches typically eaten by these lizards.

'Oh I knew you would like our cat,' I was told when I queried the cat on the island. When I explained I would have preferred to see more birds and lizards I was fixed with an incredulous and alarmed stare. 'But without the cat you will have rats. The cat is your friend.'

Vanua Rapita, like lodges and farms and houses around the world, had introduced a cat to control one of mankind's most destructive pests. But in doing so the cat had also lessened the eco-experience. Introducing a cat to a tiny island was an easy way to keep rodent numbers down, but was not the only solution. Havilla Ecolodge on the other side of Marovo lagoon stored food in cockroach- and rat-proof cupboards, and threw vegetable waste into the sea each day – as they had done for eons. Havilla had no rats and few cockroaches but did boast a family of geckoes that entertained us in the flicker of the kerosene light at night. On nearby Tetepare Island we had an even better experience.

Tetepare is the largest uninhabited island in the South Pacific and, like Marovo's forests, oscillated between World Heritage nomination and the threat of unscrupulous logging. In response, the Tetepare landowners established their own ecolodge in the forest. No cats were allowed on Tetepare, nor cane toads, dogs, or chickens. Instead intricately marked and harmless 'sleepy' snakes and brown tree snakes coiled in the rafters of the traditionally constructed leafhouses, waking at night to perform their rodent control duties. Once the initial shock of sharing sleeping quarters with a benign serpent was overcome, we enjoyed the geckoes, and even small microbats and fireflies zooming through our open rooms. The telltale bulge in the snake's belly attested to their ability to keep rat populations down without impacting the geckoes' ability to control bugs like cockroaches.

On a subsequent visit to Vanua Rapita, after I relayed the tale of cat-free ecolodges, I was asked to take away their cat. 'Take it where?' I enquired. 'It does not matter but we don't want it on our island anymore.'

In the same week, Katherine and I were invited to return to Nusa Simbo to kill more cats, two years after our initial visit, because the villagers did not want to control cats themselves. We declined both offers.

Strong, independent, sometimes brutal men, who pragmatically killed turtles, fish and possums, would not entertain the thought of controlling the unowned cats threatening their livelihoods. The parallels with our own society were striking. The first response of many cat owners or even those who have adopted some degree of responsibility for stray cats, is that 'their' cats are not causing problems. When the economic, conservation or health costs of these cats are demonstrated, we typically expect or ask someone else to solve the problem. Few people enjoy killing cats. Rather our default position, once we have accepted that something needs to be done, is to expect someone else to address the problem. Cat shelter staff, council officers, park rangers, veterinarians, even Uncle Billy from the farm, are typically expected to deal with a litter of kittens or a cat no longer desired. Just as most of us outsource the slaughtering of livestock for our meat, we don't want to confront the unfortunate consequences of owning or acquiring free-roaming cats. But unlike the production and supply of meat, which is an established and sometimes lucrative commercial trade, no one benefits directly from non-commercial pest control. Euthanasing cats is a thankless, sometimes even soul-destroying task, especially when the influx of cats seems endless.

Even when cat management is willingly outsourced, views on the desired methods of control are often parochial and intransient. So, just how should the problems of managing unowned cats be addressed? This is the controversial subject of the next chapters.

Chapter 10

TRAP, NEUTER, THEN?

Feeding a cat that is not yours is not caring for it.
Dr Carole Webb, Feline Association of Australia

'Pest control', whether the management of annoying insects or lamb-killing foxes, is typically code for 'killing'. Occasionally large pests are relocated and some nuisance animals are temporarily deterred, but our preferred means of dealing with unwelcomed animals is to destroy them. Around the world, every day, pests are sprayed, baited, shot or trapped in a relentless and sometimes futile attempt to make our lives more comfortable or our farms more productive. It is ironic that some of our most successful pest control activities involve introducing modified fruit fly to stricken orchards, or malarial mosquitoes to mossie-infested swamps. This seemingly perverse technique has also been recently touted as the most efficient way to manage unowned cats.

Sterile Insect Technology has successfully controlled crop pests for many decades through the release of thousands of sterilised males into the pest population. Male flies, rendered sterile by careful radiation therapy, mate with wild females, which lay infertile eggs. If enough sterile males are released at precisely the time the females are looking for a mate, the best part of a whole generation of fruit flies will not breed. With generation times measured in days, successive failed breeding opportunities can rapidly decimate fruit-fly populations. Swamping the fruit flies with libidinous but impotent males is a tried and tested alternative to using chemicals for pest insect control.

Another even more elaborate technique used by pest entomologists also employs randy males, but this time unsterilised. Whatever we feel about the technology, genetic engineering has opened the doors for impressively sophisticated pest control that belonged in the realm of science fiction only decades ago. Researchers Anthony James from the University of California and Luke Alphey from the Pirbright Institute in the UK have identified the genetic switch responsible for flight development in female mosquitoes. It is the female *Aedes aegypti* mosquito that bites humans and spreads dengue fever to tens of millions of sufferers worldwide. Exactly how flight development in females was identified as being different from males, and could then be altered by changing the genetic makeup of unaffected males, could be the subject of a whole book in itself. Suffice to say, James and Alphey were able to incorporate a mutant gene into the males, which spread it to their female progeny. Millions of genetically altered male mosquitoes have been introduced to the Caribbean, Brazil and Malaysia, leading to 80% reductions in deadly mosquito numbers.

Even if 80% of the males and/or females in a population could be removed by pesticide, the high reproductive rate of survivors would quickly compensate for the control. But Sterile Insect Technology is so effective because female insects breed quickly, and typically only once. By swamping the virile males with faulty individuals, the reproductive success of the entire population is affected, hence the impressive control statistics.

Much the same logic has inspired a new technique to attempt to curtail the burgeoning populations of unowned cats. With the exception of Antarctica, aggregations of unowned cats live within and on the margins of cities, towns and farmhouses on every continent. Hundreds of thousands of cats are estimated to live outdoors in each of Canada's largest cities and Los Angeles alone is thought to harbour at least three million feral cats out of a national figure of around 100 million and growing. Just ponder these figures for a moment. The sheer number of unowned and typically unloved cats is truly staggering – and shameful. It's little wonder that those who are charged with addressing this bourgeoning scourge are looking to their pest insect colleagues for inspiration.

I don't use the term scourge flippantly. These unowned (feral) cats are not pet cats that occasionally stray from a safe and loving home. They are typically sick or starving, walking a tightrope between eking out an existence and falling victim to a tortured early death. Some are fed directly by well-meaning individuals or indirectly through access to poorly managed food waste. An objective way of gauging the morals and ethics of a society is how we treat our companion animals. In the case of semi-dependent cats, our track record is deplorable and little better than the treatment of the pseudo pet cats of Simbo.

Animal welfare advocates, conservationists, public lands administrators and some devoted stray cat carers are united in their desire to reduce the numbers and enhance the welfare status of unowned cats. They live shorter, less humane and more troublesome lives than cats that are owned and cared for. Free-roaming cats also host more diseases, kill more wildlife and are responsible for more nuisance behaviours than indoor pet cats, which has not gone unnoticed by lawmakers. Although the target of fewer and healthier cats is almost unanimously agreed, the optimum path to this milestone has been one of the most hotly contested aspects of animal management.

Ad hoc trapping, shooting or baiting of unowned cats is seldom effective long-term. Oftentimes this so-called 'solution' can exacerbate the situation by alienating feral cat carers, who have more time and inclination to find a solution than most municipal workers or self-confessed cat vigilantes. Targeting cats maintained by cat carers by short-term trapping and euthanasia may encourage the carers to relocate their feeding to safeguard 'their' animals. More importantly, the cats will most likely rapidly breed up again, or immigrate once the trapping spate concludes.

As the biased genetic competition between wildcats and domestic cats demonstrates, modern moggies possess extraordinary breeding potential. A single female can produce over a hundred cats in her lifetime and once her kittens and grand-kittens are all breeding, the rate of increase can be truly phenomenal. From no more than four or five domestic cats released on Grand Terre Island in the 1950s, feral cat numbers exploded to around 7000 by 2007. Estimates suggest in excess of 90% of cats need to be removed from populations every year just to account for the birth rate.

Just like those addressing fruit fly and mosquito risks have discovered, it may be smarter to concentrate on reducing the breeding potential than the more challenging and controversial tactic of increasing the kill rate. Promoted by people who feed stray cats and can't bear to see 'their' cats euthanased, Trap-Neuter-Release, or TNR, has been recently embraced as the technique of choice for the management of unowned cats in some US states, and increasingly in other countries.

The most compelling argument for the adoption of TNR is that killing or removing individual cats just allows others to move in to vacated territories. TNR advocates claim neutered cats defend their food resources from interlopers, stemming immigration rates of other cats. Similarly, TNR theory claims desexed toms should continue to defend their local queens and chase away virile suitors. Hyper-alert and exceptionally motivated neutered toms can hypothetically prevent queens in their 'colony' from breeding. The key concept in this attractive paradigm is 'colony'.

Colonies are groups of highly interacting social animals, think meerkats or honeybees, with an established social order and a high degree of cooperation that enhances their fitness. But with the exception of lions, cats typically fall well short of this definition. Several cats lounging around in the sun outside a barn, or even feeding from the same bowl, are evidence of mutual tolerance at a shared resource, not a deliberate collaboration to increase their survival or breeding potential. Domestic cats may coexist but they seldom cooperate; the exception being the 'communal breeding' among related domestic female cats documented by pre-eminent UK cat researcher David Macdonald, whereby queens may assist in the birth and nursing of their siblings' kittens.

However, aggregations of cats do not maintain 'pecking orders', like chickens or wolves, to govern access to food or mates. Sara Ash found, in her study of managed colonies in Texas, that cat-feeding stations were not defended by original colony members but actually attracted new cats. I had assumed that the protracted, noisy and sometimes vicious cat fights that disturb sleep around the world were evidence of dogged territorial or mate-defence by resident toms. Yet researchers from Rome who have studied the mating behaviour of stray cats found apparently dominant males rarely interfere when subordinate toms mate with a queen. Most toms quickly move on after mating, preferring to seek out another queen than defend their short-term partner. This means that over 75% of urban stray litters are sired by multiple fathers.

Unlike colonial animals, clowders of cats like these on Tashirojima Island, Japan, don't defend food resources or even mates, which explains why over 90% of these cats need to be neutered before natural attrition exceeds kitten birthrates. Reductions of TNR cat clowders typically only occur when high percentages are rehomed and recolonisation is restricted. (Photo: Thomas Peter, Reuters Pictures)

Making a distinction between an 'aggregation' and a 'colony' to describe a high-density cluster of cats may sound like splitting hairs. But Stephen Spotte, author of *Free-ranging Cats: Behaviour, Ecology, Management*, goes to great lengths to demonstrate that referring to a 'cat colony' is misleading, and is responsible for confusing stray-cat management policy. The evidence Spotte has compiled from multiple studies around the globe suggests neither cooperation nor defence are particularly accurate or relevant to domestic cats. Carol Haspell's study in New York was one of several that reported resident cats don't keep immigrants away. In fact, Spotte argues that because even non-desexed (known as 'entire') toms don't guard females on heat, and rarely even defend food resources, it is implausible to believe that groups of neutered cats would behave anything like a colony. Clowder, the collective term for a group of cats, is a less loaded and more appropriate term. Informed animal behaviour theory therefore challenges the notion that TNR would be successful for cats because, unlike their insect counterparts, cats breed more than once and desexed tom cats do not prevent females from breeding with entire males.

Stephen Spotte (2014) offered the following evidence to refute that cats form colonies: with the exception of mother cats with their kittens, free-ranging cats are typically solitary; small wildcats typically spend less than 1% of their time interacting; and even in dense aggregations around food resources, cats tolerate rather than form social hierarchies with other cats. Spotte concludes from his extensive literature review on clowder cat behaviour: 'Food is not highly motivating. Small groups of cats, whether captive, feral or stray seldom fight over food or anything else.'

Putting aside the shortcomings of neutering, TNR does allow clowder carers to capture a percentage of 'their' cats for veterinary treatment. Treatment of injuries, vaccination against some debilitating diseases, and neutering to reduce aggressive behaviour are benefits available to cats living in TNR clowders that are not available to independently roaming cats.

Ironically, the International Society of Feline Medicine claims TNR programs are a well-documented and effective method of population management. By contrast, opponents feel TNR unfairly compromises the welfare of neutered cats placed back onto the streets, and deny that TNR provides a useful, sustainable or affordable tool for reducing stray-cat populations. Far from being an applied science or even veterinary debate, assessment of the role and success of TNR typically hinges on a complex suite of logistical, behavioural, psychological, ecological, animal welfare and legal constraints. This complex casserole of issues led me on a tour of cat management projects to determine the rationale and success of different approaches.

One of the most sustained and successful TNR programs I encountered was spearheaded by Julie Okamoto. Julie had been teaching at Yamate Gakuin School in the Japanese city of Yokohama for 16 years before Cosmos the cat came into her life. Prior to adopting Cosmos, Julie had recognised one or two stray cats hanging around the school, but with heightened awareness she soon realised there was a group of 12 cats near where she parked. By the time she got out of her van, a group of hungry cats was eagerly anticipating the handouts she hid under her van so the ravens wouldn't monopolise the food.

Having been made aware of Trap-Neuter-Release through a television show, Julie initiated a similar project on these dozen cats. After observing her valiant efforts to catch the cats, Julie was approached by a couple from the neighbourhood who had initiated a TNR program on two other groups of cats, making a total of 37 cats on campus. Julie and her main collaborator Mikiko established 'Yamate Necology'; the website included photos, genders and medical histories of all the known cats on campus. With the support of a growing group of TNR proponents, Julie was comfortable that most of the cats on campus had been neutered.

Integral to this success was upgrading from using laundry nets to Tomahawk traps to trap the cats. The group received permission from the school to install small kennels and to allow their members to access the school grounds to care for the cats.

Julie is satisfied her TNR program has been successful and is confident few kittens have been born at the school in the 14 years since the program started, a source of obvious pride. I was interested in how her team had succeeded in apparently reducing the number of stray cats on campus when most other TNR programs had been less successful. Julie felt rehoming and adoption of cats was as important as the neutering program. Both Julie and her friend Mikiko have adopted several cats from the school and encouraged others to provide a home. After witnessing the suffering of outdoor cats they also encourage pet owners to keep their cats indoors. At Yamate Necology, the TNR acronym more correctly refers to Trap-Nurture-Rehome, which should be the ideal for all stray cat management where rehoming facilities are available

Scientists assessing the success of TNR claim even the closely monitored Yamate Necology program in Yokohama lacks the rigour required for accurate assessment. Although she knows her program dramatically improved the health and reduced the numbers of the school's cats, Julie was unable to confirm the fate of many of these cats and hence the value of the neutering program. Since one of the main motivations for embarking on TNR is to reduce suffering, tracking individual's fate is integral to determining the success of this strategy. Fortunately, several detailed TNR studies following the fates of individual cats have been reported.

An 11-year seminal study conducted on the campus of the

University of Central Florida is often cited by TNR advocates as evidence of the success of releasing neutered cats back into the wild. From 1991 to 2002, veterinarian Julie Levy and co-workers reported that TNR and associated activities resulted in a two thirds reduction in cat numbers. However, when the fate of individual cats was tracked, the reasons for this reduction were clarified. Nearly half of the cats were adopted, 6% of the 'colony' cats relocated to nearby woods, the same percentage were found killed on roads, and another 15% simply disappeared. Of most concern to the cat carers was a further 11% of the group were euthanased, often because they were suffering from feline leukemia or other diseases. Therefore the reduction in numbers was largely attributed to adoption, premature death or emigration, rather than natural senescence through the neutering program.

In another closely studied TNR program, this time in two southern Florida parks, the original population of 81 cats declined by 20% during the study year. However, immigration more than compensated for this decline; by the end of the year the population had risen to 88 cats. Along with more stray cats discovering the feeding station, the presence of well-fed cats encouraged the abandonment of unwanted pets.

Other TNR programs in the United States have also been thwarted by abandonment or immigration. Cats can be highly mobile and readily seek out mates or food in other areas. For these reasons the largest TNR program in the US, which neutered and released a whopping 180,000 cats, is not expected, even by its proponents, to reduce the number of feral cats in California. Sitting at a rubbish dump or cat-feeding locality, patiently wishing a single wary cat into a trap, then transporting it to a vet, fundraising for its neutering and finally releasing it back to its clowder is a laborious task. Repeating this 180,000 times is truly mind boggling. Imagine the sinking feeling of those poor Californian TNR workers when their data were analysed.

> From 2010 to 2014, 10,080 feral cats were neutered and released by the San Jose Animal Care and Services at or near their point of capture in the southern San Francisco Bay area. Although this practice was deemed 'successful', the City of San Jose and National Pet Alliance acknowledge: 'There was no follow-up on the welfare or status of the returned feral cats', nor changes to the size of the cat population or their impacts. A Florida case study at Ocean Reef claims its vaunted TNR program has been successful because 'only' 350 cats remain.

Studies describing the ineffectiveness of TNR are not restricted to the US, where release of neutered strays has reached its zenith. Amanda Jones and Colleen Downs reported the effects of sterilisation of unowned cat groups at five campuses of the University of KwaZulu-Natal, South Africa. Sterilisation rates of 63% had been achieved at six of the eight cat clowders and had reduced population increases compared to the unsterilised groups. However, the researchers concluded these rates, achieved through considerable and sustained effort by many volunteers, would still result in a slight increase. Sterilisation rates would have to be increased to 90% to reduce the population in the long term and to offset any increase in breeding or immigration of non-desexed cats. Judging by the challenges of extreme trap shyness that Katherine and I have experienced attempting to catch all feral cats in an area for research, consistently trapping 90% of a stray population for sterilisation seems unachievable.

In perhaps the largest detailed assessment of TNR programs

anywhere in the world, Eugenia Natoli and co-workers tracked the success of a decade of neuter release programs in Rome, involving in excess of 10,000 cats. Cat numbers decreased as a result of this sustained and expensive program in 55 groups but remained stable or increased in 48 other areas. In keeping with the Florida and South African studies, Natoli reported the decrease in cat numbers through TNR was nullified by a nearly comparable increase through immigration. It's little wonder the authors concluded 'all these efforts without an effective education of people to control the reproduction of house cats (as a prevention for abandonment) are a waste of money, time and energy'.

> The Greek Cat Welfare Society deceives their members that 'Trap, Neuter and Return is now recognised to be the only humane method of decreasing the stray cat population, which over time will work providing TNR is carried out on a regular basis several times a year'. No evidence is provided for these claims; indeed no evidence exists that TNR programs alone sustainably stabilise feral cat populations (Zaunbrecher and Smith 1993; Castillo and Clarke 2003; Natoli et al. 2006; Lepczyk et al. 2010). Despite the overwhelming weight of scientific evidence to the contrary, Lisa M. Chassy from Ally Cat Allies still writes: 'Until a better solution is viable, TNR is the only way to reduce the numbers of feral cats in a given colony. I applaud efforts to scientifically assess the effects of TNR.'

Robert McCarthy and Mike Reed from the Department of Veterinary Clinical Sciences at Tufts University set out to mathematically compare the population outcomes of cat clowders subjected to TNR with both euthanasia and trap-vasectomy-hysterectomy-release (TVHR) programs, like a three-year project performed at the Rio de Janeiro zoo. After crunching the numbers the Tufts University team determined lethal control was the most effective technique at reducing cat numbers if 90% of cats could be caught, but with lower trapping efficiencies hysterectomies outperformed both neutering and lethal control at reducing cat numbers. When the increase in kitten survivorship in TNR groups was factored into their models, TNR was often counterproductive and cat numbers actually increased compared with no intervention at all. The authors recommended TVHR over TNR.

Somewhat surprisingly, given their new models discredited TNR as an efficient tool for reducing cat clowders, the Tufts University study galvanised opposition from other cat management researchers. Dr Chris Lepczyk and a host of co-authors from around the globe took exception to the claims that vasectomies and hysterectomies be advocated as an effective technique for controlling unowned cats, believing the Tufts model did not consider the humane aspects, economics or even conservation outcomes of TVHR. Furthermore, just as TNR looked better on paper than it performed in real life, the assumptions of TVHR had not been thoroughly tested in the field.

Having worked at the University of Hawaii, Lepczyk is well placed to comment on the impacts of feral cats and the effectiveness of TNR. Hawaii is the unofficial epicentre of the impacts, debate and management of unowned cats. Dozens of Hawaiian wildlife species have been driven to extinction by feral predators, including cats. Cats continue to present the major threat to endangered nesting seabirds, shorebirds and forest birds. Other wildlife, including marine mammals and the endemic Hawaiian crow, are suffering from toxoplasmosis transmitted from feral cats. Even the day-care centre at the University of Hawaii's Manoa campus was closed temporarily due to disease risks posed by flea infestations from a cat clowder that had, according to the university's website, grown from 100 to over 1000 cats, despite a TNR effort.

Among his inventory of concerns with the TVMR paper, Lepczyk considered the modellers failed to account adequately for immigration. Studies from Rome, Florida, Japan and South Africa had all found that new cats, dumped or wandering into feeding areas, dramatically reduced the success of programs to reduce numbers of cats in areas where they are fed. Lepczyk also claimed the hysterectomy process took too long to reduce numbers and still maintained attractive sites for dumping of additional cats. The detractors also challenged the very high costs of TVHR compared to lethal euthanasia. In an early study co-authored with associate Cheryl Lohr and Linda Cox, Lepczyk found TNR programs were more costly than trapping and euthanasing programs, even if the TNR used solely voluntary labour whilst the euthanasing trappers were paid professional rates. With tens of thousands of feral cats in Hawaii alone, costs need to be factored into any management decision that has a hope of significantly reducing numbers of unowned cats.

The biologists, modellers and vets were howling in unison that TNR was at best ineffective and at worst an expensive and counterproductive waste of time. Yet despite the overwhelming scientific evidence, TNR proponents around the world continue to passionately advocate their ideology to policymakers and cat-care organisations. The multitude of authors of the 2010 article 'What Conservation Biologists Can Do to Counter Trap-Neuter-Return' in the prestigious *Conservation Biology* journal argue their fraternity needs to be more outspoken in publicly challenging TNR in the same way they have challenged Creationism. But these scientists are fully aware that facts have little influence on the perceptions of most TNR supporters. Nils Peterson and co-workers, largely from North Carolina State University, objectively surveyed 338 cat 'colony' caretakers from just about every US State. He concluded most caretakers were either ill-informed or were deluding themselves about the objectives and consequences of TNR. A staggering 70% believed TNR actually eliminates cat clowders, despite compelling contrary evidence.

This alarming lack of awareness of the problems associated with unowned cats cannot be blamed on cat carers not listening to information. Rather, the informed messages from their vets, health-care professionals and scientists are drowned out by the incredibly well-resourced campaigns of organisations with vested or misguided interests in maximising the number of cats on the streets. Alley Cat Allies, for example, spent over US$3 million in 2010 alone advocating for the nationwide legalisation of TNR in the US. Best Friends Animal Society trumped their Ally Cat 'allies' by investing a staggering US$11 million a year promoting their 'Focus on Felines', which also promotes TNR. These campaigns are supported by pet food giants, which profit from more cats in the same way as Alley Cats and Best Friends benefit from increased donations, 'how to' seminars and grants for operating municipal TNR programs. Sadly, this 'alliance' means cats, wildlife, property rights and human health suffer in homage to the TNR cash cow.

The influence of pet food companies on public policy was strikingly evident when the legislators from Athens, Georgia, voted in March 2010 to legalise a TNR program to manage the county's cat overpopulation. Buoyed by a $600,000 grant from pet food retailer PetSmart to Best Friends, and influenced by a long-running TNR advocacy campaign, the Athens legislators voted 9:1 in favour of legalising TNR. The purported objective of this grant was to sterilise 6000 cats over three years, a figure that neither Best Friends nor councillors could either verify or be confident would be successful in reducing cat numbers. Exemplifying the degree to which the PetSmart deal won them over, the Athens council then voted to establish another $10,000 annual budget to support the TNR program. Around the country many scientists and animal rights organisations shook their heads in disbelief.

Four years later, with no corroborative evidence of reductions in stray cats from Athens, a similar project was initiated in nearby Columbus. It too involved a $600,000 grant funded by PetSmart and administered by Best Friends to deliver 'No More Homeless Pets'. Ironically, the focus on reducing euthanasia and increasing cat release rates directly results in more homeless cats. Furthermore, about half the grant money was to be spent on administration and 'promoting non-lethal approaches to cat management'.

When she learned about the Columbus program, Sarah Rowe, the local state-licensed wildlife rehabilitator, was astounded that a city government had legalised the TNR program. By stitching together information from council minutes, phone conversations, interviews, internet sites and social media, Rowe discovered the evidence contradicting the claims of TNR advocates had been withheld from city officials.

The TNR ordinance, funded by citizen taxes 'to protect public health by controlling animal populations', redefined feral cats as 'community' cats and cat feeders as 'caretakers', who were exempted from legal responsibility for the personal injury and property damage the cats registered to them would create for citizens. Additionally, the ordinance didn't require caretakers to maintain records demonstrating the effectiveness of the campaign to reduce cat numbers, nor to clean up the waste their cats deposited in the backyards of citizens, and in civic areas. Rowe felt she had 'uncovered a conspiracy between the pet food industry, Best Friends, and city officials, discovered how they benefited financially or personally, and how they reject the volumes of scientific study, and personal testimony by former TNR supporters and disenfranchised citizens that dispute their claims'.

In 2008 alone, Alley Cat Allies took in more than US$4.8 million and spent US$3.8 million on public education and outreach – largely by promoting TNR management of unowned cats. The 2014–15 Best Friends annual report reveals the main expenses of their billion dollar business was 'campaigns and other national outreach', costing almost US$58 million. Centred on their 'Save Them All' mantra, the sole measure of success of their vaunted TNR programs was a reduction in cats euthanased. Despite impressive statistics on their website of numbers of pets rehomed and over 50,000 'community cats' neutered and returned to the wild, there is no information about changes in free-ranging cat numbers or suffering as a result of their TNR campaigns.

Rowe's TNRFactCheck.org website is slowly gaining traction. Councilman Jerry 'Pops' Barnes describes his change of heart about Columbus' TNR program in a revealing blog on his own website:

> In 2013 the city approved a program to trap, neuter cats, and return them to the community. Initially, I thought this was a good idea, however, my position has changed because I began to hear the roaming cat population is increasing rather than decreasing like the proponents

of the program promised, and the cats are creating a nuisance for residents by raiding trash cans, defecating in yards, and the smell of cat urine. After hearing these complaints, I researched the program and what I learned made me, a health care professional, very concerned about the potential of the program to adversely affect the health of the community.

Pops was particularly concerned about the increase in rabies transmission from stray cats to humans. Best Friends claims that a single injection provides cats with three years of immunity from rabies, whereas vets, vaccine manufacturers and public health guidelines insist that a booster vaccination must be administered a year after the initial vaccination to enable full immunity. Pops was concerned that the mayor bent the rules so as not to jeopardise the TNR program, particularly since she acknowledged that 'it is nearly impossible to re-trap the cats a second or more times, and too costly'.

Pops' concerns about rabies risks might include his personal liabilities as well as his passion for public health. In a landmark case in Utah, the family of a boy killed by a bear was awarded US$1.95 million in damages, largely covered by the Forest Service as landowner, because the bear had been habituated to scavenging for food and hence was not considered an exempt 'natural condition of the land'. Following this precedence, individuals contracting rabies, bird flu or toxoplasmosis from cat clowders could also potentially sue those individuals and authorities permitting or feeding stray cats on public land.

Pops confessed that at first glance the no-kill target the mayor was pursuing, 'seems to be admirable, but closer examination reveals no-kill is cruel to humans and animals, and it radically changes the mission and activities of a municipal animal control agency'.

Of most interest to me was not the developing spat between the mayor and her councillor, but the outcomes of this program. Was Best Friends achieving its stated objective of 'No More Homeless Pets'? When I read Pop's blog I realised I was not alone in asking these questions:

> Another problem with this program is that no one can access records related to the program. How can a citizen-funded governmental agency not be subject to the open records act?

The reluctance of TNR advocates to disclose the outcomes of their programs reinforces scientific conclusions that TNR is seldom an effective tool for reducing the numbers or suffering of unowned cats. Openly flouting science follows a recent troubling societal trend highlighted by the ascension of populist politicians who refute overwhelming scientific evidence and, worse still, set out to diminish the role that science plays in informing public policy. Each Christmas, my standard wishlist given to my children and in-laws includes a couple of books that I eagerly anticipate. The Best American Science Writing compilation for the year, and its Australian equivalent, offer an eclectic range of stories, from medical and biological discoveries to astrological and innovations breakthroughs. The introduction for the 2016 Australian edition, penned by Jo Chandler, lamented this erosion in public appreciation of science by citing Atul Gawande, surgeon and staff writer for the *New Yorker*.

Even where the knowledge provided by science is overwhelming, people often resist it – sometimes outright deny it. Many people continue to believe, for instance, despite massive evidence to the contrary, that childhood vaccines cause autism (they do not); that people are safer owning a gun (they are not); that genetically modified crops are harmful (on balance, they have been beneficial); that climate change is not happening (it is).

To his list Gawande could have added: 'TNR is an effective and ethical means of reducing suffering and effects of cat clowders (it is not)'.

Despite the amazing scientific discoveries I read about each year offering previously inconceivable opportunities to improve our lives, I'm boggled and frustrated that even educated people are turning away from facts and rationality in favour of untruths that are either more palatable or more convenient. In a 2018 article in the prestigious *Biological Conservation* journal, Scott Loss and Peter Marra lament the modus operandi of such 'Merchants of doubt', who deliberately swamp the public with 'misinformation to minimize cat impacts and overplay TNR's effectiveness'. But before I followed my scientifically tuned instincts and believed the overwhelming tide of facts and logic, I needed to meet others at the frontline of the unowned cat issue. Many intelligent and compassionate individuals were devoting their time, and often their savings, feeding stray cats. Many also supported TNR under the expectation, or hope, they were acting in the best interests of stray cats by reducing the suffering. Maybe there were positive attributes of TNR not captured in formal reviews? I set out to find out for myself at one of the world's more remote TNR sites in Canada's Haida Gwaii islands.

Chapter 11

WHEN GIVING IS TAKING

Cats are marvellous creatures – they either adapt to circumstances, or make circumstances adapt to them. Either way, they win. Will Advise

With more than a little trepidation, I approached the house on the steeply sloping side street in the seaside village of Queen Charlotte, the capital of the Haida Gwaii islands. I wondered how best to introduce myself, but became distracted by little warblers flitting energetically through the trees. First I assumed the little balls of feathers might be black-throated warblers but on closer inspection convinced myself the high-pitched excited calls were those of female and juvenile Townsend warblers, a new tick in my field guide. A pair of spectacular red-breasted sapsuckers also hopped up the same tree.

I was visiting Haida Gwaii because Canadian wildlife ecologists considered the islands, separated from the British Columbian mainland by the 48-kilometre-wide Hecate Strait, could well represent an environment where feral cats may proliferate as the climate inevitably warmed. In his calculation of approximately 1.4 to 4.2 million feral cats in Canada, Peter Blancher from Environment Canada excluded the vast northern areas of the country considered too cold to support feral cats. Despite lying just south of Alaska, the maritime climate of Haida Gwaii placed it near the northern limit of where feral cats could, in the future, survive long winters. The larger, milder Vancouver Island to the south was even more suitable climatically but also supports larger predators like coyotes, wolves and cougars. But the dominant predators on the 10,000-square-kilometre island province of Haida Gwaii were black bears, which were unlikely to prevent the proliferation of feral cats.

Islands have been at the epicentre of wildlife extinctions caused by feral cats. The oft-cited poster-book example is the endemic Stephens Island wren, whose entire population is believed by some to have been exterminated by a single cat, Tibbles, within a year of being brought to the remote New Zealand island by the lighthouse keeper in 1894. Other cats may have contributed to the demise but the irrefutable fact that one or more cats caused the rapid genocide of this species is entrenched in conservation folklore. This unfortunate wren is by no means unique. In his ground-breaking review of the effect of feral cats, Manuel Nogales from the Canary Islands and co-authors determined feral cats were the main culprits in the extinction of no fewer than 32 other island vertebrate species, an inventory poised to increase further. Island wildlife evolving without cats was pathetically ill-equipped to cope with cat predation. Just as the dopey dodo was defenceless against rampaging sailors or pigs, most island animals are notoriously vulnerable to introduced predators. Haida Gwaii could well mirror other isolated locations worldwide where cats were having a devastating effect on the naïve local fauna.

It's important to clarify here that cats do not threaten wildlife on all islands. For example, on some Mediterranean islands without endemic vertebrates or breeding seabirds, feral cats provide valuable service by controlling rats and rabbits. High numbers of rats that predate nests and nestlings, or rabbit plagues that raze vegetation, can threaten island environments.

Removing cats from these islands can cause greater problems for wildlife than retaining some. A global review forwarded to me by co-author Karl Campbell identified six species that declined after eradication of introduced mammals from islands. The same review reported 236 native species that benefited from removal of introduced mammals. On most islands that either host nesting seabird colonies or endemic wildlife, cats represent a major threat.

Domestic cats were introduced on Isla Isabel, Mexico, by fishermen in 1930 and by 1991 an estimated 113 cats/km^2 were killing 23–33% of nesting sooty terns annually. The tern population declined from 150,000 to roughly 1000 individuals but eradication of cats resulted in tern survivorship increasing by over 80%. Steffan Oppel from the RSPB found that following removal of 56 feral cats from St Helena Island, survival of St Helena plovers also increased more than threefold in semi-desert habitats. However, presumably because of an increase in rats that also predate on nestlings, plover populations only increased marginally in pasture habitats.

But of even more interest to me than whether feral cats represented a threat or net benefit to Haida Gwaii wildlife, was the opportunity to test the efficacy of TNR. One of the main drawbacks cited by TNR opponents was feral cat aggregations are not closed systems. Individuals motivated to feed cats could seldom be certain they had treated all of the cats in their clowder and that other cats wouldn't immigrate or be dumped there. This risk is particularly prevalent in environments that support truly feral cats, independent of human handouts or shelters. Haida Gwaii presented a best-case scenario for TNR to limit breeding and reduce feral cat populations because, from what I could ascertain, the feral cats were largely restricted to the fringes of the islands' small towns. Equally importantly, the low number of residents and remote access means few new pet cats are brought to the far-flung islands. In small towns most people knew their neighbours and their pets. By all these criteria, Haida Gwaii represented an optimal location to determine the theoretical potential of TNR to reduce the size, misery and impacts of feral cat clowders.

The red-breasted sapsucker stirred my memory. Days earlier I had contacted Margo Hearne, local bird authority and author of the definitive guide to the birds of Haida Gwaii. Hearne was most concerned about the impacts of logging to birds on her islands. The felling of an iconic golden spruce tree by a disturbed environmental activist brought the destruction of local logging practices to worldwide attention back when Hearne's islands were known as the Queen Charlottes. Clear-felled swathes of forest behind the coastal fringe attested to the continued role of forestry as the mainstay of the local economy. In addition to the logging, Hearne acknowledged feral cats were prevalent around the towns and were also threatening local species. Low-nesting birds like Swainson's thrushes were especially vulnerable to cats. Hearne was particularly upset that a song sparrow family, another low-nesting bird that had inhabited her Masset yard for 30 sparrow generations, had recently been wiped out by cats.

It wasn't the birds, the Smart car or the immaculate garden decorated with driftwood that convinced me I had the correct address. It was the cats. A content Russian grey with an unusually short tail lazed in a sunny patch of grass, while a rather beaten-up black-and-white tom strode confidently up the driveway in front of me, holding his tail aloft like a flag. Fortunately neither cat was showing interest in the sapsuckers or flitting warblers. The other cats I had seen in Queen Charlotte had slunk away nervously but these were confident and cared-for pets. I was by now convinced I was at the home of Dorothy Garrett, the mainstay of Haida Gwaii's Society for the Protection of Cruelty to Animals (SPCA). I was about to meet the local 'cat lady'.

'Cat ladies' can be understandably apprehensive about opening the door to unfamiliar men wearing binoculars and clutching a notebook. To my relief I rapidly decided Dorothy may well be the world's nicest lady. Her white hair was pulled back efficiently but not meticulously into a ponytail, and her blue-grey eyes shone with interest, not fear, at my enquiry. A 35-year veteran of Queen Charlotte, Dorothy was passionate, frustrated and eager to devolve her opinions on what she openly described as 'the cat problem'.

As the backbone of the local SPCA branch for decades, Dorothy was exasperated the cat problem was far from being solved. Her primary concern was the animal welfare issues of feral cats living around the margins of every settlement on Haida Gwaii. These cats were typically malnourished and diseased, with starvation or death from exposure or injury their most likely fate. But Haida Gwaii's cat problem extended beyond their welfare, Dorothy told me. The impact of cats hunting wildlife and the community disturbance through fighting and attacking pets were also serious issues. But it was not just feral cats she was attempting to deal with. Dorothy was often overwhelmed by the number of 'pet' cats either dropped off at her door, or simply abandoned when their 'owners' left town.

Fortunately Haida Gwaii's cat problem has lessened since the Masset naval communications base closed. Like other military installations, this radio station base led to a rotation of residents through the town. Often acquiring pet cats once they arrived at

Once-stray Jem playing laser-chase with Dorothy Garrett in Queen Charlotte Village. Finding homes for abandoned and feral cats, including flying them to mainland Canada, is the main focus of cat management groups on the Haida Gwaii Islands. (Photo: Debra Gardiner)

Masset, most military families believed 'island' cats should stay on the island. Dorothy considered their philosophy flawed, and a demonstration of a tenuous attachment to their 'pet' cats. Other pets accompanied departing residents; cats were left to fend for themselves.

Even after stemming the tide of ex-military cats, last year Dorothy took in 12 adults and 54 kittens, brought by people unable or unwilling to care for cats they had inherited. But these surrendered cats did not represent the bulk of her workload or concerns. Dorothy's most intractable problem was the feral cat clowders fed by mostly well-intentioned souls. The typical clowder was relatively small and seemingly manageable at nine to 12 cats. However a Sandspit clowder of about 55 cats had increased over 15 years. These cats occupied a neighbourhood of half-acre blocks backing onto the woods, which made it ideal for cats but challenging for trappers. Like many cat carers around the world, Dorothy took cats she managed to trap to the vet and had them treated for parasites, neutered and adopted out where possible. 'How do you pay for the vet fees?' I asked. Dorothy sighed and ran her fingers through her hair. 'I think I had better get you a drink,' she replied.

Much of Dorothy's energy and that of her fellow SPCA volunteers is spent on fundraising for the treatment and care of unowned cats. Raffles and fundraisers, applications to the Gwaii Trust Fund, and occasional funding from Queen Charlotte and Skidegate municipalities enabled the SPCA to cobble together funds for both the veterinary bills and a community cat spay-neuter program to encourage low-income pet owners to fix their cats. Without the subsidies, cat owners were charged $185 to spay their queens, $110 to neuter their toms and $80 to vaccinate their cats. Such expenses represented a considerable and prohibitive impost for many locals.

'But the vet treatment is not our major problem,' Dorothy admitted. Finding sufficient suitable adoptees was not possible, mostly due to the small local population and the unrelenting tide of new cats for adoption. Dorothy extolled rehoming feral cats rather than releasing them. Although I had thought I was investigating a conventional TNR project, Dorothy never used that acronym, instead referring to her work as 'spay-neuter'. Just like Julie had in Yokohama, Dorothy passionately extolled the Trap-Nurture-Rehome (rather than Release) moniker for feral cat management. Fortunately for the SPCA, supply meets demand for rehoming dogs. But most residents who wanted, or were prepared to care for cats, already had enough pets. Dorothy was grateful to Pacific Coastal Airlines who in recent years had flown cats for free from small isolated communities like Haida Gwaii to Vancouver, and a greater pool of potential adopters.

Despite her challenges, Dorothy was openly and justifiably proud of her achievements. She showed me a video of two of the feral cats she had trapped, trained and rehoused. The new owner had kept Max and Bella exclusively inside and their thank you video to Dorothy showed them happy and healthy, playing inside with the pet dog. But Dorothy was realistic enough to acknowledge successful adoption of pets and neutering and vaccinating ferals was simply applying bandaids to the problem. 'We need to stop the relentless birth of kittens by pet and feral cats ... and that is even more challenging than the fundraising and adoption.' She advocated bylaws stipulating mandatory registration and spay-neuter of pet cats. Again demonstrating her pragmatic side, Dorothy acknowledged cat owners, not the cats themselves, were her main nemesis. Still using the contentious term 'colony', Dorothy explained, 'Every feral cat colony can trace it roots back to an unfixed domestic pet and once a colony is established, the money, time and dedication required to fix it, is beyond most individual's resources.'

The local authorities considered feral cats to be pests that should be put down. But neither the councils nor private individuals opposing the feral cat clowders invested the time or resources to trap and euthanase these cats. Neither shared the passion or determination of the cat feeders who vowed to stymie any attempts to euthanase 'their cats'. Dorothy recognised cooperation of the cat feeders was integral to solving the ever-growing feral cat dilemma.

Dorothy was confident some of the smaller clowders with nine to 12 neutered cats were now stable or in slow decline through the attrition of older cats. But success had not been as tangible in larger clowders, like one on Copper Bay Road. Although she conceded immigration and dumping were also a local problem, lack of adequate resources was probably a more serious limitation on Haida Gwaii. Despite the determination and persistence of the trappers, there were more cats than first estimated so, disappointingly, there was never enough money to fix all the cats.

Dorothy aligned herself with the 'rational' cat feeders but acknowledged there were also . . . and she paused searching for the most appropriate term . . . 'other' cat feeders. When I involuntarily finished her statement with 'crazy cat ladies' Dorothy recoiled.

'No!' she stated. 'I'm really careful not to use that description because it is very much the exception. Most feeders are compassionate regular folk.'

Dorothy considered categorising all cat feeders as crazies let the real culprits off the hook. Many feeders she worked with would be comfortable, and some relieved, if their clowders gradually declined to extinction. But she did concede 'other' feeders were primarily motivated to feed cats to satisfy their desire for companionship or worth.

Such a yearning to patronise or pamper animals and, particularly, to appease their apparent hunger is a near universal trait. I recently castigated myself after slipping an inquisitive dolphin a fish despite just reading a sign at a local wharf imploring the public not to feed

> Ethicist Michael Shermer describes a rational thinker as one wanting to know what is really true, not just what he or she would like to be true. He concedes, however, that cognitive psychology research has shown 'we are not the rationally calculating beings we would like to think we are but instead are very much driven by our passions, and blinded by our biases'. Psychologist Leon Festinger, who describes the mental tension experienced by someone simultaneously holding conflicting thoughts as 'cognitive dissonance', reflects on the likely response when an individual who utterly believes in something is presented with unequivocal and undeniable evidence that his belief is wrong. Festinger concludes that the individual 'will frequently emerge, not only unshaken, but even more convinced of the truth of his beliefs and indeed may show a new fervour about convincing and converting others to his view'.

the dolphins. Who hasn't occasionally thrown a chip to a gull or bread crusts to a duck or pigeon because they have appeared needy or because we just valued the interaction? But we know it is wrong. We know our food is not healthy for these animals, it encourages them to be less wary of people, boats or cars, and more likely to fight and transmit disease. It is therefore not surprising socially isolated or lonely people will feed feral cats despite being informed of the welfare and health consequences of their actions. A particularly tragic example occurred not far from Dorothy's house.

Just down the road lived Gerry, a lonely man who had encouraged a timid visiting black bear to return to his house by feeding it. Before long the occasional visitor became a regular, first anticipating, then expecting food. Gerry took solace in being able to assist the apparently needy animal. The bear provided an escape from the tedium and troubles of his insular life, a much-anticipated high point of his day. In time the increasingly brazen bear was followed by other bears, until a posse regularly entered town, delighting Gerry but causing fear and concern to other residents, the council and wildlife authorities. No fewer than 14 black bears ambled through the regrowth forest on the outskirts of Queen Charlotte to his house and then became so blasé they eventually used the main street to access their smorgasbord.

On numerous occasions the hermit was informed, then instructed, that his feeding of the bears was not only illegal but detrimental to their health. Bears should be gleaning a diverse diet from the forest, not relying on handouts. Gerry was warned the habituated bears may need to be destroyed. Dozens of examples demonstrated that bears, whether the black bears of Haida Gwaii or grizzlies or polar bears elsewhere, become dangerous when they lose their instinctive fear of humans. Once bears started expecting to be fed, the interaction usually ended in tears.

But so great was the misplaced compassion for his adopted bears that Gerry kept feeding them, until they were eventually destroyed. The killing of the bears was a tragedy for the unfortunate gluttonous beasts and the ironically named 'conservation officer', whose passion was for protecting wildlife, not shooting it. And it was a calamity for Gerry. Weeks later, consumed by anger and remorse, he died when his house burnt to the ground. The overgrown charred house block remains as a poignant reminder that when feeding wildlife our giving can actually be taking. Whether they are bears ambling in from the woods, dolphins following fishing boats to the wharf, or feral cats congregating around feeding stations, the short-term benefits to the hungry animals typically lead to long-term animal welfare, environmental or societal problems.

Since Dorothy had only needed to deal with two kittens for the year so far she hoped the message of responsible cat ownership was finally getting through, but her wry grin suggested the battle was far from won. Despite the alarming local story about the bears, Dorothy and her fellow SPCA volunteers continue to face a stalemate with the wild animal feeding fraternity. Single-minded feeders of feral cats were pitted against those intent on stopping the suffering and gradually removing the cats. While feral cats continue to be fed, the problems will persist.

Dorothy's considered and passionate middle-ground position on cat management presented a real opportunity for reducing the impact and suffering of Haida Gwaii's feral cats. And one of her most important allies was Don Richardson.

As a fifth generation inhabitant of the Queen Charlotte Islands, Don Richardson was known by just about everyone I met on the four-hour ferry ride to the islands and on Haida Gwaii itself. Repeatedly I was informed, 'You've got to see Don,' when I mentioned I was researching local cat issues. Dorothy drew me a mud-map to Richardson's practice, the Queen Charlotte Veterinary Hospital, located on his Poll Hereford cattle ranch near the sparsely populated community of Tlell. Bearded and bespectacled, Richardson graciously offered me time to discuss the island's cat issues before heading out to cut silage on a rare 'hot' day, when I was just considering removing my jacket.

When Richardson started his veterinary practice on the islands 33 years ago, there were as many kids as dogs with scabies. 'Haida (the archipelago's First Nations peoples, from which the islands took their name) were not pet owners culturally,' Richardson explained, 'and they had little knowledge of how to care for their pets or the risks posed by their pets to their health.' I recalled our experiences with the Solomon Island villagers who broke the wings of their 'pet' pigeons to stop them flying, and bore no responsibility for their hordes of semi-domestic cats. Education and treating the dogs for scabies had nearly eliminated the condition on Haida Gwaii. Similarly, before his veterinarian hospital was established, ringworm was endemic in local cats and children, but nowadays cats were better cared for. Richardson cited the horror in the local community when a rare contemporary case of ringworm was detected, compared with the widespread historic acceptance of the disease.

Although truly feral cats are rarely sighted, Richardson knows they are out there. His experience suggests if a female cat is left outside a remote house she will inevitably fall pregnant. Richardson has seen cat tracks in snow many miles from towns on the northern Graham Island, but concedes the feral population is not large. Racoons eat kittens and he is often brought a cat that has made the mistake of taking on a racoon in a dispute over access to a food bowl. Rather than a large self-sustaining feral population, Richardson reckons the feral cats on Haida Gwaii are largely tied to towns. He confirmed Dorothy's assertion that irresponsible cat owners and uncooperative cat feeders are the core of the problem.

Richardson told me of an old spinster at Port Clements whose affection for feral cats was only recognised after her death when 30 to 40 hungry cats descended upon the neighbours. Two cat clowders in Sandspit were also of concern to Richardson. Despite neutering kittens in a hastily conceived TNR program, a continued tide of kittens were being born because the Sandspit cat feeders were either not determined enough, or successful enough, to neuter all the breeding females.

However, where neutering is more comprehensive and feeding and dumping of new cats restricted, Richardson has noticed a reduction in feral cats. The landfill that services the islands was, in keeping with many refuse dumps around the world, the epicentre for a dense population of feral cats. Through the work of the SPCA all the 'resident' adult cats were neutered. Most importantly according to Richardson, both cat feeders and dumping of unwanted pets had been prevented by fencing around the landfill. Richardson knows of no kittens recorded there for the past five years.

Richardson attributes many of the cat issues in Haida Gwaii to a philosophical difference between owners' attitudes to cats and other pets. Locals typically make a decision to get a dog or other pet; cats 'just happen'. Few cats are brought to the islands by plane or ferry, most are picked up on the way to the grocery store or find their own way to their eventual 'owner's' house. Richardson applauds SPCA's success in educating the public about responsible cat ownership and dealing with some of the feral populations. But, like Dorothy, Richardson considers his biggest challenge is to target those individuals who repeatedly bring in kittens for adoption without committing to desexing their pet; or continue to feed feral cats without taking on the time-consuming role of trapping and neutering 'their' feral animals.

Richardson's views on cat management mirrored Dorothy's. But I wondered how Parks Canada viewed the feral cat problem in Haida Gwaii, and how this rated against other threats? Several of the ecologists and the resource conservation manager agreed cats were scarce in the more remote forests, particularly the iconic Gwaii Haanas National Park. Despite their concerns about the environmental and social effects of feral cats around communities, Parks Canada is careful to not interfere with land management outside their jurisdiction. Some particularly vulnerable species, such as the birds Hearne had identified and the tiny weasel-like Haida ermine, could well be threatened by these cats. The local museum featured amazing photos and examples of ermine headdresses worn by Haida chiefs, each garment made up of a dozen or more pure-white skins. These diminutive predators are exceedingly rare these days and listed federally as a Species at Risk. Despite being imperilled primarily through understorey reduction by introduced deer, some of the last specimens recorded had been killed by pet cats.

The Haida people, and their inspirational leader Guujaaw, had drawn worldwide recognition and admiration for opposing logging, eventually having their South Moresby Island incorporated into the cooperatively managed Gwaii Haanas National Park Reserve in 1993. After decades of logging, their convoluted archipelago of ancient cedar and spruce forests were spared. The local economy turned to tourism based on the culture and unspoilt wilderness that defined the Haida and their islands. But all was not rosy in paradise.

Exotic black rats and Norway rats have decimated colonies of important ground-nesting seabirds such as the rhinoceros auklets, Cassin's auklets and fork-tailed storm petrels. Of particular concern to local ecologists was the survival of one of the most diminutive of the auk species, the ancient murrelet, of which half of the world's population breeds on Haida Gwaii. In response, Parks Canada embarked on an ambitious program to eradicate rats from several of the key islands of the park reserve to restore seabird populations and improve the ecological health of ecosystems.

A larger and more intractable problem was caused by the Sitka black-tailed deer, first introduced from the mainland by one of the early missionaries as a food source in the late 1800s, and again in 1911 by the provincial government for game hunting. So numerous were these alien deer that beachside forests sported a horizontal graze-line that looked like it had been created with string lines and hedge cutters. The lower branches of trees and any shrubs or saplings had been stripped away. Small deer exclosures, like the ones I visited near Yakoun Lake on Graham Island, dramatically demonstrate the impact of these herbivores. Sapling trees and shrubs produced a dense and diverse understorey inside the tall fenced compounds compared with the park-like desolation outside.

Despite the deer representing a blatantly obvious threat to the magnificent forest and wildlife of Gwaii Haanas National Park, pressure from local hunting enthusiasts was a serious challenge to proposed deer control programs. Hunting limits of 15 deer per season ironically, perhaps deliberately, ensure deer numbers are maintained at levels that prevent forest regeneration. Rather than attempting to control these pests, deer permits similar to that used for the local salmon and crabs are used to ensure the proliferation of deer throughout all of the islands, not just the area accessible to hunters. Deficiencies in public policy and the determined stance of a minority of intransient stakeholders are undermining control of deer and feral cats on the islands.

Despite the concerns of many island residents, local ecologists believed deer and rats, closely followed by ecological damage of past clear-fell forestry practices, posed more of a threat to ecosystems of the Haida Gwaii environment than feral cats. Feral cat impacts are largely limited to the outskirts of towns, with the cold winters and predation by racoons restricting them from establishing clowders in the forests. But with warmer winters due to climate change such climatic barriers may soon be lowered and the feral cat problem exacerbated. Until then the feral cats on Haida Gwaii will mainly remain a problem for Dorothy and her SPCA volunteers, for Hearne and the birds inhabiting her garden and sanctuary, and for vet Richardson who manages the pointy end of cat welfare.

As I reluctantly departed Haida Gwaii after an enlightening week, I conceded spay-neutering of feral cats could prevent expansion of isolated clowders, especially where rehoming was far more prevalent than release. But my overwhelming conclusion was that focusing on management of feral cats was missing the point. Only by stopping ad hoc feeding could humane groups and local authorities reduce the relentless renewal of cat clowders.

Dorothy's rescued and rehomed Max and Bella are inspirational examples of the positive outcomes for feral cats that can be trained and rehomed. Unfortunately most 'rescued' cats can't expect the same fairytale ending, as we learn in the next chapters.

Chapter 12

PROTECTING CATS OR DUPING CAT LOVERS?

She's lived outside for seven years. She's not homeless.
Alley Cat Allies poster

The English rural landscape was improbably green and immaculately tidy, its small quilt-like paddocks spotted with white Dorset sheep. Dairy cows had recently moved on in the face of cheap Spanish milk imports. The border and seams of this quilt were hedgerows, enclosing the fields of Devon. These living fences represented a complex microcosm of the wooded forests that once grew here.

At the centre of hedgerows was an unexpected core of earth, maybe waist deep, that presumably represented the original land surface prior to erosion of the paddocks and roads, supplemented by soil and litter accumulated in the dense hedges over the centuries. Bonsaied oaks and hawthorns formed an impenetrable tangle with brambles and berries. Grasses and wildflowers, especially the brilliant-purple foxgloves and saffron buttercups tended by enormous bumblebees, twined through the sunlit edges, along with nettles and thistles, pruned more by sheep and passing vehicles than by hedge trimmers.

Shrews and squirrels, rabbits and foxes coursed through tunnels in these otherwise impenetrable hedgerows. The wren, apparently with a case of 'little bird syndrome' and with no regard for its droll-sounding name, *Troglodites troglodites*, was a plucky vocal species. Although typically reluctant to show themselves for more than a glimpse, I learnt to recognise their calls along with several other birds. What they lack in colour compared with their brilliant Australian counterparts, British wrens and other small birds make up for with their songs. As if to help the novice birdwatcher, the chaffinch effectively announced its name with its repeated *chiff chaff chiff chaff* call. While not the most beautiful call, the mistle thrush arguably boasted the cleanest and most confident call from the hedgerow. I stood motionless with an involuntary grin as I marvelled at the repertoire of this amazing hidden bird.

It was not only the complex living fences and exquisite vocalisation of the thrushes that impressed me. I was also taken by how passionate and connected this rural community had remained to their wildlife. I met fanatical gardeners who carefully tended their expansive grounds meticulously designed to provide nectar and larval food plants for a staggering array of local butterflies. Even the seemingly unkempt patch of long grass in Gavin Haigh's butterfly garden had been deliberately retained to provide egg-laying sites for his favourite ringlet and marbled white butterflies. Another 'open' garden boasted ponds of different depths, purpose built for local frog and toad species, and an assortment of tiles and other shelters provided cover for boldly marked juvenile slow worms, common lizards and grass snakes. Part of a farm had been converted into a badger sanctuary, complete with a below-ground viewing hide where these bumbling creatures could be observed in their underground chambers, oblivious of our presence behind perspex screens.

But it was the bird enthusiasts who were most prominent among the local nature lovers. I joined weekend bird counts on moors and in forests where great excitement ensued among the gathered throng of the Taw and Torridge Branch of the Devon Birdwatching and Preservation Society. These eager amateur birdos, who raised money to purchase and maintain key bird habitat, also ran a 'twitching' contest each year where several members regularly identified more than 200 or 300 bird species, inflated by large numbers of migratory species at certain times. On the morning I joined the group on their survey at Malmsmead I only reached the paltry total of 27 species, but these included both the grey and pied wagtails, which were new to me.

Rather than hoping to compete against these seasoned birdwatchers, I was more interested in their perceptions of the status of local birds. The decline in numbers in several species had been attributed principally to the clearing of historic hedgerows to facilitate broader-scale modern agriculture. But other threats included inadvertent killing of birds that had consumed snail and slug poisons, and predation by magpies and cats. My interest piqued, I enquired about what was being done to address the impact of cats. The responses were both consistent and defeatist. 'Even though there are plenty of us birdwatchers, the cat lobby is stronger,' I was informed. Although I assumed there was considerable overlap in affiliation between the two groups, it appeared there was little scope for compromise. The bird lovers reluctantly accepted cats were both very popular and inclined to catch their birds.

I had spent a couple of weeks becoming acquainted with not only the wildlife and wildlife enthusiasts of Devon, but also with my new bride's grandmother. Dot proved to be the very embodiment of what I expected an English grandmother to be – tiny, almost bird-like in stature, and full of warmth and cheer. Whipping up extravagant dishes on her AGA stove, or sipping afternoon wine in her flowery sunroom, Dot was an absolute delight. I was enchanted by her stories of the war and of rural life dominated by early-morning dairy farm rituals.

Although her horse riding and cow milking years were by now a fond memory, Dot retained a keen interest in the farm animals and wildlife on her farm in the rolling green hills of Devon. Strategically positioned in view of her sunroom window was a bird feeder that provided me with far better view than I achieved along the hedgerows. Indeed the ticks in my UK bird guide came more readily while idly enjoying the sun-warmed vestibule and consuming scones decked in double clotted cream than by stalking the cold hedgerows and forested patches.

Dot's old bird guide in her sunroom attested to the British

Until the mid-1990s the Heard and Sendell Farm Supplies business at Tiverton where Dot sourced her bird food sold only a few bags of peanuts for local birdwatchers to hang in stockings for their backyard birds. But in recent years their trade has exploded into a 10–15 tonne per annum business, such has been the growth in the backyard bird-feeder market. In his seminal book *Living on the Wind: Across the Hemisphere With Migratory Birds*, Scott Weidensaul describes how backyard bird feeders have drastically changed migration patterns of North American birds. Hummingbird feeders in the south-eastern US now enable rufous hummingbirds to overwinter there instead of flying south to Mexico. Backyard bird feeders keep purple finches, pine siskins, other seed eaters and the hawks that prey on them further north than their original winter haunts. Because the forests they once depended upon have been largely cleared, these birds are now largely reliant upon the feeders, which ironically leave them more vulnerable to outdoor cats.

obsession with encouraging songbirds to their gardens. The descriptions of each species paid greater attention to the types of feeders and food preferred by each species than the habitat information more typical of bird guides from other countries. Although Dot's most popular and prominent feeder suspended peanuts from a branch, she also put out seed for other birds.

Keeping an alert eye on the feeder while listening to stories in the sunroom, I was hoping to observe a bird that had aroused my interest ever since I started reading ornithological journals as an adolescent. *Parus major*, I had been reliably informed, was one of the most common attendees at English backyard feeding stations. As I ticked off the common birds at the feeder I knew I must be getting closer to my prize. I had distinguished between the singing sparrows and their more vocally challenged house sparrow cousins. In time I learned the 'sparrows' revealing a bright white rump when they flew off were, in fact, bullfinches. Whenever the sun appeared out from the clouds I could make out the olive colouration of the greenfinch and the pastel hues of the chaffinch. The plump little bird that snuck into the top of the peanut feeder and made off with a nut, like a naughty schoolboy, was a nuthatch. Its ability to shimmy down the feeder to extract its prize could well have annoyed the beautifully marked greater spotted woodpecker, which was industrially but messily hammering away at the nuts, sending chips scattering in all directions to be picked up by the dunnocks on the lawn below.

Among the frenetic activity at the peanut feeder a couple of small birds arrived that I thought might be *Parus major*. Slightly smaller than a sparrow they sported a yellow breast and greyish cap. A ray of sunlight illuminated the pair, turning the grey cap to blue, and revealing them as blue tits. With the sun still peeking out through the clouds another pair of slightly larger birds arrived with darker caps. Quickly I turned the page in the field guide to confirm the diagnostic dark stripe down their underparts. Bingo! I'd now recorded 40 species from Dot's garden and seen my first great tits.

Eager to help the recent widow but having neither the skills nor the pluck to offer assistance in her kitchen, I was assigned outdoor jobs that helped to burn off the relentless tide of calories that Dot bombarded us with. Once the leaves had been raked and the firewood stacked, Dot asked me if I would mind setting a trap for a stray cat she had noticed lurking around. She had been watching the development of a couple of treecreeper chicks in a cavity within the exfoliating bark of a dead tree in the garden and had been saddened to find a scatter of feathers and a silent nest on her morning inspection. Knowing I had a passion for animals, Dot assumed that I would be reluctant to trap the black-and-white cat she held responsible for predating the treecreeper nest. And I had been careful not to give her reason to think differently.

Katherine's relatives were all devoted cat lovers. Her parents had a pet cat named Moshie and fed stray cats at the small engineering factory they owned in suburban Adelaide. Dot doted on Puss, her long-haired grey cat resplendent with white stockings that had free rein of her house and garden. Puss was a pretty cat, but on close contact I developed a runny nose and itchy eyes. It was a constant battle to keep our bedroom door closed to keep Puss out, and on those cold English nights I knew Katherine would have otherwise encouraged Puss to curl up at her icy-cold feet.

The best way of dealing with stray or feral cats represents one of the most emotive and divisive decisions faced by any cat lover and wildlife enthusiast. Around the world, in gardens and parks, in forests and on farms, the most appropriate, compassionate and effective way to treat feral cats provokes more angst than almost any other animal challenge. These are not wandering pet cats, fed and valued by cat devotees, but unwanted pests. But they are still cats.

Maybe Dot had been forewarned of my pragmatic attitude towards feral cats in the Australian desert or my interest in studying their diets and was now setting a trap for her new grandson-in-law. There was no way I wanted to risk our congenial sojourn with an emotional debate about stray cats so I 'forgot' her request and busied myself with unnecessary gardening instead. But after a couple of days Katherine raised the subject again, concerned the stray cat was catching birds in her grandmother's garden.

Stray or feral cats are often difficult to trap but my bigger concern was what to do with the cat if we did manage to trap it. I doubted Dot would stroll out with a pistol and put the cat down. But it turned out Dot and Katherine had other ideas, an option not available in the remote areas where I lived. If we could trap the cat we would take it to the local Cats Protection League, and they would deal with it.

Within hours of setting the trap that Dot had used for trapping other strays over the years, the suspected culprit was in the cage. Dot came out to confirm its identity and jumped backwards when the frightened and cantankerous cat lurched towards her, bashing into the cage as it hissed. Even the calming words of the octogenarian cat lover did nothing to pacify the enraged coil of muscle and fur that had obviously been contained for the first time in its life. Standing back so as not to alarm the trapped cat further, I wondered aloud what the Cats Protection people would do with a cat that was so obviously feral. Quietly I also worried how Dot would respond when we inevitably had to inform her the cat had been put down. Overhearing my thoughts, Dot reassured me. 'Don't worry, John,' she said, 'of course Cats Protection will take the cat. They look after *all* cats and won't put it down.'

Katherine dutifully contacted the local branch and we were invited to bring in the spitting monster. Careful not to expose a finger we draped the cage with a towel and placed it in the back seat of Dot's little white Honda Accord. Half an hour later, after descending from the hedgerow-lined hill farms of middle Devon, we located the Cats Protection facility in Exeter. The first sign I noticed at their facility was the distinctive logo of the Royal Society for the Protection of Birds. Then I noticed a bird feeder, just like Dot's, hanging from a low branch in the front yard. As we hauled the still hissing caged cat down the path to the front door, we stepped around a cat snoozing in the sun, within easy reach of the bird feeder. I was struck by the irony. Pigeon fanciers don't attract falcons and shepherds don't keep wolves, so I couldn't understand why a cat refuge would attract birds to their garden.

The neatly dressed middle-aged woman inside asked me to put the cage down, still draped in a blanket, in a quiet room where their staff would assess the cat before deciding its fate. Despite Katherine's warning over the phone, the Cats Protection staffer did not seem at all alarmed by the unsociable behaviour of the cat. I assumed this inferred the uncontrollable cat would be euthanased, maybe even in time for us to take Dot's cage trap back to her. When I suggested this would be more convenient than for us than returning I was fixed by an incredulous stare.

Cats Protection, I learnt in a hurry, pride themselves on never euthanasing cats unless there are strong medical reasons for doing so. This no-kill policy makes them a particularly attractive organisation for cat lovers like Dot to patronise. I was intrigued as to how Cats Protection, which typically hosts a minimum 5000 homeless cats across the country, in addition to over 100 cats they rehome every day, could maintain this open-door but no-kill policy. Every cage and pen in the Exeter facility housed a cat awaiting adoption. Nationwide, Cats Protection neuter 163,000 cats per year. Given only a third of these cats are rehomed, and even less can be humanely housed in their shelters, a black hole was emerging in their accounting system.

With tens of thousands more cats brought in than homes for them, surely cute tame cats would be prioritised while old, injured or downright antisocial cats would miss out. Despite Dot's misplaced fears, I was comfortable, indeed even supportive, of this cat being quickly and painlessly euthanased. But I was relieved it was not my task to perform this unfortunate duty and pitied the volunteer cat lovers, of the 10,000 nationwide, who decided the fate of the cats brought to them. I had a fair inkling of what was going to happen to the terrified cat when we returned home.

Back at Dot's farmhouse I read the leaflets from Cats Protection and was astounded to discover that Trap-Neuter-Release is their policy of choice for dealing with feral cats. It seems to follow logically that feral cats brought to their full-capacity shelters will also be neutered and released. Unlike at Simbo, or in the deserts at home, where controlling cats had a direct conservation outcome, I had no strong feelings about the impact of cats in rural Devon.

Two mornings after taking the black-and-white cat to Cats Protection I had nearly finished my pre-breakfast walk around the boundary hedgerows as the morning fog lifted. Suddenly a black-and-white cat slunk off into the hedgerow. It must have been a sibling, I initially thought, another feral Dot might ask us to trap and rehome. But then I thought back to some of the feral cats we had fitted transmitters to at home. One male cat had covered more than 30 kilometres in a night. Maybe Dot's treecreeper killer had indeed returned home, although we would have next-to-no chance of trapping it again to confirm.

Ten minutes later a short-haired black cat with a white blaze and chest snuck into a hedgerow as I approached. Then I walked past a handwritten notice for a long-haired black cat that had gone missing from nearby Frogwell. I was musing over the abundance of cats and their apparently seamless transition from pet to feral, and maybe cat shelter to feral, status in rural Devon as I walked back to Dot's house. Right next to the feeder Dot had just topped up, I disturbed a black cat with white socks I'd not seen before. The countryside was literally crawling with free-ranging cats. I doubted whether we could dent the regional population even if we were to trap all the cats on the farm and take them to Cats Protection. And I started to wonder whether the cat refuges could paradoxically be perpetuating the numbers of free-ranging cats. Not only were some of the cats released by refuges, the notion Cats Protection provided a humane service to deal with all unwanted cats effectively let irresponsible cat owners off the hook. Don't bother desexing the family cat, or itinerant farm cats, because excess kittens could be 'cared for' by a cat shelter. Maybe this rural community had been conned into believing all unowned cats were being treated humanely.

What became clear as I researched cat management around the world was most cat refuges faced the same overriding dilemma. Irrespective of whether they had the capacity to provide humane refuge for four or 400 cats, the relentless supply of unowned cats

> The Green Valley Paws Patrol I visited in Arizona found the average cost of sterilising a cat and providing vaccines is US$100, not counting budgets for traps, crates and food. Hence trapping just 200 ferals a year accrued costs in excess of US$20,000. Even though Green Valley was a far more affluent region than most dealing with feral cat control, the impost of these ongoing expenses was limiting the effectiveness of their TNR program.

nearly always exceeded their capacity to rehome or accommodate them. So what to do with the hordes of cats they cannot house? There were two very different pathways to resolving this quandary, I learned, advocated by compassionate versus sentimental cat carers.

Chapter 13

'MISPLACED SENTIMENTALITY'

Domestic house cats kill more fish than all the world's seals put together. Paul Watson

If anyone was qualified to provide an insight into the challenges of managing unwanted cats it was the inaugural winner of the 2014 International Companion Animal Welfare Award. Elizabeth Oliver invited me to her cat and dog shelter on the outskirts of the Japanese megacity of Osaka to demonstrate first-hand the difficulties she faced and to explain her award-winning philosophy.

From the outside, the Animal Refuge Kansai, better known as ARK, more closely resembled a colourful, manicured garden than an animal refuge. Tucked away on a quiet winding street in the foothills on Osaka's margin, there was little indication from the street of the frenetic activity inside the leafy grounds. Only when I walked past the volunteers' car park, packed with little cars bearing dog, cat and whale stickers, was I given an inkling of the scale of the abandoned pet sanctuary inside.

Summoned from her rounds by a volunteer, Oliver invited me in to her busy office-cum-meeting room, issuing instructions to two other staffers on the way. Bespectacled and slightly hunched, Oliver may have lost a little of her mobility but none of her passion since she established ARK 25 years ago. Originally volunteering at an organisation that euthanased most of the animals it rescued, Somerset-born Oliver decided to start her own refuge and improve those odds. Although her cat refuge was an International Associate Member of the Royal Society for the Protection of Cruelty to Animals, Oliver was an independent free spirit.

Elizabeth Oliver was justifiably proud of her achievements. She pointed to a chart on the wall that tracked the number of dogs (3320) and cats (1358) ARK had rehomed since opening its doors in 1991, and informed me that an Englishwoman operating an animal shelter in the mountains of a far-away country is not unusual. 'You find us animal lovers everywhere,' she said. Her motivation for ARK was to provide a compassionate option for Japan's homeless dogs and cats. Unlike in England, there had been no government department to oversee the management of stray cats. Japan didn't even have animal welfare laws prior to 1973, when the impending visit to Japan of Britain's Queen Elizabeth led to the hastily convened *Animal Control Law*.

Before she invited me on a tour of her refuge complex nestled into the forested hillside, Elizabeth went to pains to distinguish between her own views and the attitudes of many of the cat lovers in her adopted home.

'Japanese are very sentimental people,' Oliver explained, describing their typical response to being presented with a sick or homeless cat as 'you poor thing'. 'They tend to make decisions based on how they think the animal would like to be treated at that particular time,' she explained. By contrast, Oliver framed her decision-making on a 'compassionate' approach that considered the bigger picture and the likely future prospects for the animal. Oliver acknowledged she could not help every cat or solve every animal welfare issue; she was limited by funds, space and staff.

While I struggled to comprehend the difference between sentimentality and compassion, Oliver cited the difficult decision

> There are millions of stray cats in Osaka,' explained compassionate animal refuge manager Elizabeth Oliver. 'Count as many street cats as you can by day and night and then triple that number.' A cat shelter rapidly fills to capacity and the manager needs to be selective about those cats they can help. Oliver observed, 'Sentimental cat carers attempt to take all unowned cats into their care, but in doing so they risk inadvertently harming the welfare of both incoming cats and their increasingly crowded resident cats.'

cat refuge managers typically have to make: which cats they can or cannot accommodate or assist.

She developed a simple test. When encountering a stray cat in a park or on the street, Oliver tried to coerce it to approach, with kind words and sometimes food. If she could convince the cat, it was likely to be lost or a stray. If the cat fled, Oliver considered it a feral. By Oliver's reckoning, Dot's evasive and hostile black-and-white cat was not a suitable candidate for rehoming or refuge life. She typically only brought in stray cats because they were most likely to be suitable for rehoming and were most vulnerable to abuse by cat haters, who could rarely get close to feral cats.

The main reason Oliver did not take in all cats was she felt strongly about the minimum standards she had adopted for cats in her care. Accepting truly feral cats, would result in overcrowding within days, exposing the residents to stress, disease and potential injury. Rather than further explanation, Oliver walked outside into the driving rain to demonstrate.

Garden paths fringed by beautiful flowers and shrubs led to a network of closely nestled buildings. Despite the unavoidable feline aroma, I was impressed with the facilities. An average of seven and maximum of nine cats, carefully segregated by gender and temperament, lived in bedroom-sized rooms equipped with shelves and steps, ramps and boxes. Most cats were lazing on individual cushions in their favoured position as we walked through. Rosters of busy cheerful staff and volunteers fed each of the hundred or so cats awaiting adoption, carefully measuring servings of pet food.

All cats, even kittens four months of age, were desexed on arrival. Others requiring specific medical attention were quarantined in specialist facilities. Both feline influenza and feline AIDs were prevalent among local stray cats, so all were blood tested on arrival and volunteers were vigilant for signs of these debilitating diseases. Routine vet inspections and strict quarantine and treatment procedures for any cat seen sneezing or otherwise unwell had proven successful. Vet checks were particularly important when the shelter received unsolicited boxes of kittens dropped outside the gates or when they received major intakes, such as the influx of abandoned cats that survived the Fukushima earthquake, tsunami and nuclear meltdown tragedy.

Although compassionate to cats herself, Oliver had surprisingly strong views on some of her fellow cat keepers. She considered 'cat people' as often socially isolated and lonely indoors people, as distinct from more outgoing and outdoorsy 'dog people'. Oliver also explained the 'no-kill' policy of cat refuges like Cats Protection in the UK was popular among her Japanese friends. Perhaps, she thought, this sentimentality, rather than compassion, was 'a Buddhist thing'. Yet it made it difficult for Japanese, even Japanese vets, to take personal responsibility for pragmatic decisions like euthanasing incurable cats.

Neutering was prohibitively expensive for most Japanese refuges. Most local vets also opposed early neutering to limit birth

Elizabeth Oliver, inaugural winner of the International Companion Animal Welfare Award, with one of about a hundred cats enjoying climbing towers at her ARK pet refuge in Osaka, Japan. Oliver condones ethical euthanasia, rather than overcrowding her shelter, for cats unlikely to be adopted to safe homes. (Photo: J. Read)

rates and euthanasia. Again Oliver felt it was a cultural thing not to administer lethal injections, although she said the workers at the Hokensho, or Public Health Pound, seemed to harbour no such misgivings about gassing multitudes of cats with carbon monoxide in a big room, or even allowing feral cats to suffocate in polythene bags. Apparently although quick painless euthanasia by injection was considered abhorrent, 'indirect' deaths, despite the suffering, were kosher.

Despite being a 'nice' and culturally appropriate objective, Oliver was frustrated 'no-kill' was neither realistic nor necessarily humane. In particular, she deplored shelters boasting they 'looked after' all cats, including those with tumours that would be euthanased in most other countries. But ARK needed to be careful about openly acknowledging they euthanased cats. An active blogger, vehemently opposed to euthanasing cats, would give them a bad rap and stop the public bringing in strays.

With ARK at full capacity, despite recent expansions, I could not understand why Oliver was so concerned about the no-kill advocates not bringing more cats to her. Oliver abruptly stopped our tour and fixed me with a stare to ensure I took heed. 'I started ARK out of concern for the animals, not to make my own life easier,' she explained. 'These no-kill shelters can either keep new cats in increasingly crowded and squalid conditions or return them to the streets. At least ARK offers hope of a better outcome for cats that can't be rehomed.' As we resumed our tour of ARK she muttered 'misplaced sentimentality!' under her breath.

Oliver's philosophy of euthanasia in preference to keeping cats in cramped conditions was supported by the International Society for Feline Medicine: 'Long-term caging or permanent confinement in a homing facility or "sanctuary" is not acceptable.' Instead these vets advocate neutering and release, either at the point of capture or to another more appropriate location. Importantly, though, the International Society for Feline Medicine acknowledge the pragmatic but nonetheless controversial caveat: 'Where resources and/or options are limited, euthanasia may have to be considered to avoid long-term confinement.' Oliver argued that numbers of unowned cats exceeding resources for their appropriate care were unfortunately the norm, resulting in the inevitable but appropriate widespread euthanasia of cats.

Despite electing not to cuddle the cats like many of the

volunteers, I was pleasantly surprised by how healthy and content they looked. It was little wonder ARK had such success in adopting out their cats and little trouble in attracting devoted volunteers. Like Dorothy at Haida Gwaii, I applauded Oliver's devotion and success. As Oliver had pointed out, there were cat carers, mostly women like her, in nearly every city of every country. With my interest in the different approaches taken by cat shelters piqued, I decided to further investigate their issues and challenges.

I was attracted to the Rainbow Friends Animal Sanctuary in Hawaii by its reputation for being another well-organised model cat refuge and their moniker of 'Compassionate Care'. Like Oliver's ARK sanctuary in Japan, Mary Rose Krijgsman's sanctuary also operated in beautiful garden surrounds. The similarities between the two refuges were striking. I was most interested in whether Oliver and Netherlands-born Krijgsman shared similar definitions of compassionate care. The ex-scuba diving instructor, who first developed empathy for whales, dolphins and sharks, has built up a large and renowned cat and dog refuge and adopting centre since opening on a small scale in the 1990s.

Krijgsman fitted the mould for many cat shelter managers I had met, and reflected the norm from the US survey of cat care workers. Many were middle-aged woman with little or no scientific or veterinary training but boundless emotional investment in their cause. Like Oliver and many others, Krijgsman oozed the charisma integral to attracting and maintaining the dozens of volunteers who assisted at her shelter. Despite my ambition to keep an open mind and critical eye, I found it difficult not to get swept away by the content-looking cats, and the confidence of staff and management that Rainbow Friends indeed offered the most compassionate outcomes for those cats lucky enough to be admitted.

On my tour I was struck by the vertical complexity of the cat rooms, with many of the cats lying on or investigating elevated shelves and ramps. Most of the standalone cattery buildings allowed free access to outdoor pens through open doors. Krijgsman permitted no more than 25 cats in each of her ten 24-square-metre rooms, which seems like almost battery-hen densities until the multi-storeyed denning and vantage points are considered. Although tempted to increase densities to accommodate more of the island's strays, higher numbers were a challenge to room cleaning and ensuring food quotas.

A roster of 50 zealous volunteers visited about three times a week to feed and groom the cats and clean out their rooms. My 10-year-old daughter Elke, who joined the tour, commented on how Rainbow Friends was like a holiday camp for cats. Her older sister Layla thought it more of a cat hotel, with the staff moving from room to room with clean bedding, food and a little pampering.

We were all taken by Miracle House, providing quarantine conditions for cats with feline influenza, and Zanny's Wing for cats too old for adoption. These cats were treated by the staff with even more care and devotion than the healthier members of the main cat camp hotel. I was relieved to note all the cats in the Miracle House appeared to be pain free and Krijgsman assured me that cats with untreatable painful afflictions were compassionately euthanased by one of the two local vets who made regular visits. All Rainbow Friends cats were desexed, tested and immunised against feline leukemia, and dewormed at a cost of approximately $200 per cat. Some of these costs were recuperated by adoption donations. Sponsorship certificates pinned to walls in the cat hotels revealed which of the resident cats were sponsored to the tune of $20 a month.

As we walked around the spacious grounds my eye was caught by a spectacular saffron finch alighting on a long grass stalk and riding it to the ground where it pecked at the seed head. These aptly named birds were so bright a single feather dislodged when preening could conceivably colour a steaming cauldron of rice. Unlike the Cats Protection branch at Tiverton, birds were not encouraged by feeding at Rainbow Friends, but the gardens attracted them nonetheless. Pointing out the brilliant bird in a vulnerable position on the ground, I enquired whether any of the Rainbow Friend cats lived outdoors, or had access outdoors. Krijgsman knew where my line of questioning was headed. 'We do have a couple of outdoor cats but they are so well cared for they don't chase the birds or roam beyond the refuge grounds,' I was told. I had no way of checking this claim but an outdoor cat owner acknowledging to a biologist that their cat might catch birds would be as unlikely as a mother sympathising with her daughter-in-law about her son's perceived faults! I thought back to the Peterson study that revealed only 9% of cat care workers conceded feral cats harm bird populations and let the matter slide.

I tried to raise the issue of euthanasia for the unowned cats Krijgsman was unable to cater for, but she deftly dodged the subject. 'Rainbow Friends advocates no killing of healthy cats,' I was reminded. I persisted, asking how she responded to the tens of thousands of Hawaiian cats that could never be housed at Rainbow Friends if she stuck to her philosophy of no euthanasia, no overcrowding or adopting cats out unless they would be treated better than at the Sanctuary. These resolute protocols inevitably

Miracle House, reserved for quarantined cats with feline influenza at Rainbow Friends Sanctuary, Hawaii. This debilitating disease spreads rapidly through poorly managed or overpopulated cat refuges.
(Photo: J. Read)

forced Krijgsman to turn back as many as 80 calls a day for cats and dogs she could not accommodate. Although she was valiantly fundraising to increase her capacity to offer respite for more cats and even employ and accommodate an in-house vet, Krijgsman was clearly exasperated she couldn't do more.

But Krijgsman could never get close to providing care or adoption opportunities for more than a fraction of the island's cats. Hawaii's mild climate and absence of large predators make it a perfect environment for feral cats to breed and prosper without dependence on humans. According to the Hawaii Humane Society, which has the unenviable task of euthanasing cats in the island state, roughly 22,000 cats are euthanased each year, similar to the tally for all of Australia. As deplorable as this statistic appears, it is nowhere near the number required to effectively manage outdoor cats in Hawaii. Not surprisingly, the Hawaii Humane Society takes exception to Rainbow Friends, which they consider does little to ameliorate the burgeoning and ethically unacceptable toll of stray cats. On this telling criteria, Rainbow Friends clearly took a sentimental approach, rather than offering compassionate euthanasia for the excess stray cats.

Although she couldn't accommodate unlimited stray cats, Krijgsman did not ignore these other cats. Rainbow Friends team also helped coordinate TNR activities at Lilio Kalani, where about 80 unowned cats were fed. This large feral population was difficult to manage because, as has been found in other TNR clowders, people kept dumping cats there, assuming they would be looked after. And, like Dorothy had described on Haida Gwaii, 'crazy cat ladies', according to Krijgsman, considered they owned the cats in 'their' clowder and would not cooperate with the trapping and neutering program. Without the willing participation of all of the feeders, TNR amounted to little more than an expensive, exhausting waste of time. Kerrie Anne Loyd and Jayna DeVore from the University of Georgia found providing food to cat camps may actually lead to hyperpredation of adjacent wildlife by allowing cats to persist at high densities even when their prey is scarce or in decline.

A further challenge to large TNR programs was the need to treat all of the cats in the clowder, which could take Krijgsman and her volunteers years to achieve. Her challenges mirrored those of the Hawaii Humane Society, who claim to be able to neuter approximately 15% of the registered 'colony' cats per year. Originally reliant upon relentless perseverance to achieve saturation neutering, Krijgsman now attempts to trap the whole colony at once, using her artillery of 100 cage traps baited with canned tuna or mackerel. I remarked on how expensive such an operation must be and Krijgsman acknowledged it would not be possible without sponsorship from PetCo and PetSmart Foundations. She also pointed out the valuable contribution made to Rainbow Friends by major grocery stores and other pet food manufacturers and distributors. As seen worldwide, companies profiting from the sale of pet food often make sizable donations to cat welfare organisations.

Mary Rose Krijgsman outside her Rainbow Friends sanctuary in Hawaii. Commercial cat food suppliers that donate to cat sanctuaries might also support stray cat clowders 'managed' by typically counterproductive Trap-Neuter-Release policies. (Photo: J. Read)

US cat food sales ballooned from US$4.2 billion a year in 2000 to a staggering US$11.4 billion in 2017. Donations of cat food to TNR programs represent promotional opportunities for the pet food companies to increase their share of this enormous and growing pie. Anyone who can remember the barrage of deception by DDT manufacturers, which extended sales for a decade after the risks were widely recognised, or similar strategies employed by big tobacco, pharma, asbestos or coal, may question the brazen promotion of TNR by pet food giants in the face of evidence that TNR is flawed and often counterproductive. And as Councilman Pops Barnes learned in Columbus, Georgia, the welfare outcomes of major Best Friends/ PetSmart TNR programs are either not recorded or are closely guarded secrets of their complicit sponsors.

My previous impression of large pet food companies donating cat food to refuges and particularly clowder feedlots was one of corporate responsibility, framed not too subtly by a targeted marketing opportunity. However, Krijgsman's mention of her donated tuna and mackerel now resonated in a different way. I had just read the enlightening book *The Ocean of Life: The fate of man and the sea* by marine biologist Callum Roberts.

The global impact of the hundreds of thousands of tonnes of cat food manufactured each year became apparent to Roberts when he investigated the source of the ingredients. All foodstuffs can be categorised to a trophic level based on their position in the food chain. Plants, the primary transformers of sunlight to energy, sit at level one, whereas strict herbivores that eat only plants are at trophic level two. For every hundred units of energy produced by grass, only about 10 are captured by level two herbivores like cattle. The rest of the energy consumed is used up by respiring and metabolic processes through flatulence, defecating, moving, fighting and breeding. First order carnivores, those that only eat herbivores, sit at trophic level three, again losing another 90% of the energy originally captured and so on. Level four carnivores eat smaller carnivores and use about 100 times the raw energy used by herbivores.

Strict vegetarians consuming homegrown vegies rank at about two on this trophic scale alongside rabbits and squirrels, but the average human slightly exceeds trophic level three due to the mix of different meats and vegies in our diet. Lions, as befitting the kings of the jungle, command a trophic level approaching four, which is pretty close to the sustainable limit of land-based ecosystems. However, Roberts noted incredibly productive marine ecosystems can expand this trophic cascade, with small fish eaten by progressively larger and then larger fish. Atlantic salmon and bluefin tuna rank at about 4.4, whereas some large sharks may exceed this figure.

Roberts made a startling and alarming discovery. Due to the high proportion of salmon and tuna in commercial cat food, most domestic cats feature higher than lions and way higher than humans on the trophic ladder. No other pets and few other animals have such high protein requirements as cats. Unlike dogs, which can survive quite well on a mixed diet of meat and vegetables or grains, cats are obligate carnivores and their predilection for predatory fish like tuna and salmon makes them among the highest-ranking consumers on Earth. Adult pet cats require 800–1200 kilojoules of energy each day, with nursing queens requiring closer to 3000. Domestic cats, weight for weight, consume more biological energy than obese junk food addicts.

The extraordinary protein and energy dependency of over 200

million pet cats worldwide has major implications for the world's fisheries. This energy drain also presents an ethical challenge for cat feeders, many of whom have adopted a vegetarian or vegan diet to lessen their own footprint on our increasingly crowded and resource-depleted planet. The bowl of food they place out for the stray cat, let alone the bags of food left out for a feral clowder, likely place a larger dent in the Earth's food resources than their choice of evening meal. And most cat food manufacturers, especially those who donate tonnes of food for unowned cats, are also complicit in this extraordinary depletion of marine resources exacerbated by the recent explosion in cat clowders. Robert's concerns about unsustainable fishing are exacerbated if fussy consumers select gourmet cat food, which is typically marketed as being derived from energy-intensive predatory fish like tuna and mackerel.

The Best Friends Animal Society distributed 80,000 tonnes of cat food to unowned cats in the US in 2009. Gregory Okin from UCLA calculated that pet dogs and cats in the US consume about a fifth of the dietary energy consumed by humans and constitute over a quarter of the environmental impacts from animal production in terms of the use of land, water, fossil fuel, phosphate and biocides – with trends towards 'premium' pet food exacerbating this trend. Okin's research did not consider the quantity of cat food fed to unowned cat clowders, including the 1200 registered cat 'colonies' that support over 16,000 cats on the Hawaiian island of Oahu alone.

Since Hawaii has both one of the highest feral cat densities and numbers of vulnerable wildlife in the world, the isolated archipelago is the epicentre of cat associations. Krijgsman was one of the spearheads behind HAWC, the Hawaiian Animal Welfare Coalition, which aims to improve the welfare and management of Hawaii's cats and dogs. HAWC concentrates on managing unowned cats and dogs on the Big Island, AdvoCATS operates on the west. Along with the Hawaii Humane Society and the Humane Society of the US, these cat advocate groups formed an uncomfortable but necessary allegiance with wildlife supporters who want all cats off the streets to help protect the unique wildlife of their formerly idyllic islands.

The Hawaii Coalition for the Protection of Cats and Wildlife was formed to help broker deals with nervous yet recalcitrant cat feeders to relocate their cats away from key wildlife refuge sites, identified by the coalition's biologists. Importantly the coalition also campaigned for more appropriate statewide cat management laws, modelled on the Honolulu County Ordinance that mandates sterilisation and improves the legal status, identification and appropriate care of cats. However, the increasingly ineffective and fractured coalition ultimately withered and failed without milestone successes.

I pushed Krijgsman on her perspectives as to why the coalition failed to endorse or achieve the restrictions on breeding and containment of pet cats. Just as she has campaigned against the backyard breeding of dogs, an obvious source of strays, the Rainbow Friends founder also supports registration of cat breeders to reduce the influx of ferals. However cat containment was clearly not high on her list of priorities, either for Rainbow Farm or society in general. 'Responsible cat ownership is a huge problem but we are so busy we haven't the time to even begin with the owners.'

Cat containment could have been a defining circuit breaker

for the Hawaii Coalition for the Protection of Cats and Wildlife. Although they claimed more pressing concerns prohibited their advocacy of containment laws, Krijgsman and Cathy Swedelius, president of AdvoCATS, found compulsory cat containment unwarranted. Like other cat carers, growing up with seemingly content outdoor cats had left them accustomed and accepting of cats' free-roaming behaviour, despite Swedelius lamenting, ' We have found cats we adopted out after owners moved off island and abandoned them again.' If outdoor cats in their care were well fed and received regular veterinary treatment, Krijgsman and Swedelius didn't consider they represented a major health, welfare or wildlife predation problem.

The second, and even more intractable sticking point for Hawaii's cat and wildlife coalition was the emotive and divisive issue of unowned cat management. They had shared minor victories by erecting a cat-proof fence around a seabird rookery and relocating some cats short distances away from threatened wildlife. But the hundreds of thousands – perhaps millions – of feral cats in Hawaii remained the elephant in the coalition's room. Biologist Chris Lepczyk summed up the situation eloquently when I visited him at the University of Hawaii. Unless the coalition dealt with the influx of new cats, 'all our management actions are essentially triage'.

Although wearing sandals and an aloha shirt, Lepczyk was earnest and frustrated. Direct predation by cats on threatened birds, like the almost unpronounceable ahu 'elepaio and palila, understandably ranked at the top of his concerns, but he was also collecting information on the prevalence of toxoplasmosis affecting both wildlife and, probably, cat carers. Another irritation of the academic biologist was that although cat numbers had not

Although feeding unowned cats had been banned from the nearby Chaminade University due to the welfare and health risk they posed, University of Hawaii academic Dr Chris Lepczyk could not even convince his own university to follow suit. As he walked me around the campus' cat feeding stations that frustrate him every day, Lepczyk revealed he has two cats, and once owned three. 'They are desexed and adored indoor pets, the way cats should be. Not like these miserable stray cats or true ferals.' Lepczyk is not alone in being a cat-owning biologist. Most of the 239 bird conservation professionals included in a US-wide survey conducted by the North Carolina State University identified themselves as also being 'cat people', with nearly half owning a cat at the time of the survey. But like Lepczyk, the vast majority of these cat-owning biologists kept their cats indoors and favoured proven and humane euthanasia over TNR for unowned cats.

declined noticeably at TNR clowders like Lilio Kalani, the Humane Society of the US received more funds for ineffective TNR than scientists could muster for conserving or studying Hawaii's threatened fauna.

Lepczyk pointed out both public opinion and scientific modelling supported euthanasia, rather than TNR as the most effective and appropriate management for Hawaii's feral cats. More than eight out of 10 Hawaiian residents didn't support outdoor cats and felt euthanasia was preferable to returning neutered cats outdoors. Lepczyk's main beef was that euthanasia, which he considered both humane and effective for the tens of thousands of Hawaiian cats that can't be rehomed, was vehemently opposed by the small but vocal cat lobby.

Lepczyk reminded me of a scientist who, despite compelling

data, had failed to gain political support for the unambiguous link between smoking and health risk, or carbon emissions and accelerated climate change. His students repeatedly found compelling evidence that unique Hawaiian ecosystems were being decimated by feral animals, especially cats, and their ineffective and naïve management. Rachel Carson had exposed the dangers of pesticides to ecosystems and ensured multinational chemical companies changed their ways. But Lepczyk was not pitted against chemical, nicotine nor oil barons in his battle to contain pet cats and control feral cats. Instead his intransigents were mainly middle-aged women, who he otherwise admired for their passion and dedication.

Cat owner and ecologist Dr Chris Lepczyk advocates humane euthanasia over ineffective Trap-Neuter-Release for feral cats fed at these stations at the University of Hawaii. (Photo: J. Read)

Instead of acquiescing to Lepczyk's suggestion to euthanase cats beyond the capacity of adoptees and shelters, Krijgsman proposed increasing the capacity of shelters. In particular, she advocated for cat shelters to be built in all suburbs to help attain her vision of a 'no-kill' Hawaii. 'No-kill', the very exemplar of sentimentality, reigns supreme for cat care individuals and organisations on Hawaii.

After reviewing these perspectives from the frontline of feral cat management, I sought the perspectives of other groups involved with the challenges posed by unowned cats. The next chapters complete my quest for determining the most pragmatic, compassionate and effective strategy for managing unowned cats.

Chapter 14

COMPASSIONATE CONSERVATION

Compassionate conservation is neither. Dr Peter Fleming

Elizabeth Oliver had raised the distinction between the 'sentimental' ideology of 'no-kill' cat shelters and the 'compassionate' ideology she espoused at her ARK shelter. The sentimentalists advocated a black-and-white approach. Euthanasing a cat brought to their shelter was both immoral and implausible to the sentimentalists, even when they were deciding the fate of a mortally sick cat where the alternative was to house the creature in cramped conditions or release it back to the wild. Sentimentalists believed, with good reason, that some cat lovers would not bring a suffering cat to them if there was a chance it would be euthanased. Others avoided confronting the question altogether.

By contrast, compassionates assessed individual incoming cats for their health and rehoming potential before deciding their fate. Elizabeth, for example, had made the gut-wrenching, but in her eyes responsible and compassionate, decision to peacefully euthanase cats with untreatable debilitating illness or injury, or with poor prospects of rehoming.

Both approaches allowed the cat refuge manager to justify their actions based on their perspective of the how the cat should be treated. Presumably a sentimentalist opposed to euthanasia of stray cats would also oppose facilitating the empathetic end of life of a terminally ill relative for whom living has become a painful, valueless battle. Such a personal viewpoint is bound to be influenced by the unique life experiences of the decision-maker and the degree of anthropocentricity they infuse into their judgement. As a scientist, I sought a more robust and pragmatic decision-making tool. I yearned for a process that accommodated evidence of distress and, ideally, probabilities of an optimal outcome for not only the cat and the shelter staff but for the ongoing welfare, social and environmental issues of unwanted cats. Sentimentality and compassion are keystone emotions that I hold very dear but they can perversely challenge the actions of conservation biologists.

For this reason a symposium to discuss the compassionate treatment of animals at the 2013 International Conservation Biology biennial conference in Baltimore drew my attention. Typically conservation biologists discuss their approaches for minimising environmental threats and for protecting or reintroducing threatened species. Conservation biology is typically centred on saving habitat and killing invasive species as effectively as possible. Such a preoccupation and reliance upon killing animals initially seems contrary for field biologists, who typically found their vocation through a love of animals and motivation to help them.

The Baltimore conference organisers had broadened the scope of conservation biology and given voice to an alternative viewpoint. The animal liberation community were invited to present their case in a novel session titled 'Compassionate Conservation – Animal Welfare in Conservation Practice'. In another symposium, the imposing Michael Reed had presented modelling predicting TNR was potentially counterproductive for reducing the numbers of unowned cats. Other talks over the week-long conference presented innovative ideas on the most effective ways of controlling (that is, killing) exotic species. Therefore, even the title raised eyebrows among the milling ecologists who felt this session implied their conservation practices were uncompassionate. Compassionate conservation is a term gaining traction, especially among publicly funded lobby groups. Securing public support or funding for conservation programs that openly acknowledge their most important work involves baiting or trapping animals is far more difficult than for 'no-kill' and 'no-harm' organisations.

Compassionate conservation symposium organiser Chris Draper, from the Born Free Foundation, set out to appease concerned ecologists by claiming better welfare equates to better conservation. Although Draper conceded that animal welfare might be perceived by conservationists as a 'hindrance' or 'luxury', he claimed compassionate conservation was an increasingly rigorous science with practical implications for conservation.

Marc Bekoff, from the University of Colorado, was the star presenter and arguably the grandfather of this emerging paradigm. Bekoff's two guiding principles for scientists to adopt when planning their programs was 'first, do no harm' and 'second, individuals do matter'.

In order to place these principles into a more realistic framework the confident and articulate professor of cognitive ethnology offered the following advice. 'If you would not do it to your pet dog, don't do it to other animals. Full stop.'

Such a mantra emerged from an appreciation that animals have feelings and barbaric experiments using animals were no longer defendable. Bekoff's pet dog analogy was particularly useful for scientists planning laboratory experiments where animals were used as substitutes for humans. Crash-test dummies, not guinea pigs, should be used wherever possible for simulations and invasive trials. Every effort should be made to eliminate suffering by experimental animals.

The other scientists I was sitting with nodded in tentative agreement. There was no argument about the ability of animals to experience pain, nor the obligation of scientists to reduce suffering of research animals. But concern about where this session was headed was palpable.

Compassionate conservation aimed to recast conservation decision-making priorities. Rather than focusing on achieving the desired outcome, Marc Bekoff, from the University of Colorado, advocates concentrating on the more individualistic perspective of the pest animal. Ecologists were asked to put themselves in the position of the invasive toad, or rat, or indeed feral cat. Only through this cognitive transformation could decisions be made on what approaches, or techniques, were appropriate to deal with conservation threats. By contrast, James Russell from the University of Auckland points out: 'Deciding not to remove or control invasive species where they negatively affect native species would, in effect, be in conflict with the founding principle of Compassionate Conservation to do no harm.'

Bekoff's philosophy led to only one logical conclusion. When viewed from the perspective of the pest animal, death was undesirable. Scientists and wildlife advocates were responsible for their own actions, not those of pest species like unowned cats. In short, Compassionate Conservationists let the pest species live freely and bore little regard or responsibility for the consequences to wildlife. So-called Compassionate Conservationists could sleep soundly in the knowledge they had personally done no harm to an animal and treated all pests as they would their beloved pet dog.

Uncomfortable twitters spread like pond ripples through the audience and erupted into a tsunami of opinions and commentary in the ensuing open discussion. Draper, Bekoff and their co-presenters had their supporters, who were appreciative of the opportunity to reinforce the morality and importance of the Compassionate Conservation mantra among a scientific audience. But the detractors were equally as vocal.

Among the most outspoken was the passionate and dignified Cristian Bonacic. Not to be outdone by the compassionate conservation moniker, he introduced another term I had never heard. 'You have fallen into the "speciesism trap", he pronounced with authority to the assembled speakers who looked at him, somewhat bemused.

Bonacic implored with equal measures of exasperation and indignation, 'You are placing the rights and the welfare of one species above those of another, or many others.' Bonacic's assertion was that Bekoff and his associates were perpetrating a biological apartheid that did not consider the pain and suffering caused to prey species by introduced predators. Noticeable for its omission in the Compassionate Conservation presentation was the call for ecologists to place themselves in the position of the endangered prey species that was killed, or worse still maimed, by the invasive species. Bonacic's basic tenet was this: 'What about the bird with the broken wing or fatal bacterial infection? What about the native rodent that is tossed around like a toy before eventually dying of its experience? Why are their rights not as important, indeed even more important, than the perpetrating cat?'

Vets and conservationists are not alone in recognising the

ethical inconsistency in preserving the life of a feral cat that directly threatens the lives of many other animals, especially wildlife. Although he describes it as a 'morally dumbfounding problem', renowned psychologist Michael Shermer ultimately countenances euthanasing pest animals to protect native species from an ethical perspective, acknowledging that pest control results in the killing of fewer (wild) animals than those that would otherwise succumb to starvation or predation.

Bonacic also eloquently reopened the divide between animal liberationists, whose main concern was for the rights of individual animals, and conservationists, whose emphasis was on the fate of populations, species and ecosystems. So intransigent is the disconnect between the two mindsets that philosopher Mark Sagoff argues confrontationally but pragmatically that 'an environmentalist cannot be an animal liberationist. Nor may animal liberationists be environmentalists'.

It was unclear whether Draper and Beckoff had set out to reconnect the two disparate groups, or to promote their philosophy to their nemeses. What was apparent was neither objective had been particularly successful in the Baltimore lecture theatre.

At the conclusion of the symposium I introduced myself to the outspoken man who had introduced the issue of feral cat management into the Compassionate Conservation spotlight. Associate Professor Cristian Bonacic is a Chilean vet and director of the Ecosystems and Environment Department at the Catholic University in Chile. Aside from several academic postings, Bonacic has served as a member of the Wildlife Trust Alliance and associate researcher of the Wildlife Conservation Research Unit at Oxford. He has managed a Darwin Initiative project and received a Whitley commendation for his innovative work in conservation science from HRH Princess Royal at the Royal Geographical Society of London.

Bonacic had clearly been agitated by the symposium and was still seething 30 minutes later. 'People who claim it is not the cat or dog's fault are missing the point. We humans caused the problem and we can't sit back and let the problem get worse. It's our responsibility to take action,' he exclaimed, exasperated.

I soon learned this vet's concerns about Compassionate Conservation were measured compared to his outspoken views on Animal Rights organisations that perpetrate TNR. 'TNR is the cruellest thing you can do to a cat. It lowers their social status and increases their chance of being beaten up. TNR also exposes them to operation-related diseases.' And Bonacic does not hold back his disdain for complicit vets either, claiming, 'Vets undertaking TNR should be stripped of their accreditation.'

Although not as resolute as Bonacic, the American Veterinary Medicine Authority supports actions to eliminate the problem of free-roaming abandoned and feral cats, including consideration of euthanasia for clowders that are not 'achieving attrition'. The AVMA consider 'the almost inevitable suffering and premature mortality of free-ranging cats from disease, starvation, or trauma' constitutes 'a national tragedy of epidemic proportions'.

Another outspoken vet, David Jessup from the Santa Cruz Marine Wildlife Veterinary Care and Research Center, echoed these concerns. Jessup recoined TNR as Trap-Neuter-Re-abandon and urges his fellow vets to work towards a time when it is just as socially unacceptable to abandon a cat on public or private property as it is to abandon a horse, cow or dog. Jessup advocates trapping and neutering of all unowned cats but never re-abandonment. Where possible, trapped cats should be rehomed, as he and his family have done with 11 cats.

Far from being a 'cat hater' this compassionate yet pragmatic man still keeps four once-feral cats in his home. Another alternative that Jessup supports is the establishment of fenced sanctuaries where neutered and vaccinated cats are cared for but kept apart from feral cats and wildlife. But Jessup does not shy away from the third option for feral cats when homes or enclosed sanctuaries are not available. Like Cristian Bonicac, Jessup considers the most compassionate choice is to euthanase feral cats, rather than re-abandon them to 'an almost certain painful death'.

My first dog boasted a mixture of beagle, poodle and terrier, although I'm doubtful whether breeders of any of these pedigrees would claim a contribution. Saudi was a Christmas present, sourced from an animal shelter. He was the consolation prize for my two siblings and me after our planned year-long adventure to Saudi Arabia for Dad's work had been cancelled at the last minute. Little Saudi was more than compensation and provided countless hours of entertainment and affection. Saudi went everywhere with us perched on the back of the bench seat in the family station wagon, but as he grew older and more infirm, our trips to the vet became more frequent. Mum had told us that the vet was the best judge on whether to quietly put him to sleep or not.

I can still remember the three of us in the vet's waiting room hearing the kind white-jacketed woman tell us what we deep down already knew. We were allowed to have one last pat but the best thing for our dear Saudi was to go to sleep. Through watery eyes we agreed and complied, somewhat comforted by knowing that Saudi's pain would soon be over. Looking back on it after many decades I realise how complicit we were, accepting that the vet knew best.

I'm wondering now whether I would have agreed to the wise and compassionate vet's opinion if the situation had been different. What if my pet cat had given birth to two more kittens than I could find homes for and the local animal rescue and pet stores were unable to take any more? What if Mum and Dad had already said that we couldn't keep more pets and our vet had informed me that the most responsible, and compassionate, action would be euthanasia, to save them from a life of suffering. I could take the cats to a local park and let them take their chances. I could take them to a friend's farm where there were already a few cats living around the sheds to eat mice. I could let them go in a patch of bush, where they could hunt their own food, or in the back garden in the hope they would find themselves another home. If I took them to the vet she might charge me to euthanase them and probably give me another lecture about getting their mother desexed.

Healthy kittens would not be in pain, so unlike Saudi's predicament there would be no urgency to take action. But of even greater consequence is the fact the decision regarding the fate of unwanted kittens falls with the cat owner, not the vet. Whereas the default decision for an ailing pet in the vet's care is euthanasia, the easiest and superficially most compelling decision for unwanted kittens is to dump them somewhere they have a chance of survival. No one need know. If the cats were caught and euthanased, or if they were run over on the road or succumbed to a fatal disease, the kitten's 'owner' would be none the wiser.

To my surprise, opposition to euthanasia of unowned cats is neither as entrenched nor as common as outspoken critics would have us believe. In his survey of 1388 Hawaiians about their preferred technique to reduce cat populations, Chris Lepczyk found that live capture and lethal injection was the most popular. Despite the protests of a vocal minority, Hawaiians were sufficiently informed and pragmatic to support the most efficient and ethical management for unowned cat colonies. Across the Pacific, Mark Farnworth and his co-workers found that irrespective of whether they were cat caregivers or not, lethal control was also considered an acceptable, even desirable, outcome for unowned cats in New Zealand. However, Farnworth did concede a semantic twist, suggesting cat caregivers still harbour doubts. The cat feeders remained less likely to support lethal control in cats that were categorised as 'stray', rather than 'feral'. Although not covered in either questionnaire, I bet that most respondents were more likely to embrace euthanasia as a desirable outcome if the decision, along with the act, was out of their direct control.

If we as a society are serious about reducing the suffering of stray cats, we need to slow their birth rates back to typical levels experienced by their wild cousins, that is one small litter a year. The easiest, cheapest and most effective way to do this is to stop providing surplus food. But our sentimental instincts often conflict with our logic. Around the world I routinely encountered cases where well-meaning individuals were unconsciously exacerbating the issues. One pertinent example was revealed to me on the Greek island of Naxos in late 2016.

Dimtri was a short wiry jeweller specialising in crafting ornate miniature bicycles for the passing tourist trade in the shopping precinct of sun-drenched Naxos Island. As my daughters inspected Dimitri's handiwork and recounted for the umpteenth time what was left of their pocket money, I noticed a sleek black cat slide through the open door of his shop and dart under the counter. Seconds later the sound of the cat methodically crunching cat biscuits competed with the sounds of silver ornaments blowing in the breeze. Making conversation with the patient jeweller as my girls satisfied their shopping desires, I asked Dimitri the name of his cat. 'Oh its not my cat,' Dimitri acknowledged, 'I just feed it.'

Throughout the Greek islands I had been astounded by the number of stray cats at al fresco tavernas, along breakwaters, in ruins, on backstreets and main roads. On my morning jogs I counted dozens of cats jumping out of rubbish bins or the backs of cars, or lazing in the morning sun. In the evenings we usually had at least two or three cats pleading for scraps from our plates, even jumping onto restaurant tables.

Dimitri fed any cat that looked hungry. Having already observed the diminutive jeweller in his crowded shop for what seemed an eternity, I could sympathise. The cats wandering into his store for a quick feed offered company or distraction when the shop was quiet. Dimitri probably had no other interactions with animals, indeed with nature, in the crowded tangle of tourist shops linked by narrow cobbled paths. 'Does anyone else look after these cats?' I asked. 'There's a group that used to neuter some of them, but I don't see them much since the economic crisis,' the jeweller replied.

Dimitri was referring to the Naxos Animal Welfare Society, one of thousands of small volunteer groups that care for stray cats around the world. I had tried unsuccessfully to contact the society prior to my visit and had found their office vacated when I visited the Greek island. Despite not being able to make contact with NAWS, I had noted their outcomes. Five of the nine stray cats outside the Naxos Town Hall and one of four in our hotel lobby exhibited the characteristic ear notch that signified they had been neutered. A few minutes earlier I counted ear notches on three of the eight cats on the steps outside Dimitri's store. My quick tally suggested despite the efforts of NAWS, fewer than half of the stray cats in downtown Naxos had been neutered, well short of the 90% level believed to be required to reduce numbers.

Once a trinket had eventually been purchased for a school friend we left Dimitri and his black cat. Outside, one woman was feeding a marmalade kitten and two large tabby cats. Another lady was coaxing a diminutive black kitten torn between approaching her outstretched hand and bolting for cover through the fence. Asking the women if they were from the elusive Naxos Animal Welfare Society, I was informed in a cultured Dutch accent that they were just tourists feeding the cats.

Conny Salden, known to her friends in Holland as the 'cat lady' explained she fed cats whenever she travelled to the Mediterranean, devoting as much time to that as she did to shopping and sightseeing. She didn't see lots of stray cats like this in Holland, but there were many in Spain, Italy and Greece. 'Turkey is the worst; there are so many starving cats there.'

I commented that apart from the skinny black kitten, the other cats looked reasonably healthy. Conny explained that the cats usually look good at the end of the tourist seasons but in a month or so they will be starving. Conny surprised me, 'It's terrible really. These cats should all be neutered and rehomed. I try very hard not to judge the way locals treat cats and birds in small cages through my Western perspective. But we wouldn't tolerate this suffering back home.'

It was unlikely Conny's black kitten would survive the winter, not because it was too cold but because Dimitri and other shop

Conny Salden, the self-professed Dutch 'cat lady', later acknowledged that this little black kitten she was feeding on the Greek island of Naxos would probably starve to death at the end of the tourist season. (Photo: J. Read)

owners could not maintain the feeding rates supported by seasonal tourists. Conny was well aware she was not solving the problem nor easing the long-term pain for the kitten. Her handful of biscuits provided temporary respite for the cat and a fleeting sense of satisfaction for the cat lady. When I informed Conny that I was researching cat management for a book I was writing she, at last, diverted her attention from the cats. 'This is really important,' she conceded. 'We need to find ways to stop this suffering.'

We swapped contact details and Conny offered to share her considered thoughts on how best to limit the suffering of bourgeoning numbers of stray cats, while I shared published information on trials of different management approaches and sample chapters from this book. A month or so later, Conny replied. 'I have read everything you sent me attentively. I can honestly say I had to think about it. I have also spoken with people in the Netherlands who work in animal shelters. Here opinions are divided as well, some are in favour of euthanasia, others against.'

Conny confessed she hadn't appreciated that sterilisation programs fail on such a big scale, but acknowledged that the alternative, euthanasia, was not initially acceptable to her. She then turned her attention to the key question I had posed: how can we stop the needless suffering of these stray animals?

'A maxim in my culture is that no animal should suffer needlessly. When an animal is ill without chance of recovery we put it down, don't we? Suffering is also lack of food, shelter and medical care. To cull their numbers through euthanasia to give the survivors a better chance, I cannot exclude that possibility.'

I admired her rational yet troubled perspective in not discounting euthanasia as a compassionate option, despite her initial abhorrence. But Conny went on to state that euthanasia alone would not solve the problem of the constant influx of new animals. 'We are the ones responsible. I think that education, like you are doing, and a change in mindset is essential to convince people to make considered pet choices and sterilise their pets and maintain an open mindset to dealing with issues.'

After months of researching and visiting TNR and other cat management approaches around the world I felt I had come almost full circle, to a dead end. Euthanasia is the most humane and responsible outcome for feral cats that cannot be rehomed. We know the claim that neutered cats prevent immigration is fiction.

Euthanasia, when combined with ceasing of supplementary feeding, is the most effective means to reduce the population of unowned cats, the stated objective of most cat management plans. However, outspoken clowder feeders and some shelter operators and public officials continue to reject lethal control as an option. Although the dichotomy between the sentimental and compassionate approaches intrigued me, I couldn't help but conclude both camps might be missing the point.

Compassion and sentimentality are deeply personal traits, unlikely to be influenced by discussion or even facts. Hence there is little worth in public debate, nor likelihood of reaching consensus, on the pros and cons of compassionate versus sentimental approaches. More value and reason would enter the debate by discussing ethics, a more structured and mature methodology dating back to Roman philosophers. Ethicist Peter Stemmer argues that unlike the emotions, ethics have a strong scientific influence and hence serve as a more useful framework for debate. What, therefore, I wondered, is the most ethical solution for the problem of unowned cats?

Chapter 15

GOODNIGHT KITTY

Cats are connoisseurs of comfort. James Herriot

In my attempt to determine the most ethical approach for managing unowned cats, I consulted the outspoken US-based animal rights organisation, People for the *ethical* Treatment of Animals (P*e*TA). Its members worldwide are champions of the animals they believe are being treated unjustly. P*e*TA is renowned for their relentless exposure of animal suffering perpetrated from factory farms to circuses, private backyards to scientific laboratories. I wondered which camp of cat carers, the no-kill sentimentalists or the pragmatic compassionates, would be supported by these outspoken animal welfare campaigners?

The most impressionable employee in the Norfolk, Virginia, headquarters of P*e*TA is Bubbles, the director of office companionship. Yes, that's right, this band of ethically focused animal lovers have some unconventional job descriptions. What's more, Bubbles is a cat.

A smoky grey mixed-breed with flecks of marmalade and salt, Bubbles has a distinctive cream-coloured sock on her back right foot and her nose is half pink and half grey, as is her chin. But it's not only her distinctive colouration that sets Bubbles apart from your average moggie. She is quite possibly the most content and influential cat in the world. Bubbles supervises the affairs of her human co-workers in between amusing antics and writing occasional blogs about her life as a truly content feline. Her Christmas wishlist includes, among other aspirations, a cat tower for climbing, nesting and surveying, because, as Bubbles' blog explains, 'all cats covet supervisory duties'.

But life was not always so rosy for the pampered moggie. She had been a stray, living life on the streets. Like her fellow feline co-workers Brandi and Marshall, who is missing half a leg, Bubbles' luck changed when she was adopted by one of the worlds' largest and most determined animal rights organisations.

Over half of the six to eight million animals handled by animal shelters in the US each year are not reclaimed or adopted and cannot be retained by increasingly overcrowded shelters. Being adopted by PeTA was the cat equivalent of Annie being invited off the streets by Daddy Warbucks. With the possible exception of Dorothy from Haida Gwaii, Bubbles could not have hoped for more informed or compassionate adopters.

'Our three cats have the sort of exciting, full lives we wish all cats had,' Jenny Woods, senior communications administrator for PeTA, explained. 'They have constant human companionship, toys, and special perches that allow them to see out many windows. We even play them YouTube videos including their favourites of pigeons or other birds.'

Being natural and accomplished hunters, cats like Bubbles who grew up outdoors, must surely prefer having unfettered access to the stimulation of an outdoor life?

I challenged Woods whether the indoors life that PeTA advocated was really ethical for cats, or rather satisfies the aspirations of cosseting cat lovers at the expense of a cat's instincts.

Woods was adamant. In stark contrast to 'old school' cat

ladies unconvinced about the necessity for containment, all PeTA employees, many of whom also have their own cats, disagree with the outdated assertion that cats belong outdoors. But now to the more vexed issue. 'If Bubbles had not been adopted by PeTA, or found another suitable family, what ethically should her fate have been?' I asked.

Most of PeTA's campaigns and policies are self-explanatory. Little emotional stress or in-house debate ensues about decisions by an animal rights organisation to rescue tortured animals from depraved owners, to lobby against laboratory testing on restrained but conscious animals, or to foster legal cases against trafficking of wildlife. Even PeTA's opposition to factory farms and circuses is perfectly understandable and defendable to anyone more influenced by ethics than economics.

But the suffering of unowned cats can seldom be tied to a depraved or misguided individual or organisation; their fate cannot be solved by litigation. Building sufficient animal shelters to keep up with the endless stream of homeless animals is, as PeTA describes, 'like putting a bandage on a gunshot wound'.

PeTA's animal care and control specialist, Teresa Chagrin, came to Woods' support:

'Ethically and legally there is no doubt about it. Euthansia is the right thing to do.'

Wow!

Chagrin was adamant. 'As a humane officer for many years, I've seen it all and can attest to the fact that it isn't kind to abandon domestic animals on the street. Homeless and roaming owned cats come to painful ends.' Energised by my question, she continued: 'So-called cat carers, who consign cats to a life on the streets are in denial because it makes them feel better, not because it is the most humane option for the cat.'

Woods, still stroking Bubbles behind her ear, sensed my surprise. 'All our staff, right up to the boss, agree that euthanasia is preferable to releasing cats back on the streets or confining them to a life in a cage in a crowded shelter.'

In his defence of euthanasia as an ethical outcome for animals likely to experience ongoing pain, Dr Bernard Rollin stated, 'To treat animals morally and with respect, we need to consider their mentation limits. Paramount in importance is the extreme unlikelihood that they can understand the concepts of life and death in themselves rather than the pains and pleasure associated with life or death. To the animal mind, there is only quality of life, that is whether its experiential content is pleasant or unpleasant ... for example, whether they are bored or occupied, fearful or not fearful, lonely or enjoying companionship, painful or not, hungry or not, thirsty or not. We have no reason to believe that an animal can grasp the notion of extended life, let alone choose to trade current suffering for it.'

Like the organisation she founded, PeTA's president, Ingrid Newkirk, is both opinionated and zealous. For an individual so concerned about animal welfare and animal rights that she has campaigned from India to Canada, Newkirk's promotion of euthanasia over TNR took me by surprise. Outspoken conservationists, like Wamsley in Australia, kill feral animals to help protect vulnerable wildlife. But idealistic vegetarians are not widely acclaimed for their pragmatism. How could an individual, indeed an entire organisation, opposed to unsympathetic and unethical treatment of animals, condone the killing of homeless cats?

The British-born activist carried an air of authority and seemingly revelled in being invited to justify her views. 'Euthanasia literally means "good death",' Newkirk explained before reinforcing that true euthanasia, the approach she condoned, is painless, quick and dignified.

'Because of the high number of unwanted companion animals and the lack of good homes, sometimes people have to choose a disposition that causes the least pain and suffering. The options can be life in a cage stacked in some hoarder's house; sending the cat to a laboratory to be killed in experiments; or letting them die in a slow and miserable way of disease, injury, traffic, or some other horror by turning them loose.'

In their public taxation report dated July 2015, Alley Cat Allies cite research indicating that so great is the excess of cats over houses for these cats, one cat is killed every 15 seconds in the US shelter system. The Australian RSPCA euthanased 27% of the cats brought to their shelters in 2016/17.

Newkirk's pragmatic argument mirrored that of human euthanasia campaigners. When quality of life and prospects of improvement have declined to a point where near constant pain and misery are inevitable and irreversible, euthanasia does indeed seem the kindest, most ethical, outcome.

As I was working on this chapter in March 2017, I was forwarded a Facebook post originating from the Hearthside Cats shelter in Geneseo, New York. Opening the page I was confronted with the shocking image of a bloodied and moribund ginger cat with a face so red and grotesquely swollen it was impossible to tell if its left eye was still present. Because of the severity of his facial injury and fever of 104.8°C, Hearthside was unable to vaccinate the poor creature they named Leo. The post had originated from a 'no-kill' cat shelter appealing to the hearts and purse strings of their supporters. The Facebook post suggested, 'If 60 of our supporters donated $5, we could fully cover the cost of Leo's veterinary care'.

A knot tightened in my stomach. Both the photo of the deformed and battered cat, but even more so the knowledge that its suffering was going to continue even after the poor creature was abandoned back on the streets (after it had recovered sufficiently to be vaccinated and neutered) left me shocked. When I clicked down to the comments I was heartened that I was not alone. Three comments, in particular, elucidated what Elizabeth Oliver and PeTA had explained about the flaws of both the 'no-kill' sentimental approach and also the cruelty of TNR.

> ... refusing to euthanaze a cat so obviously suffering intensely should be cause for a serious criminal investigation. TNR is cruel and selfish, but kind people are being misled to believe it somehow 'saves animals' by those who are either making money (through grants and donations), are hysterical and completely ignorant in their opposition to euthanasia, or are blatantly sadistic. This poor, poor cat deserves a humane end to his suffering and homelessness
>
> ... Knowing that things like this happen to outdoor cats, why in the world would you ever release cats back outdoors after neutering? And you plan on putting this poor cat back out? TNR is the most inhumane practice ever. Give this poor guy some comfort and euthanaze him. TNR sucks.

... 'No-kill' shelters have to pick and choose. That is the only way they can practice 'no-kill'. Shelters can either help them all, which means including euthanasia in their policy, or turn all those away for which they have no room and to allow what has happened to this cat.

Newkirk does not support the assertion of TNR practitioners that their 'colony' stabilises. 'Again this is delusional. In the best-case scenario this means feral cat feeders never see the other homeless cats. Those other cats don't disappear; they go somewhere else to breed yet more homeless cats.'

Trap-Nurture-Rehome (rather than Release) is the preference of all the cat welfare groups I've met. But what about the truly aggressive cats, like Dot's black-and-white cat from the English farmhouse? Is there ever the potential for a safe indoor future for these cats? Karen Johnson, director of National Pet Alliance in the US, categorises cats not suitable for immediate rehousing as either fearful or fractious. Fearful cats 'run away or do not approach, may hiss initially and show whale eye, are able to be handled but remain stiff'. As their classification suggests fractious cats 'frantically dart about the cage, or may stiffen in place and hiss, lunge and try to bite would-be handlers'. Cats demonstrating these behaviours are deemed unsuitable for rehousing or retention because these cats experience 'extreme stress in the shelter environment, making all cats more susceptible to disease'.

Johnson's classifications mirror those used by Elizabeth Oliver and other compassionate cat carers. Aggressive or fractious feral cats are generally considered unsuitable for retention or adoption, their fate governed by either short-term sentiments or bigger picture compassion. The next chapter profiles a particularly aggressive Japanese cat and a most improbable outcome.

Chapter 16

MICHAEL THE WONDER CAT

The key to a successful new relationship between a cat and human is patience. Susan Easterly

As far as rags to riches transformations go in the animal world, Michael's story challenges Bubbles' astounding transformation. His conversion from the worst-of-the-bad-arse feral cats to the pin-up boy of the feline world has been remarkable, almost implausible. Without evidence from secret footage and a documented series of events, Michael's story would not be believed by anyone except the most forgiving, even delusional, of cat lovers.

Michael first came to the attention of ornithologist Kazuo Horikoshi in May 2005. The middle-aged biologist has retained a youthful passion for his work, alongside the Japanese traits of earnestness and meticulousness. Horikoshi was keen for advice on how best he could deal with the last of the cats threatening rare birds on remote Japanese islands. His heartfelt sense of both hope and frustration as he explained his challenges to me were deliberately concealed by respectful and polite control.

Horikoshi had been investigating the unexpected decline of a breeding colony of brown boobies on the remote Hahajima, one of the Bonin or Ogasawara islands cast out into the Pacific a thousand kilometres south of Tokyo. Working for the intriguingly titled Institute of Boninology, Horikoshi is responsible for studying and protecting the unique wildlife of the World Heritage listed subtropical archipelago. Predation by cats was recognised as the principal threat to the ground-dwelling and critically endangered red-headed wood pigeon, whose numbers had dwindled to only 40 survivors and hence was precariously close to extinction. Cats had been held primarily responsible for the extinction of over 30 island-dwelling vertebrates worldwide, so their threats to the wildlife of Ogasawara came as no surprise. Horikoshi and his team of Japanese ornithologists were determined not to let any of the birds on their watch join this tragic inventory.

Even the local community shared their concerns about pet cats destroying the local wildlife. In 1999, Ogasawara prefecture became the first Japanese local government to enforce an ordinance on responsible cat ownership. All local cat owners in Ogasawara are required to register their cats and are encouraged to keep them indoors. However, despite these new initiatives and the sterilisation of hundreds of strays through a government sanctioned TNR program, cat numbers did not noticeably decrease. The endemic Bonin white-eye soon also joined the growing list of birds threatened by both feral and pet cats. Faced with the unenviable task of protecting the islands' rare birds from continued cat predation, Horikoshi and his co-workers built a two-metre-high fence to exclude cats from a shearwater colony on the island of Hahajimi, yielding immediate benefits for that species. But birds outside this haven were still vulnerable. Particularly interesting to Horikoshi was the perplexing recent deaths of boobies.

Although cats were recognised as the key threat to the smaller birds of Ogasawara, it seemed inconceivable they could be responsible for recent deaths of mighty boobies. These birds, nearly the size of a pelican, dwarfed any predators Horikoshi and his fellow biologists knew of on the 2000-hectare island. Brown boobies boast more than a memorable name. Weighing in at over a kilogram and sporting a 1.5-metre wingspan and a long pointed beak resembling a sharpened carrot, a lone booby – let alone a colony – should be able to instantaneously peck the eyes out of a cat unwise enough to approach them.

In an attempt to identify the culprit predator, Horikoshi set a remotely activated camera near the booby colony. Within a few days he had identified the perpetrator. Enter, from left of stage, the star of the story. The flash, coinciding with his glance at the camera, obscured the look in the villain's eyes. Was he proud? Nervous? Or annoyed by the unexpected flash? Whatever the emotions, Horikoshi was certain of one thing. The mighty ginger

'Michael' the killer cat, caught on camera dragging a freshly captured booby past the carcass of an earlier kill on Hahajima Island, Japan. (Photo: Institute of Boninology)

cat staring at his camera was the offender he was pursuing. Grasped firmly in the cat's jaws was the neck of a brown booby. Only the head and front right leg of the ginger tom's body could be seen, the rest of his body concealed behind the bulk of the booby carcass. So large was the bird that its beak was longer than the cat's head; the kill so fresh that Horikoshi could see where the neck feathers had been parted by the killer bite.

To reinforce the significance of this unexpected evidence, Horikoshi noted that the muscular ginger cat, which was almost inevitably a male based on its colour and size, had dragged his most recent victim to the site of an earlier kill. Subsequent investigation of the other carcasses in the area also revealed the telltale serrated feather stems indicative of cat predation. Horikoshi had uncovered a disturbing example of an emerging trend in studies of cat predation on threatened species. 'Catastrophic' predation sounds like a tautology, when viewed from the perspective of the prey. Of course all predation is catastrophic, or final. But the term gaining currency with wildlife biologists refers to the propensity of some predators to target specific prey and potentially drive them to extinction. The systematic targeting of Katherine's quolls by certain cats was just one of many recent examples of this phenomenon.

On an isolated rocky ridge in Central Australia, one cat is believed to have systematically killed half of the young and several adults of a rock wallaby colony over a nine-month period. Despite the allied rock wallabies coexisting with cats for over a century, one cat learnt to hunt these large prey, weighing nearly as much as the offending cat, and target them with disastrous consequences for the colony. A mighty tomcat was believed responsible for killing 14 radio-collared brush-tailed bettongs at Venus Bay on the South Australian coast over a five-month period. Despite other cats being recorded before and after this predation spree, no other bettong deaths had been attributed to cat predation since the nearly six kilogram cat was trapped.

Of even more relevance to Horikoshi was that survival of the iconic kākāpō parrots on New Zealand's Stewart Island increased dramatically after a concerted effort resulted in the removal of the few cats that had learnt to predate these rare ground birds. Both before and after this catastrophic predation spree, other cats present in the area were seemingly not significant predators. These few cats, possibly only one or two, had killed half of the tagged kākāpō over the space of a year, a far higher predation rate than the kākāpō had experienced since cats were introduced to Stewart Island over a century earlier. The big ginger tom on Hahajima was fitting a pattern that had tormented threatened wildlife, and their worried managers, around the world. This propensity for targeted and repeated killing of unusually large prey is by no means unique to domestic cats. 'Man-eater' bears or tigers, crocodiles or sharks are feared because they are far more likely than their naïve siblings to 're-offend'.

And it's not only the targeting of certain prey that signifies a catastrophic predator. Surplus killing, exemplified by the carnage resulting from a fox in the henhouse, occurs when predators start killing indiscriminately, overindulging in frenzied attacks far beyond their dietary needs. Such predatory debauchery, although less recognised in cats than in their canid cousins, typically results in both mass killing and maiming, and an irate farmer or wildlife manager. Those well-fed cats displaying uneaten trophy kills on the front step are doing just that. They are satisfying their hunting urges, or perhaps showcasing their exploits to their master or other cats, by stalking, catching and killing. Maybe cats are hardwired to hunt whenever potential prey is encountered, and show a predilection for live prey over carrion, as a result of their high protein requirement.

The innate hunting instincts of cats in breeding bird colonies may trigger surplus killing. Island nesting seabirds that have evolved without mammalian predators are even more naïve and defenceless than captive hens. When nesting they are typically clustered and vulnerable, providing an irresistible target for cats. And despite their size, boobies are no exception. Indeed their name is thought to have been derived from their naivety in the face of human marauders. It is therefore of little surprise dopey island-nesting birds have proven to be among the most vulnerable animals to cat predation. For example, the soft plumage petrel, grey petrel and the (once) common diving petrel were hunted to extinction by cats on Marion Island, midway between South Africa and Antarctica. It's little wonder why when you consider ornithologists sent to investigate these losses calculated that nearly half a million burrowing petrels were killed each year by up to 2000 cats on the island. Without predators or disease, these cat numbers had grown from five founders in only 25 years. On Kerguelen Island, over 2000 kilometres to the east of Marion Island, the cat toll was even more extreme. A staggering three million seabirds were killed by tens of thousands of cats each year. This disastrous situation also originated from only four or five cats released on the island less than three decades earlier. Horikoshi knew if he did not act quickly and decisively, more seabirds on his beloved Ogasawara islands were also destined to join the growing global list of extinctions caused by cats.

The strategy of neutering cats had failed to protect the nesting seabirds, so Horikoshi planned to remove all cats from Hahajima, starting with his known killer. But as anyone who has tried to catch a master hunter could attest, removing dozens or hundreds of feral cats from an island presented a formidable challenge. Fortunately for Horikoshi, there was a readymade template he could follow from New Zealand. About the same size as Hahajima Island and also a conservation hotspot, Little Barrier Island near Auckland had just been cleared of cats.

The feral cats of Little Barrier Island had already contributed to the total extinction of the Little Barrier snipe and the local extinction of the North Island saddleback before control was attempted. Painstaking and heartbreaking surveys of nesting colonies on Little Barrier in the mid 1970s indicated more than 7000 Cook's petrels alone were killed by cats each year. Urgent action had been taken by the New Zealand authorities to protect these tiny oceanic migrants and their even rarer cousins, the grey-faced and black petrels, also threatened by cat predation. Starting with a release of cat specific feline enteritis that killed at least half the cats, the New Zealanders then turned to toxic baits. Over 26,000 poisoned meat baits were laid around the island. Then, to mop up the survivors, an arsenal of traps, shooting and concerted 'dogging' was employed to remove the remaining 151 cats over a four-year period. Following removal of the cats, Cook's petrel breeding success skyrocketed from five to 70% and the fast declining population rebounded.

The much publicised eradication of cats from Little Barrier not only yielded benefits for the local petrels, it also took the wind out of the sails of naïve or deluded naysayers, who had claimed cat eradication had never proven successful. To legitimise support for cat neutering or relocation programs, opponents of programs to eradicate feral cats often repeat their erroneous claims that long-term control of free roaming cats by eradication had not been achieved. The spectacular success of Little Barrier clearly refuted these claims. Karl Campbell and co-authors then documented 83 successful cat eradication campaigns worldwide.

Although cats had been cleared from many smaller islands, it was also the recent successful eradication from Little Barrier Island that gave Horikoshi confidence. Had he been an ornithologist protecting nesting seabirds almost anywhere else in the world, Horikoshi would have followed the Little Barrier model and unleashed an arsenal of disease, baits, traps, dogs and firearms on the recalcitrant cats. But Horikoshi was an ornithologist with a compassion for cats and little experience in the plethora of control techniques apparently necessary. So he consulted Yasushi Komatsu, vice-president of the Tokyo Veterinary Medical Association, to enquire about the best method to euthanase his feral offenders.

Unlike many vets in other countries, Dr Komatsu was strongly opposed to euthanasia. Like many other Japanese vets, Komatsu felt his mission was to protect the lives of all animals, challenging the accepted paradigm that lethal cat control was the only way to ensure the conservation of endangered wildlife. Dismissing the fatal techniques used by ecologists in New Zealand and elsewhere, Komatsu felt only veterinarians could understand and operate programs to appropriately control cats.

Before considering how he would achieve the feat, Komatsu committed to supervising the transit to Tokyo, training and rehousing of any cats that Horikoshi and his team trapped on the Ogasawara Islands. This formed an unlikely alliance that set the stage for the amazing transformation of both the wildlife of the Ogasawara Island chain and the life of their once-feral cats.

Rather than resorting to viruses or lethal trapping, Horikoshi set out to live trap the booby-killing cat and then find a way to give his nemesis a new life in Tokyo. And this is where we once again take up the story of Michael.

Within a few days of setting a trap near the booby kills, Horikoshi faced the biggest cat he had ever seen, the imposing ginger cat he had photographed. It was one of those rare but savoured moments a field biologist experiences when they have their quarry. Although Horikoshi knew he had fulfilled his primary objective of removing the killer cat from the booby colony, he pitied Komatsu's challenge in subduing and training the snarling, angry beast spitting at him and charging at the sides of the cage.

As he had promised, Komatsu travelled to the Ogasawara Islands when Horikoshi commenced cat trapping. Although the quiet vet was accomplished at handling unowned cats from the streets and parks of Tokyo, the cat he dubbed Michael was different. So vicious was the king of the Hahajima cats that Komatsu had to anaesthetise Michael to transfer him to the pet cage for the 1000-kilometre voyage to his Shin-Yurigaoka animal hospital in western Tokyo.

Knowing that taming malicious cats presented a unique challenge, one that would be under the cynical scrutiny of Japanese ornithologists and ecologists, Komatsu devised a novel training schedule. Through his 30 years' experience with pet or stray cats he would routinely desex them to improve their behaviour and reduce annoying yowling and spraying behaviour. But Komatsu had a hunch his priority was to first gain the trust of these cats. Later, all going well, he would consider neutering to add the finishing touches. So Michael, without vaccinations or desexing, commenced his training.

How this remarkable domestication unfolded can best be described in the words of the dedicated vet himself:

> I put Michael's pet cage at the place where the staff of my animal hospital frequently pass. It is important the cat would be provided no place to hide. Hiding them away in the quiet will prevent the cats from being tamed.
>
> Upon the arrival of feral cats at my animal hospital, I immediately name them and I named this first big cat Michael. Whenever I passed by Michael's cage I called him saying 'I will always care for you, Michael.' Although Michael was not adorable at first, I called him in a sweet voice at least ten times a day.
>
> At first, I used leather gloves on my hands when I pulled the tray out of his pet cage to exchange his food, water and pet sheet. But in time the threats and punches of Michael were gradually decreased to the point where eventually I could take his tray out with my bare hands. At the same stage of taming, I sometimes touched Michael's body with the round tip of my ballpoint pen through the mesh of his cage. At first when I thrust a pen under his nose, he became angry and punched and bit at the pen. Slowly he understood that he did not need to be frightened, and he started to sniff the pen.
>
> When Michael became calm at sniffing the pen, I persistently touched the nape of his neck and his forehead, those spots cats like to be rubbed. After I evaluated the safeness, I touched his body thoroughly. Through these steps, Michael was tamed just like a house cat. After two-and-a-half months I could hold him in my arms.

The sight of Komatsu cuddling Michael, now more closely resembling a rotund Garfield than a buff booby killer, speaks volumes. And it seems as though Michael's transformation was no fluke. Each of the nearly 400 feral cats have been tamed through this sustained and patient process. I now have little doubt the snarling black-and-white cat caught at Dot's farm in Devon could also have been tamed by Komatsu and his team, had the resources and motivation been available.

Each of the vets responsible for the taming of the Ogasawara feral cats selected a family to adopt their graduates on the strict

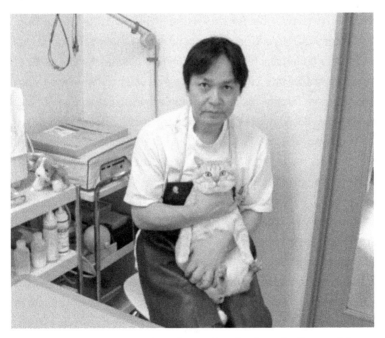

Dr Komatsu with the content and rotund Michael, gradually tamed from a wild seabird killer to a Tokyo Veterinary Hospital mascot. (Photo: Yasushi Komatsu)

condition they were raised and kept exclusively indoors. Not surprisingly, given the effort they devoted to these cats, many were adopted by the directors or their staff. Michael, favourite at the Shin-Yurigaoka animal hospital, will stay there for life with his doting owner, Komatsu.

Many cat owners, even many vets, claim a cat used to the stimulation of an outdoors environment cannot, or should not, be confined inside. Some claim it is cruel to keep cats inside or that they cannot adapt to an indoor environment. But Michael and his compatriots are given no choice by the pampering staff. The vets understand the cats have been given a second chance and do not want to be responsible for transferring their wildlife killing from the islands to Tokyo. Komatsu is confident these rehabilitated cats will not be let outside because their owners also realise the perils of the outdoors for cats. He proudly shows off Michael, who by now has become quite famous in Japan, as ample evidence that, like Bubbles in Virginia, outdoor cats can adapt to an idyllic indoors lifestyle.

In Tokyo, like any other city, wandering cats are killed and maimed on roads, are injured by other cats or dogs, or inflicted with a range of incapacitating diseases. Unfortunately for the stray cats of Tokyo, Komatsu concedes the Ogasawara cats are afforded special treatment because of the risk to the birds of the World Heritage islands. His veterinary association is unable to provide this extraordinary treatment to the city strays or feral cats from other Japanese regions and has yet to grapple with the best outcomes for the thousands, perhaps millions, of unowned cats in Japan beyond the scope of his intensive feline decorum classes. A more pragmatic vet may have transferred the euthanasia to Ogasawara and instead tamed an equivalent number of local cats that are currently euthanased due to the overcrowding of Tokyo's animal rescue centres. But that should not tarnish what they have achieved in homing the feral cats of the Ogasawara Islands.

While Komatsu rightfully basks in the success of his finishing school for errant cats, his friend Horikoshi is recording a response in the birds he set out to protect. The cat removal program, reinforced by a cat-proof fence around the shearwater colony, brought immediate success. The year the cat removal commenced coincided with the first recorded breeding of wedge-tailed shear-waters for many years, and the population has been increasing ever since. This heartening response mirrors the recovery reported from Little Barrier Island, and an even more impressive response from the subantarctic Macquarie Island. Prior to the eradication of cats from Macquarie, an estimated 60,000 seabirds a year were killed by up to 500 cats. Following a lengthy but even-tually successful cat eradication program, burrows of grey petrels, which had not been recorded breeding for over a century, were reported in the summer of 1999–2000. The population of these threatened birds slowly but steadily increased to over 90 chicks fledged in 2011.

Back in the Ogasawara Islands, forest birds also benefited from the cat control. Populations of the critically endangered red-headed wood pigeon increased fivefold to 200 following the removal of more than 160 cats from Chichijima Island. Importantly, Horikoshi has also recorded an increase in nesting frequency from once a year before cat control was initiated, to four times a year. This response suggests to Horikoshi that as well as pigeons being killed, the fear of cat predation was interfering with their foraging. Now free to feed without the threat of cat predation, the pigeons breed in the open, whereas previously they had nested under the cover of thick scrub.

Karl Campbell and co-authors found that successful cat eradications from islands typically use two to three methods, including leg-hold traps, hunting, primary poisoning, cage traps, and dogs. These eradications can be invaluable for wildlife. For example, 25 feral cats on Natividad Island, Mexico, killed on average 37 black-vented shearwaters *each month*. Shearwater survivorship increased by over 90% once these cats were eradicated. Seabirds have naturally re-colonised Ascension Island in the South Atlantic and four mammal species extirpated by cats have been successfully reintroduced to Faure Island, Australia, following eradication of cats.

The brown booby, Michael's prey of choice, has been slower to respond. Finally, eight years after Michael started his indoor life in Tokyo, the first pair of boobies successfully bred in the Ogasawara islands. Horikoshi is keen to point out that although they are celebrating these victories, the battle is far from won. A handful of trap-shy cats still remain on both Chichijima and Hahajima islands and their capture is proving challenging. Horikoshi knows only too well if these remaining cats are not captured they could rapidly breed and the temporary gains in his threatened birds will be lost. These cats have learned to avoid traps and may yet prove to be the nemesis for the inspirational relocation and taming program that has delivered promising results. Horikoshi is pondering what other techniques will be needed to remove these savvy cats, especially given his countries aversion to lethal control or euthanasia. His answer may well come from the other side of the Pacific Ocean.

A hundred kilometres off the Californian coast lies the 5896-hectare US Navy-owned San Nicolas Island, an important breeding site for seabirds threatened by feral cats. In 2005, the US

Navy and Fish and Wildlife Services, in collaboration with other stakeholders, decided to eradicate cats to protect the island night lizard, western snowy plover and Brandt's cormorant. But due to the presence of an endemic endangered fox, poisoned baits used in most successful cat eradication projects were not an option. San Nicolas authorities needed to eradicate cats without baits, making this the largest island on which cat eradication without toxicants had been attempted.

Initially the authorities on San Nicolas proposed cages, like Horikoshi had used, to trap their cats. But initial trials showed most cats were reluctant to enter these traps. Fortunately, concealed padded leg-hold traps set near scented lures were found to be at least 12 times as effective as cage traps. Just as with cages, foxes caught in these buried leg-hold traps could be released unharmed as long as reached quickly. In contrast, cats would be swiftly and humanely dispatched. But before the cat trappers could start, their intentions were reviewed by a public environmental assessment.

The proposal to eradicate feral cats from a remote naval base received nearly 6000 submissions. Most were from members of the Humane Society who suggested alternatives to euthanasia. As had been done on Ogasawara, the Humane Society offered to arrange and manage the live transfer of all cats from the island to the mainland. Importantly for the biologists in the team, the cats were to be maintained in a fenced enclosure on the mainland and not able to contribute to feral populations.

The team started setting 236 traps with a state-of-the-art alert system that informed staff when a trap was activated. It took over seven months and 30,000 trap nights (number of traps multiplied by the number of nights operated) to cover the island. Fifty-one

Island fauna, including Japan's rare Amami rabbit,
are often highly vulnerable to cat predation.
(Photo: Amami Wildlife Conservation Center)

cats were caught and transported from San Nicolas but eventually the cat trapping team faced the dilemma of diminishing returns. Cameras revealed cats avoiding traps, and with the reluctant approval of the Humane Society, lethal techniques were employed. Teams of trained dogs located some cats; spotlight shooters accounted for the last two. Eventually, after removing 66 feral cats, the island was declared cat free in December 2011 at a cost of a staggering US$2.9 million.

At $500 per hectare, removing cats from San Nicolas Island was more expensive per hectare than any other feral cat eradication. Biologists noted eradication from Faure Island in Western Australia, using poison baits, was completed at approximately $4 per hectare. The United States Humane Society, which had instigated and conducted the off-island transport of the feral cats, raised concerns about the ethics of the live removal program in their final review of the San Nicolas cat removal project.

Review authors concluded, ironically: 'Consideration must be given to the welfare of captive wild animals when being held in, and transferred from, a remote location', stating it in some cases it may be more humane to utilise lethal methods of control.

Because feral cats can rapidly breed to replace removed animals, the inability of live capture to remove all cats from Hahajima will prolong the time and expense of eradication, as well as the number of cats that need rehousing. The San Nicolas team eradicated cats by taking the pragmatic approach to use lethal control for the last handful that couldn't be trapped. Had they continued with the trapping program there would still be cats, probably an increasing number, trapped and stressed on San Nicolas. A considered assessment of the best technique for reducing the suffering of feral cats on Hahajima would likely recommend lethal techniques to humanely control the last few cats. Paradoxically, the impressive rehoming of Michael could blindside the Japanese into relying on inefficient, and possibly unethical, live capture.

Due to their isolation from natural colonisation or inadvertent recolonisations, islands showcase the most extreme impact cats make to wildlife and the most dramatic recovery stories once they have been removed. But in recent years the reliance upon island sanctuaries for vulnerable wildlife has been broadened to include refuges on mainland too.

Chapter 17

WHILE THE CAT'S AWAY . . .

The man who carries a cat by the tail learns something that can be learned in no other way. Mark Twain

'*Wati wara!*' the men called out in genuine excitement, unusual among the typically reserved Aboriginal rangers. Ever since I had started working with the isolated Indigenous communities some two decades earlier in the mid 1990s, I had been dubbed '*wati wara*', or 'tall man' in the Pitjantjatjara language of Central Australia. 'We got oil up in the *puli!*'

Jacob and Bronson, resembling unlikely modern-day oil sheiks, were particularly excited about their discovery of oil in the rocky hills above their settlement in one of the remotest parts of Australia. From Dulgunia Hill, overlooking the tiny Aboriginal settlements of Kalka and Pipalyatjara, the rangers could look from South Australia over the Western Australian border to the shiny roofs of Wingelina. In a helicopter surveying the ranges for rare rock wallabies we could just make out the glowing orange domes of World Heritage-listed Uluru and Kata Tjuta to the north-east.

But their attention had been focused in the crevices. Jacob and Bronson weren't searching for oil, but for warru scats. Warru were small rock wallabies, once an important food source for their grandparents and described in the 1930s by pioneering outback naturalist Hedley Herbert Finlayson as 'swarming on every hill' in Central Australia. But by the turn of the 21st century introduced foxes and cats had decimated their numbers. The rocky range Bronson and Jacob were searching hosted one of only two remaining small populations of what had become South Australia's most endangered mammal.

Like plump black spidermen, the rangers inched their way along a narrow ledge, scarcely wider than a boot, to a horizontal crevice. Enthusiastically, and totally unconcerned for my safety, they urged me along as well. They pointed out the shiny black tar inside a deep crevice in the granite hill. Bright white teeth emerged from their smiles when they saw my expression change from fear to surprise. Indeed they had found tar, but it was not a sign of untold oil riches. Their beaming smiles turned to disbelief when I informed them their glossy black bubbles were, in fact, *tjuwalpi kuna*, or old rat shit.

Although only distantly related, stick-nest rats construct similar multigenerational nests to the pack rats of the United States deserts. These industrious Australian endemics collect sticks sometimes twice the length of their bodies and drag them back to their nests. Over the years a family of these chubby inoffensive rodents accumulate impressive structures, which are often adorned with grass, flowers, bones or stones. Protection from predators and the searing summer heat is their motivation for building what resemble massive eagle eyries under bushes, in warrens or in crevices and caves.

Unlike most other animals, which go to great lengths to separate their living quarters from their toilet, stick-nest rats defecate and urinate in and around their nest. Pete Copley from South Australia's National Parks and Wildlife Service, an expert on these rats, suspects their waste may be used for territorial marking or to help cement their stick fortresses together. Anyone who has ridden a horse or an elephant will be aware that a diet of leaves results in copious quantities of '*kuna*'. What Jacob and Bronson had located, high on the cliff in Central Australia, was amberat, the accrued excreta of maybe centuries of rats. Like the amberat tar accumulated around old pack rat nests, the stick-nest rat tar comprised plant material bound together by faeces and urine. Copley suggests the tar-like sheen may be attributed to the rats very concentrated urine, produced by their disproportionately large kidneys to help them deal with the high salt content of their forage.

Bronson and Jacob's surprise, tinged with disappointment, was twofold. Firstly they took considerable convincing that the shiny hard black oil they had found was actually rat faeces. Eventually I was able to break off a chunk and the cross-section revealed unmistakable semi-fossilised rat scats. But even more difficult for the traditional owners of this desert country to comprehend was that tjuwalpi had been living up on this cliff, within a dingo howl of their homes on the plains below. Like many other animals known only to their generation through stories or ceremonial dances, tjuwalpi, and their larger relative wopilkara, straddled the realms of recent history and the ancient Dreamtime. According to Copley, who painstakingly sorted through the records of Australia's two species of stick-nest rats, both species declined rapidly once domestic livestock and cats and foxes arrived in their land a century or more ago. Along with a host of other Antipodean animals that had not evolved with exotic predators, stick-nest rats were pathetically vulnerable to cats and foxes. Their main traditional predators, goannas and snakes, were active primarily by day, so by keeping an eye out for owls, the rats were able to forage safely most of the night. But that all changed when cats and foxes could patiently sit outside their fortresses all night, waiting for the hungry and naïve occupants to emerge.

Although Copley still harboured hope of finding extant rat colonies on the mainland as late as the 1970s, a flurry of fieldwork in the ensuing decades confirmed their earlier demise. The last live tjuwalpi known to science was collected in 1933 near Mt Kintore, a couple of hundred kilometres from where Jacob and Bronson had shown me their tar find. Anthropologist Norman Tindale filmed Anangu collecting rats from a large stick-nest built around the base of a mallee at Mt Kintore by burning the nest, their dogs chasing an escapee and an Anangu digging for another beneath the nest. Copley reckons tjuwalpi's larger cousins, the wopilkara or greater stick-nest rat, survived on the Nullarbor until about the same time. Now only their nests remain, serving as poignant, and sometimes pungent, reminders of their former abundance and widespread distribution.

Knowledge of other recently demised species was largely limited to Dreamtime stories. Ninuku Spring in the valley below us was named after the greater bilby that was also immortalised by a series of landmarks making up the Ninu dreaming. Brush-tailed possums and bettongs featured in other local stories but, like bilbies and stick-nest rats, had been exterminated from many Central Australian deserts. Of all the medium-sized mammals, only the warru remained locally, clinging precariously to survival on isolated and rugged ranges. Just before climbing up to verify the old rat tar, I'd been shown a photo of an eviscerated warru carcass discovered when Ethan, another Anangu ranger, had shot a cat the previous week. Ethan also placed the stomachs of feral cats he shot into a freezer for me to dissect when I visited. In one particularly alarming dissecting session we found warru remains in four cats. The warru rangers harboured grave concerns that these agile and attractive wallabies would join the 15 other small mammals on the sorry inventory that made arid Australia the world epicentre of mammal extinctions since European colonisation.

Wopilkara, the greater stick-nest rat, barely survived this catastrophic wave of extinctions. Safely tucked away on a tiny island ark off the South Australian coast, a small colony survived, oblivious to the catastrophe that had wiped out their compatriots on the mainland. Franklin Island, a tiny dumb-bell-shaped speck in the Great Australian Bight, was too small to sustain a permanent farming family, hence the vegetation was spared the ravages of livestock and rabbits that often followed even temporary colonisation. Even more fortuitously for the nest-building rats, the absence of a farmhouse also meant house cats had not been brought the 20 kilometres from the mainland, or the far greater distance from the nearest port of Ceduna. It is likely a single cat let loose on Franklin Island would have replicated the fate of the doomed Stephen's Island wren and spelled the death knell for another genus of small mammals. Yet Franklin Island was just large enough to sustain a viable population of rats for the eight millennia since sea level rise had isolated the island from the mainland.

To reduce the chance of a calamity extirpating this last population, Copley and a team from the South Australian National Parks and Wildlife translocated stick-nest rats to neighbouring islands. Island protection of remnant threatened species populations was far from unique. Worldwide there are dozens of animals, from parrots to bandicoots, that have only survived on islands not reached by introduced predators. These island sanctuaries were the inspiration for John Wamsley, of the feral cat-hat fame, to create cat-proof continental 'islands'. Species teetering on the edge of extinction flourished inside his reserves, providing many Australian and international tourists with their first experience of hitherto unknown species.

Feral cats are recognised by the Australian Threat Abatement Plan for Predation by Feral Cats as a potential threat to 74 mammal, 40 bird, 21 reptile and four threatened amphibian species. The plan also notes that the impact of cat predation is not restricted to these threatened species. In a recent review, Sarah Legge and co-authors tallied 38 mammals threatened by cats that are largely dependent upon 17 cat-free fenced and 101 island havens for their survival.

Wamsley's initial Warrawong Sanctuary in the wet and fertile Adelaide Hills was a world away from the arid interior of the continent where many of the locally extinct or critically endangered mammals hailed from. Protecting species out in these dry unproductive regions would require huge sanctuaries, which in turn were extremely difficult to clear of cats. Eventually an opportunity presented itself to develop a landscape-scale reserve near the affluent mining town of Roxby Downs in the South Australian desert. In 1996, a rabbit-specific virus, known as rabbit haemorrhagic disease (or RHD), that had decimated valuable native rabbit populations in Europe, was introduced into Australia. Rabbits were estimated to cause in excess of AUS$200 million losses to agricultural production each year, as well as being one of the most serious environmental pests in Australia. As well as that, their periodic plagues supported large populations of predators, which then turned to the vulnerable native prey, like stick-nest rats, once rabbit numbers inevitably crashed.

Within months of its release in Australia, RHD wreaked havoc on the rabbits across the continent. Warrens that had housed dozens of rabbits only weeks earlier, now lay barren, with only the sounds of blowflies buzzing around bloated carcasses. Once reptiles became inactive in the autumn, cats and foxes ran out of food. I had been studying the wildlife in the desert near Roxby Downs for over a decade and was stunned by the dramatic impact this rabbit virus had on the native and introduced animal populations. Long-term counts at several other research stations confirmed the lowest ever recorded numbers of cats and foxes. Soon after, rarely seen native rodents, marsupials and ground-nesting birds started to flourish. If there was ever a window of opportunity to create a safe haven for stick-nest rats and other vulnerable desert mammals, post-RHD 1997 was the time. Katherine and I, along with Peter Copley, the stick-nest rat man, and bird bander David Paton, pioneered the Arid Recovery Project at Roxby Downs, which set out to achieve just that.

Type 'exclosure' into your word processor and chances are you will be met by a squiggly red underline indicating a spelling error. Clicking on the underlined word prompts the alternative and far more commonly used term 'enclosure'. Why? Enclose is what we typically do to animals, whether they are pets, curios or livestock; we don't want them to escape. Even the burgeoning science of conservation biology typically relies on enclosures to breed threatened species. But Arid Recovery was different. The fence design prohibited entry by cats by a simple yet ingenious floppy overhang. Not being able to support the weight of a cat, the wobbly overhang prevented cats from climbing over or gaining purchase for a leap inside the exclosure, at least that was the theory. By contrast, any climbing animals, including cats, on the inside of the exclosure without an overhang could readily climb out.

The Arid Recovery fence was built according to the best design for a cat-proof fence known at the time, and all rabbits were removed. Without their key food source the last of the cats climbed out of their own accord before we had to decide how to remove them. But before we considered reintroducing locally extinct mammals we needed to convince ourselves the fence was indeed cat proof. Katherine and I trapped feral cats around the Reserve and placed them inside a purpose-built squash-court-sized enclosure of the same design. I hope you noticed the term 'enclosure'. The floppy top of our trial pen arced inwards to test whether we could keep cats inside. The first big tomcat we released inside ran straight up the corner post and, with claws sunk into the wooden post to gain traction, took 36 seconds to leap over the 30-centimetre floppy overhang.

Our hearts sank. We had just spent hundreds of thousands of dollars and many months work building a state-of-the-art cat-proof fence that was demonstrably useless. Cats are so agile and such good climbers that the fancy floppy top had not even come into play; the cat had cleared it with ease. Although wooden posts have well served dingo-and rabbit-proof fences for many years, they clearly didn't stop climbing cats. We knew we had to stop cats gaining purchase at the top of the posts. Our first initiative was to nail iron sheets onto the wooden posts, so the cats' claws could not grip. This simple, but rather ugly, modification worked a treat for the next cat we tested. The following morning the cat was still in its pen, under a log near its food and water. The fence had worked. But the next cat we tested was smaller and more agile. It raced up the netting and actually perched, albeit precariously, on top of the iron sheet. From there it too launched over the floppy top and escaped.

After a couple more frustrating but illuminating weeks where modifications were made every time a cat escaped the trial pen, we finally felt we had perfected the fence. Two electric wires had been added to prevent cats from balancing under the overhang and finding an escape route. These wires needed to be close enough to the netting to prevent cats from sneaking underneath them, and far enough out to stop the cats stepping over them. We also extended the floppy top to a 60-centimetre arc, held in shape by short high-tensile wire rods. Finally we needed to reinforce the lower section of the fence with finer gauge netting because we found young rabbits could squeeze through 'rabbit-proof' netting. We were acutely aware that keeping all the rabbits out of the exclosure was critical to the vegetation regenerating and reducing the attraction for cats once rabbits inevitably bounced back from the virus. Our little trial pen had become an unsightly but effective hodgepodge of five different widths of netting, second-hand iron sheets, and electric wires held in position by purpose-modified insulators. To ensure the effectiveness of our larger exclosure, we then repeated these modifications over the 14-kilometre-long fence. Subsequent expansions to the reserve were built with only two wider mesh strips, joined at knee-height and supported on recycled metal-bore casing posts that cats couldn't climb. This modified fence soon became the prototype for cat-proof sanctuaries springing up elsewhere around the world.

Within two years the once degraded vegetation at Arid Recovery had recovered to the point where Copley and Katherine, who had conducted the original stick-nest rat translocations, felt they could trial a mainland release. Rat skulls at a nearby old owl roost and old nests in local cliffs indicated stick-nest rats had lived in this area only a matter of decades ago. Fittingly, this first stick-nest rat reintroduction on to cat-free mainland reserves was split between our new Arid Recovery sanctuary and John Wamsley's newly constructed Scotia Sanctuary in the New South Wales mallee.

One of my most exciting and rewarding field trips was capturing the founder stick-nest rats for these reintroductions. We loaded traps, transport boxes and a few days supplies onto an overcrowded little fishing boat for the hour-long transit to Reevesby Island, not even visible on the horizon when we set off from the South Australian fishing village of Tumby Bay. The low scrubby island proved to be a rat utopia. Untidy jumbles of small sticks spilled from a dilapidated tractor, from under the elevated flooring of the abandoned farmer's house, and from dozens of thorny bushes around the once-cleared farmland that was reverting to low shrubland. By day we set traps around the most active nests, selected by the collections of distinctive rat scats. But because we needed to catch at least 50 rats within a couple of days we supplemented our trapping by running down rats when they became active at night. And that's where the real action started.

Armed with head torches and fish-landing nets we scanned the low dunes and clearings for the faint orange glow of a rat's eyeshine. Upon sneaking to within range of a rat we then sprinted before it could evade capture into a nest, an impenetrable shrub, or down a penguin burrow. Inevitably I would end up spreadeagled, with arms and net outstretched, scrambling to reach the net and grab the rat before it escaped. A rat escaping down a penguin burrow with thrusting hand in fast pursuit resulted in the most ghoulish screeches I had ever heard. The first time I heard the penguin's bizarre screams at close range I abandoned the rat and sprang to my feet with rare agility. With nerves already heightened by face-to-face encounters with the abundant death adders and black tiger snakes, I was well and truly spooked. When a rat escaped down a quiet burrow I had no hesitation in lunging after it, even though I recognised a burrow without a penguin could harbour a deadly snake. Yet despite being determined to catch our requisite number of rats and priding myself on going the extra yard to catch any rat I pursued, I could not overcome my irrational fear of plunging my hand down a burrow from which the eerie penguin shrieks emanated.

After two nights of adrenalin-pumping chases we had our booty and commenced the boat ride then six-hour drive into the desert before nightfall. Then, for the first time in hundreds of rat generations, these little builders were once again leaving their distinctive flowery footprints on red sand. Inexplicably they ignored the special piles of sticks Katherine had carefully constructed to make them feel at home and instead pilfered the sticks to build their own nests elsewhere. When checking up on our radio-collared rats at night we found some climbing into the canopies of sandhill wattles, testing their new diet. Others sought refuge from the searing summer heat in old rabbit warrens that had been opened up by goannas. Within two years rats had reached every corner of the 1400-hectare sanctuary and their footprints ran along the exclosure fences. Young rats could easily fit through the fence and occasionally we saw their tracks outside, but they never lasted more than a week.

Inside the Arid Recovery exclosure the rats thrived. In time their nests grew to the size I had seen recorded in Tindale's video and in old black-and-white photos taken from the Australian deserts a century ago. Little pathways through the undergrowth attested to the philandering behaviour of male rats regularly visiting female rats living in their separate nests. Jacob and Bronson visited Arid Recovery to reunite with the enchanting rodents they had only known through stories. But they still harboured doubt these rats were the source of the black tar they had found near their desert homelands. The new nests were too exposed and too new to have accumulated enough scats to form the tar. But if the cats and foxes can be kept out for another century or so, maybe the tar will once again start forming in the Australian desert.

The successful reintroduction of stick-nest rats provided the confidence to reintroduce other threatened mammals wiped out by cats and foxes. Tiny western barred bandicoots were sourced from Bernier Island off the West Australian coast. The pugnacious colonial burrowing bettong, or boodie, the only member of the kangaroo family to live in warrens, was also brought back from cat-free islands. Iconic bilbies were sourced from captive-bred animals. Within a few years our desert Eden supported hundreds, then thousands of these species and we had to keep on expanding the exclosure to accommodate them. But there was, of course, a limit to the area of land we could fence and maintain cat free. Each of the Arid Recovery founding scientists had already moved onto the pursuit of our true holy grail. How could we reinstate these species outside fences?

As she had with the releases inside the reserve, Katherine led trial releases of bilbies and boodies into areas where foxes were controlled by baiting. But each trial yielded frustrating results. In every case enough feral cats evaded the intensive trapping and baiting, shooting and luring to wipe out the colonists. Cats also prevented young bandicoots and stick-nest rats, which could crawl straight through the netting, from establishing outside. Without the benefit of the ocean barrier protecting these endangered animals on Franklin and Bernier islands, cats from the surrounding desert continued to thwart releases outside the exclosure. And it wasn't only the reintroduced mammals these feral cats were affecting. There were consistently at least 10 times as many native mice inside the cat-free haven compared to outside.

Our cobbled-together fence had proven beyond doubt the overriding debilitating influence of cats on many of our native mammals. Our external trials had also shown no contemporary cat-control techniques, except exclusion fencing, were sufficient to protect threatened species from cat predation during the risky reintroduction phase. Unfortunately our depressing failure at re-establishing bilbies, stick-nest rats and other threatened mammals outside the fence was replicated elsewhere. The Australian Wildlife Conservancy, who greatly expanded John Wamsley's network of cat-free sanctuaries, was also unable to establish sustainable populations of threatened species outside their exclosures. Even low cat numbers were sufficient to prevent the reestablishment of the Australian desert to its former glory.

Whereas the doomed golden whistler in my mist net incident had focused my attention on the impacts of cats, the failed reintroductions of bilbies and boodies outside the Arid Recovery Reserve cemented the need to improve control measures for feral cats. Biologists from Ogasawara to San Nicolas islands, and from the Australian deserts to Hawaii, recognised novel solutions were necessary to reduce the devastating wildlife toll on native wildlife inflicted by feral cats. And with feral cat populations inextricably linked to free-ranging pets and supplementary fed colonies in many places, well-thought-out and sensitive measures are required to manage all free-ranging cats. But as Dorothy on Haida Gwai and Horikoshi on Ogasawara had made clear, effective cat management needs to be both ethical and palatable to the public.

Chapter 18
THE SOUNDS OF SILENCE

Imagine a world without cats: just think of the uncontrollable vermin and creepy-crawlies everywhere. Cats Protection League

When Polynesian seafarers first pushed way down south into the Pacific Ocean they were drawn by persistent telltale cloud that marked the location of Aotearoa, 'The Land of the Long White Cloud'. Centuries before the advent of hobbits on these isles, Maori ancestors settled Aotearoa and thrived on the abundant and tame game animals. Within 200 years of their arrival, every last morsel of nine or 10 species of emu-like Moa was eaten in one of the most dramatic human-induced extinction events recorded.

Ever since Maori colonisation in the 13th century, the name, like the wildlife, of Aotearoa has been in a state of flux. In 1642, Abel Tasman, the first European to sight The Land of the Long White Cloud, was unimpressed with the reception he received from the parochial inhabitants who killed four of his crew, presumably preceded by the hostile chanting, slapping and tongue-poking haka reception visiting sports teams still receive. Had he conformed to the Maori etymological convention of naming new lands by their first impressions, Tasman would perhaps have named the islands 'Land van de Lange Roze Tong', the Dutch equivalent of 'The Land of the Long Pink Tongue'. Instead Dutch cartographers named the islands Nova Zeelandia, anglicised to New Zealand by Captain

James Cook, who became the first European to set foot on the land in 1762.

Two-and-a-half centuries after Captain Cook's historic landing, Aotearoa has earned yet another moniker, the 'Land of the Long Departed Children'. Like other small nations, New Zealand suffers from the 'brain drain', where young professionals and intellectuals leave their motherland for the bright lights and opportunities in larger countries. So significant is this issue it captivated the attention of one of New Zealand's most influential scientists and social commentators, Professor Paul Callaghan. A decorated physicist and entrepreneur who was awarded New Zealander of the Year in 2011, Callaghan had a vision to make New Zealand the home of choice for young professionals; a magnet for bright minds. Once the long-departed children returned, the prosperity and sustainability of the bright-green isles would be revitalised. New Zealand's point of difference from other nations, argued Callaghan, was its clean and green food production, and its open spaces providing boundless opportunities for surfing, hunting, fishing and tramping, as New Zealanders describe hiking. Somewhat surprisingly for a physicist, Callaghan considered the barometer of Aotearoa's image to be the dawn chorus of its endemic bush birds.

Captain James Cook described the morning song from his ship *The Endeavour* anchored in the Marlborough Sounds as 'deafening'. His more erudite botanist, Joseph Banks, agreed.

> This morn I was awakd by the singing of the birds ashore
> from whence we are distant not a quarter of a mile, the
> numbers of them were certainly very great who seemd to
> strain their throats with emulation perhaps; their voices

were certainly the most melodious wild musick I have ever heard, almost imitating small bells but with the most tuneable silver sound imaginable to which maybe the distance was no small addition. On enquiring of our people I was told that they have had observd them ever since we have been here, and that they begin to sing at about 1 or 2 in the morn and continue till sunrise.

I am visiting New Zealand to experience the vestiges of this once deafening 'wild musick'. Unlike the flightless kiwis and kākāpō, for which New Zealand is internationally famous, the choristers that so defined the original dawn were small flying birds, the bellbirds and tui, the saddlebacks and yellowheads. Reliant upon native vegetation, these birds were devastated by land clearing for farms and cities. Today their traditional haunts have been usurped by avian invaders. Chaffinches, goldfinches, sparrows and yellow hammers from Europe now dominate the New Zealand agricultural landscape, while Australian invaders such as silvereyes and magpies rule the forest edges.

But the New Zealand songbirds aren't safe in the bush either. Sixty species of birds at current count have been driven to extinction by introduced mammals in New Zealand alone, and at least five of these have been lost since 1900. Cats have almost certainly contributed to the extinction of 11, and possibly up to 21 of these bird species. New Zealand and Hawaii, with its similar tragic record of bird extinctions, account for more bird extinctions than the rest of the world put together. To put this calamity in further perspective, there are only 80 resident native New Zealand bird species surviving, just over half the original tally. Callaghan had observed how the chorus of these threatened birds once more rang out on offshore islands such as Tiri Tiri Matangi, after replanting and clearing of exotic predators. Mirroring the depressing fate of our stick-nest rats that emigrated from the Arid Recovery Reserve only to be wiped out by patrolling cats outside, Callaghan despaired that the rare birds bred up within sanctuaries were quickly killed when they departed. In order to recreate the idyllic New Zealand of his dreams, Callaghan touted a predator-free New Zealand to serve as an inspiration for his countrymen, immigrants and tourists alike.

Virtually on his deathbed in 2012, Paul Callaghan bequeathed his aspiration to another unlikely hero of New Zealand wildlife. Gareth Morgan is an economist and businessman, both professions that are typically inconsistent with, and often diametrically opposed to, a passion for environmental causes. Indeed his lifelong passion for riding motorbikes in far-flung nations was not a conventional or logical pathway to adoption of Callaghan's vision. Morgan's trademark bikers' moustache concealed an erratic cluster of teeth and a lisp that belied his clear thinking and determination. He shared his mentor's passion for recreating an acoustically rich New Zealand, and possessed the drive and resources to make it happen. With the entrepreneurial enthusiasm that saw him amass a personal fortune with a number of wildly successful businesses, Gareth Morgan turned his attention to his family charity and bike riding. He embarked on a pivotal adventure, a ride on Antarctica with his mechanic wife. En route to the icy continent in 2008, Morgan called in at Stewart Island and several of the sub-Antarctic islands south of New Zealand. More than simply being a welcome stop on his rough travel, these islands provided a light-bulb moment for the adventurous entrepreneur.

Stewart Island's website acknowledges, tongue in cheek: 'The island's rainforests and wetlands are a glorious testament to our climatic conditions.' But their most prized natural asset is unfortunately no longer a drawcard for tourists to the island. Kākāpō are one of the world's most enigmatic birds. These huge, flightless quizzical green parrots the size of garden gnomes eked out an existence in some of the harshest environments of the rugged South Island. Even more so than its bizarre appearance and reproductive biology, the kākāpō's courting behaviour was unique. Observed by less than a handful of intrepid and persistent ornithologists prior to the 1970s, the kākāpō composed and choreographed an impressive display of calls from specially constructed earthen bowls, connected by well-trodden paths. These communal recitals of drumming, booming and screaming alarmed naïve explorers who feared a rapacious devil taunting them from the darkness.

Unfortunately, being a ground dweller, kākāpō were vulnerable to the introduced hordes that had laid waste to dozens of New Zealand's iconic birds, from the tiny bush wren to the oriole-like piopios. Stoats, cats and brushtail possums preyed on adults or young kākāpō. After the early settlers had assuaged their fear of the night screamers, kākāpō also provided their camp kitchens with easy meat. The once-common mighty parrot had been driven back to the seemingly impregnable Fiordland. With specially trained sniffer dogs, intrepid biologists pitted themselves against the rugged landscape and inclement weather as much as the elusive nature of the kākāpō. Repeated expeditions in the 1940s and 1950s eventually revealed a handful of birds and their network of trails and bowl-shaped depressions. A couple of translocation attempts to predator-free offshore islands to save the last of these parrots had failed. All but the most optimistic New Zealand ornithologists had farewelled one of their most distinctive species, although most had never witnessed its comical waddle or heard its booming drum beat.

Tantalising records suggested Stewart Island, that weather-beaten rainy anchor of the Aotearoa canoes, might provide the last bastion of hope for the kākāpō. Unlike Aotearoa's major islands to the north, Stewart Island was spared the introduction of mustelids by ill-informed government officials keen to reduce rodent populations. However, three species of introduced rats and the brush-tailed possum were all present by 1911, the possums deliberately liberated onto Stewart Island in 1890 for the fur trade. These predators were largely responsible for the localised extinction of several endemic subspecies of Stewart Island birds. In January 1977, the New Zealand Wildlife Service's Kākāpō Team, having all but given up on their prize in its former range on the South Island, visited Stewart Island. Within hours they had found networks of foot-beaten trails and meticulously created earthen bowls. Within days they had been mesmerised by the courting behaviour of at least 18 kākāpō on the Tin Ranges. By 1980, the Kākāpō Team had found nests. All had seemed lost, but Stewart Island proved the Shangri-la for the kākāpō.

But all was not well for this seemingly doomed parrot on Stewart Island. Spending months hunkered down in the territories of the kākāpō, acutely observing their behaviour, their diet and their habitat, the Kākāpō Team became at first aware, then concerned, about feral cats. Soon after the rediscovery of kākāpō on Stewart Island in 1997, eight cat scats were collected, one of which contained the unmistakable feathers of the kākāpō. This concern turned to alarm in the early 1980s when kākāpō remains were found in six of the 118 cat scats collected. Within a few years, horrified researchers were led to piles of green feathers, the distinctive work of cats, by radio-trackers they had placed on several of their subjects. Before long the team started finding other cat-killed kākāpō carcasses, including an increasing percentage of the leg bands they had painstakingly placed on their elusive quarry. Feral cats, descended from early seal-hunters' pets, and possibly others straying more recently from Oban, threatened the kākāpō with imminent extinction. Between their discovery in 1977 and 1982, cats had killed more than half of the kākāpō monitored by scientists.

The remains of one of the last Stewart Island kākāpō found in 1982. Pioneering conservation ornithologist Don Merton, who was instrumental in preventing the imminent extinction of kākāpō, determined that this bird, like many others, had been killed by a cat. (Photo: Don Merton)

All-night vigils by rangers at every known kākāpō nest often ended tragically when a cat slipped in quickly and quietly. The kākāpō team were losing the battle with the cats and they knew it. Being compulsive and skilled hunters, cats were less inclined than dogs, foxes or mustelids to eat carrion. As a result they were more difficult to lure into traps by meat baits. They were also less likely to consume poison concealed in a chunk of meat. Unlike their comical, almost dopey kākāpō prey, which sometimes approached, even climbed up the trousers of bemused onlookers in broad daylight, the cats were elusive and evasive.

In a last-ditched effort to save the species, the New Zealand Wildlife Service was granted permission to remove 25 pioneering kākāpō to Little Barrier Island near Auckland. Little Barrier had been one of early cat eradication success stories, serving as an inspiration for Horikoshi to remove cats from the Ogasawara Islands. By the time the authorities permitted the poisoning of cats in the kākāpō territories of Stewart Island it was too late; by 1992 their booms and screams fell silent. But apportioning all the blame for the extinction of the Stewart Island kākāpō – like the snipe, bush wren and kokako wiped out earlier – to the tardiness of the authorities is unfair. They lacked the armoury to effectively deal with the threat of feral cats in the rain-drenched forests. Lacking too was the awareness, let alone resolve, of the Oban community to ensure their pet cats did not exacerbate the kākāpō's demise.

Sitting in his mansion-like beach house in the prime location in the holiday coast town of Mt Manganui, Morgan explained it was on his southern motorbike adventure that he became aware of the plight of New Zealand's birds and the role of cats in their demise. But four years after his visit, Stewart Island still lacked a plan to rid the island of predators. Morgan was aghast. He was so 'blown away' by the ecological challenges facing these isolated islands that in 2012 he organised and part-funded a voyage for scientists and policymakers to study the risks of invasive species and climate change to these far-flung islands in the Southern Ocean. Morgan told his guests the story of the five cats introduced to Marion Island in 1949. By 1975 there were more than 2000 cats, estimated to be killing nearly half-a-million petrels a year. They had eliminated three species within 15 years. Along for the ride and listening to his laments were 40 'everyday New Zealanders' who Morgan sponsored with the hope they would return to New Zealand and spread the word about the ecological catastrophe confronting the sub-Antarctic islands. But along with this advocacy, Morgan realised Stewart and the subantarctic islands needed a champion.

'What the Stewart Islanders needed was a noisy bastard to get things happening,' he acknowledged, 'and that sounded like a good job for me.' Morgan's first task was to make the villagers of Oban aware that for Stewart Island to reach its ecotourism potential they would have to relinquish their roaming pet cats. Oban, nestled in Halfmoon Bay, was the sole settlement on Stewart Island and its intrepid residents obviously held the key to the success of the ecotourism venture. In typical cavalier style, Morgan announced his cat-free plan then called a town hall meeting to face the flak. And there was plenty. Most of the 400 occupants of the close-knit community resented being instructed by a businessman from out of town what pets they could or could not keep. The fishermen didn't want their boats searched for invasive furry cargo and the cat owners were distraught. But prepared for the reaction, Morgan put the ball back in the court of the hostile Stewart Islanders.

'When are you going to wake up to the fact that your town and your way of life is dying?' Morgan challenged them. Built around whaling, sealing, mutton birding and then fishing, Morgan stared down a resolute but regressive community, more accustomed to farewelling departing residents than welcoming parties or exciting new opportunities. 'What Stewart Island needs is a progressive silver bullet rather than harking back to the glory days of a dwindling fishing industry,' he told them.

Morgan inspired the Stewart Islanders with visions of an economic revival spurned by tourists queuing up to hear the dawn chorus, to witness the amazing kākāpō in the mountains, and see kiwis walking down the main street of town. 'They are only a ten-minute walk away, and there's no reason other than predators to explain why kiwis won't come right into town,' Morgan explained. By the end of the meeting most of the town were onside. Over 80% of the residents supported the plan to remove cats, along with possums and rats, from a sanctuary built around the town. Morgan was already fast tracking his plans to build a 12-kilometre fence across the town peninsula and remove all cats from the area. Ironically this would turn the town, once the source of the feral cats and the scourge of the Rakiura National Park, into the sanctuary for Stewart Island wildlife. Morgan did not aspire to a remote cat-free enclave in the distant forest, he was going to bring the wildlife and the tourists, who would surely flock once more to the island, right to the townsfolk.

And 2000 kilometres north, on another remote island, Morgan could point to a pertinent model of his dreams for Stewart Island. Lord Howe Island is the only breeding locality of both the aptly named providence petrel and the endemic Lord Howe Island woodhen. The quirky woodhen has been adopted as unofficial mascot of the island, much in the way Morgan hoped kiwis and kākāpō would become for Stewart Island. Like Stewart Island, largely national park, three quarters of the World Heritage listed crescent-shaped volcanic remnant of Lord Howe is a Permanent Park Preserve, hosting 70 endemic plant species. Woodhen numbers crashed to as few as 20 in 1970, even fewer than kākāpō numbers on Stewart Island at the same time. Locals were rightfully concerned their mascot was doomed to join the 10 other species of bird driven to extinction since settlement on Lord Howe. By the early 1980s, when the Lord Howe Island authorities finally bit the bullet and outlawed the keeping of domestic cats, only 15 increasingly lonely woodhen remained.

Locals arranged a grandfather clause in the new cat regulations, allowing existing desexed pet cats to remain on Lord Howe until deceased. The last pet cat passed away in 2006, and Lord Howe has been free of cats since then. Along with the elimination of pigs and control of rats, removal of cats has seen the woodhen population increase to about 200 individuals. Once again this peculiar bird is a feature of a visit to Lord Howe by one of the 400 tourists permitted at any one time on the island. And with the bulk of the local residents employed in the tourism trade, Lord Howe provided Oban with a sustainable model of how quirky endangered birds could become the centrepiece of their economy.

Another island and another idiosyncratic flightless bird provides further support for Stewart Island to embrace cat control for their own benefit. Never before had I seen so many two-dimensional animals before finally setting eyes on the real thing. On the southern Japanese island of Okinawa, car stickers, T-shirts, lapel pins and billboards all displayed the black-and-white bird with lipstick-red beak and legs; road signs featuring the bird warned about the threat of collisions. As I stood at a road intersection, scanning in three directions with my binoculars, other birdwatchers inched along the road eager to spot an elusive bird, seemingly terrified the focus of their quest would rush from the undergrowth and kamikaze into their car.

Although it was known as 'Agachi' or 'Yamadui' by generations of locals, the Okinawa rail was only formally 'discovered' and

---

Richard Trethewey is presiding member of the Kangaroo Island Natural Resource Management Board, which oversees the Australian ecotourism and clean-produce mecca. Trethewey explained when I visited KI that sarcosporidiosis infection in island sheep is so high that a major regional abattoir has refused to process their livestock. This high incidence of cyst-forming 'sarco', as well as the abortive toxoplasmosis also exclusively transmitted by outdoor cats, is largely attributed to the island supporting an order-of-magnitude higher density of feral cats than found on mainland Australia. Kangaroo Islanders have committed to eradicating cats to improve the marketability of their produce and to attract ecotourists, lured by the unique wildlife.

---

described in 1981. Birdwatchers from around the world flocked to the Yanbaru forests of northern Okinawa to catch sight of this striking bird. Locals too felt a strong attachment, even sympathy, for this critically endangered species, the only flightless bird in Japan. Farmers searched out their nests and refrained from cutting the grass until the chicks had left. Birds injured by their cats or by vehicle accidents were carefully taken to a wildlife hospital. As the knowledge and concern for their adopted mascot grew, so did their realisation that too many Okinawa rails were falling victim to pet cats. Researchers warned the Yanbaru locals the related white-browed crake from Iwo Island was believed to have been driven to extinction largely by cat predation.

Piles of black-and-white feathers and encouragement from the Department of Environment prompted them into action. On 1 April 2005, Yanbaru took the serious step of becoming the first Japanese municipality to impose a cat management ordinance requiring cats to be registered and microchipped, and encouraging desexing and containment.

A couple of years after the cat ordinance was enacted another threat loomed for the Okinawa rail. The mongoose, introduced to southern Okinawa in the futile attempt to control snakes a century earlier, pushed as far north as the Okinawa rail habitat. Now facing a two-pronged threat to the survival of the rail, authorities embarked upon one of the most incredible wildlife rescue operations on the planet. Two barrier fences were constructed across the island to hold back the invading mongoose and to help control the feral cats. Although I had read about these fences and the predator control initiatives to safeguard the Okinawa rail, I was blown away by the scale and expense when I visited the tropical southern Japanese island. The local government had funded the erection of one of the seven-kilometre-long fences, costing a staggering 100,000 Yen or US$1000 for each and every two-metre panel! But this outlay represented only the tip of the fiscal iceberg.

Up and down the fence and throughout an extensive network of trails in the Okinawa rail habitat, 40 predator busters maintained thousands of traps six days a week. The sight of 14 busloads of workers arriving back at headquarters at the end of their daily shift was mind blowing. Not relying on predator control alone, a $2 million state-of-the-art breeding facility was constructed, housing 67 rail fed individual portions of a complex diet fit for royalty. Further down the road was a million-dollar release pen and Okinawa rail visitor centre, promoting awareness and conservation for the famous bird. A staggering 16,000 tourists visited the remote outpost in the first nine months it opened and had been wowed by Kyonkyon, a charismatic female rail who delights in showing off her spacious enclosure to visiting school kids and tourists. Posters adjacent to Kyonkyon's habitat explain the cat ordinance, the importance of responsible cat ownership, and the annual location of all roadkills of rails and the equally enigmatic long-haired rat.

At yet another flash new facility, bird watchers, rail researchers and visiting authors are hosted at a modern bush hotel and conference facility. Breakfast on the balcony comes with the near certainty that rails will be heard, and the tantalising possibility one will be seen emerging from the forest. My breakfast rail sighting raised my count to eight birds, three seen sleeping in trees with spotlight the previous night and four spied on my pre-breakfast drive to their hotspot down the road. The local restaurant staff, tourism operators and even roadside pineapple stallholders were all now deriving benefits from the quirky local bird.

Challenging as it seemed to rid the Oban area of feral cats and promote kiwis and kākāpō as the twin pillars of the island's economy, Stewart Island was not enough for Morgan. The famous Zealandia sanctuary in Wellington has fenced out all exotic mammals, even house mice, from a former water reserve in the centre of town. As a resident of Wellington, Morgan was aware of the broader impacts of cats. 'Zealandia is New Zealand's most expensive cat food factory,' he proclaimed, explaining that many of the endangered birds breeding in the sanctuary were returned as cat kills once they flew the coop. Backing up Morgan's concerns, Brian Bell and his children who banded birds in Wellington

*'Kyonkyon', protected from feral cats and mongooses in her spacious
enclosure, entertains and educates thousands of tourists at the Okinawa
rail visitor centre. (Photo: Okinawa Rail Ecology Center)*

reported that 70% of their bird recoveries were retrieved by
domestic cats.

Morgan did not want birds from the cat-free zone on Stewart
Island becoming prey when they crossed the fence, nor to read
more reports of pet cats killing birds dispersing from Zealandia or
other sanctuaries. He wasn't content with a patch of the far-flung
Stewart Island being the largest predator-free enclave in his
country. A couple of hundred jobs in the Oban tourist industry
weren't going turn around the economic fortunes of the Land
of the Long-Departed Children. Instead, Morgan set to work on
his amazingly ambitious and extraordinarily contentious goal of
ridding his country of cats.

Not one to pussy foot around, Morgan 'declared war' on cats

John Flux provided alarming statistics by meticulously recording the prey brought home by a single suburban cat in the hills above Lower Hutt, New Zealand. Over its 17-year lifetime this cat's inventory amounted to 221 mice, 63 rats, 35 rabbits, four hares, two weasels, nine skinks, one frog and 223 birds, including 54 native birds – all believed to have been captured within 600 metres of his house with its half-hectare garden. Researcher Yolanda van Heezik from the University of Otago reviewed published literature including Flux's data to estimate that each year 28 million animals, including 1.2 million native birds, are killed by domestic cats in New Zealand. And van Heezik's statistics don't include the hunting toll from stray or feral cats.

throughout New Zealand. In early 2013, he initiated the 'Cats to Go' campaign, urging owners of all 1.4 million 'owned' cats to follow in the footsteps of their Lord Howe Island neighbours and make their current cat(s) their last. Predicting the indignation, Morgan's website opened with the disclaimer: 'If you are reading this there is a good chance that you are a cat owner and you are probably upset at the thought of getting rid of your beloved pet. Before you fly into a rage, have a read of some of the facts and get educated on why cats need to go.'

But rage, not considered reading, ensued. Within days the Cats to Go campaign had been joined by a 'Rich men telling me what to do to go' campaign and a more pointed 'Hands off my Pussy Mr Morgan' Facebook site that helped galvanise the cat-owning community. The media had a field day with Morgan fending off questions from scores of interviews, first from New Zealand, then around the world. A Kiwi commentator astutely reasoned that if the word 'cat' was replaced by 'gun', the feverish and emotive debate being waged in New Zealand would resemble the gun control debate raging simultaneously in the

United States. The vocal aggrieved cat owners were not prepared to give ground or listen to reasoned debate.

Morgan was not calling for the instantaneous and heartless destruction of all New Zealand's felines. Anyone reading past the headlines would see he was advocating the same desires expressed by responsible cat owners around the world: cats should be desexed, registered and kept indoors. Even Morgan's most controversial suggestion that cat owners should consider not replacing their cat was not novel to New Zealand pet owners. Perhaps initiated by the threats that uncontained dogs present to kiwis, new housing subdivisions adjacent to forest, beach or swamp habitat often came with a no-pet caveat. If intending residents wanted to move to idyllic housing estates surrounded by nature they had to relinquish their pet ownership, or in rare cases demonstrate how their pets would be confined. From Coromandel's Mahakirau Forest Estate to a cat-free subdivision at Waihi Beach, many bush-loving New Zealanders had already made the decision to make their current outdoor pets their last.

Vitriol directed at Morgan centred on his wealth disqualifying him from possessing a social or environmental conscience, or dismissed him as a 'bird loving bastard', but the T-shirt clad man casually chatting with me about his vision for his country fitted neither of those stereotypes. Despite not advertising the fact, I learned Morgan donated considerable money and time to causes as disparate as ridding the Antipodes Group of subantarctic islands of feral mice to promoting education and family planning in the Solomon Islands. Insults rolled off his back like water beads from a duck, with one exception. Morgan refused to ignore what he considered to be blatant hypocrisy of the nation's premier humane society to oppose his initiative. The SPCA claimed to improve the welfare of New Zealand wildlife, yet supported TNR for unowned cats, an inhumane but popularist initiative. Like Lepczck in Hawaii and Bonacic in Chile, Morgan opposed the releasing of neutered cats back into the wild and the public funds being used in this counterproductive process that, he argued, was bad for cat welfare and contrary to his objective of returning native songbirds to the suburbs and prosperity to New Zealand.

Morgan's advocacy for cat management seems to have been effective. A 2017 survey of over 1000 New Zealanders revealed strong support (78%) for a National Cat Management Strategy, with most respondents in favour of cat exclusion zones to protect wildlife and the public from cats. The respondents were, however, less convinced by Morgan's hard line on cat control, with only a third considering lethal control should be engaged to control feral cats, and a fifth still favouring TNR.

Chapter 19

ON A HOT TIN ROOF

The devastating consequences of a cuddly killer.
Peter Marra and Chris Santella

Harry Butler was an inspiration for many young Australian naturalists like myself in the 1970s. Like an antipodean David Attenborough, the homegrown wildlife enthusiast and star of his own television show, *In the Wild with Harry Butler*, introduced us to a world of bizarre and spectacular animals in the Australian bush. I delighted in Butler's ability to find a lizard under just about every rock he overturned and to expertly extract possums from hollows or spot birds high in trees. But one of Harry Butler's most noteworthy wildlife exploits was not captured on camera.

In March 1965, Butler was driving through the Dryandra Forest south of Perth in the botanical hotspot of south-western Western Australia. He screeched to a stop to collect a bronzewing pigeon that had collided with his windscreen. Regretting the accident, Butler did not want to waste the opportunity to investigate its diet and eat the plump pigeon. After noting the pigeon's crop contained seeds of the toxic *Gastrolobium* plant, Harry cooked up the pigeon for the family dinner. The toxic seeds came as no surprise. Wongi Aboriginals had warned the naturalist with a penchant for sampling the local fauna to be careful of eating bronzewing pigeons, particularly in spring and early summer when the *Gastrolobium* seed was set. Old timers who had been heavily reliant upon native fauna for food had also informed Butler that so-called 'poison pigeons' possessed toxic bone marrow dangerous for pets to eat. Butler carefully discarded the crop containing the poisonous seeds and figured the pigeon was no longer toxic and Butler's kids fed their puppy the leftover pigeon scraps. Within 30 minutes the beloved family dog was convulsing; 10 minutes later it was dead.

The European settlers of south-west Western Australia recognised as early as the 1830s that toxic plants were the cause of many deaths in their pioneering sheep flocks and cattle herds. One of the first colonial botanists, James Drummond, was tasked with the challenge of determining which plants were responsible for these deaths. Drummond's investigations revealed most deaths were associated with consumption of native legumes in the *Gastrolobium* genus, plants that quickly became known as 'poison peas'. These plants produce fluoroacetate, a highly toxic compound, as a defence against being eaten. Before long, settlers were also reporting cats and dogs dying after consuming the remains of their owner's dinner of pigeon, possum or bettong. Subsequent investigation confirmed these native animals had been feeding on the flowers or seeds of poison peas.

War was declared on poison peas in the interests of domestic livestock and pets. Within a few decades the incidence of poisoning had been reduced considerably. But then locals reported another discovery. Populations of bettongs, possums and intricately striped numbats used to supplement the settlers' diets were decreasing, even in remote forests. Cats and foxes, which had recently invaded the area, inflicted carnage upon the naïve marsupial prey. The last refuges were the remote scrub blocks where *Gastrolobium* had been spared the bulldozers and tractors. Fearing these increasingly rare mammals would join the catastrophic inventory of mammals driven to extinction, scientists developed an ingenious local solution. In a 'back to the future' program, the same toxin employed by the poison peas was used to replicate the eroded natural chemical defences of these now rare mammals.

After the outbreak of World War II and the loss of regular supplies of rat poisons such as red squill, chemists in the US undertook a series of trials. The rodenticide they numbered as chemical number 1,080 was fluoroacetate. Coincidentally, the toxic component of poison pea seeds is the same colourless salt. Fluoroacetate disrupts the intracellular Krebs cycle and deprives cells of energy, leading to death. Sodium fluoroacetate was manufactured as the synthetic compound now known as 1080, which is highly toxic to cats and foxes but far less so for wildlife that evolved with poison peas. Meat baits laced with 1080 were deposited around relict colonies of rock wallabies, bettongs and numbats with often spectacular results. Near-extinct colonies bourgeoned once again and spread out as far as the 1080 baiting allowed, while foxes continued to decimate unbaited populations.

Hundreds of kilograms of 1080 baits are now dropped from planes, hung from wires and buried in shallow holes over thousands of square kilometres. Grandiosely named schemes such as 'Western Shield' in Western Australia, 'Southern Ark' in Victoria and 'Bounceback' in South Australia, all recorded dramatic recovery in the populations of rare wildlife that had been driven almost to the point of extinction by foxes. Many proponents of this wonder poison also believe the effects of 1080 are more humane than alternative toxins like strychnine or arsenic previously used for fox and dingo control. However, 1080 is not without its critics.

I've watched, distressed, as my own poisoned dog Ninti yelped and ran around manically, his nervous system affected by the toxin.

Despite appearances, pioneering 1080 researcher Laurie Twigg argues 1080 poisoning is unlikely to result in undue pain or distress. Twigg attributes the short bursts of hyperactivity or convulsions observed in poisoned dogs to metabolic changes in the cells, including the nerves, of the poisoned animal, rather than pain. A New Zealand government review concluded that these intracellular metabolic processes might account for the nausea, lethargy, sickness and breathlessness experienced by some poisoned carnivores.

It's only when the non-toxic fluoroacetate (or 1080) has been converted into fluorocitrate by mitochondria that it becomes toxic, which explains why poisoned animals might not show symptoms for several hours. Fluorocitrate inhibits both the production of energy, which shuts the body down, and nerve and brain function. Rather than indicating pain, the spasms and hyperactivity observed in poisoned dogs (but not cats) likely result from interference with neurotransmitters that communicate between muscles and their nerves. This same inhibition of neurotransmitters possibly explains why humans often have no recollection of the adverse effects of 1080 intoxication.

In the 2010 volume of the journal *Animal Welfare*, Twigg explained why 1080 was likely a humane toxin but did concede due to the complex effects of 1080 'that it was not currently possible to assess the extent to which impairment of a poisoned animal's pain receptors and pathways decreases the ability of animals to experience painful stimuli'. Twigg was responding to a 2007 article in the same journal where Miranda Sherley questioned the humaneness of 1080, concluding, 'a poison that caused death more rapidly, or with less opportunity for injury, would clearly be more desirable from a welfare perspective'.

New Zealand toxins expert Dr Charlie Eason cites another reason that 1080 has been given an unfair rap when it comes to selecting effective and ethical toxins for cat control. Describing the death of 24 cats in his pioneering 1080 poisoning trial as 'humane', Eason then elaborated. 'The symptoms were far less severe than anticipated . . . the cats became lethargic and immobile for several hours before death.' Eason, along with subsequent researchers, reported that cats do not exhibit hyperactivity after 1080 poisoning and hence are not subject, as Sherley was concerned, to increased opportunity for injury.

Unfortunately for wildlife advocates, 1080 has been far less effective for controlling cats. Rather than numbers declining in the large areas systematically baited, feral cats numbers typically increase. Another Western Australian ecologist, Dave Algar, recognised the problem. Unlike dogs and foxes that typically derive a considerable amount of their protein from scavenging and moisture from consuming plant material, cats are almost obligate hunters. Their high protein requirements and need for the amino acids taurine and arginine impose a strictly meat diet. Having evolved in desert areas without consistent access to drinking water, feral cats also derive most of their moisture requirements from their prey. The cats he was targeting, Algar stresses, are truly wild feral cats, living remote from houses and totally reliant on wildlife for their food. Dry jerky-like meat baits neither satisfy their water requirements nor stimulate their hunting instincts, and hence are typically ignored by all but the most desperate of cats during times of food shortages.

With a mindset reminiscent of Colonel Sanders, Algar trialled and improved a secret blend of scents and flavours to improve the palatability of specially manufactured moist cat baits. Trials of Algar's thumb-sized chipolata sausage baits, trademarked as 'Eradicat baits' proved effective for cat control on islands. Periods when cats were particularly hungry, for example when seabirds were not nesting and reptiles were not active, proved to be prime opportunities to target cats with the new baits.

Ecologists battling feral cats on mainland Australia were keen to trial the baits as well. The Arid Recovery team had already witnessed the dramatic response of native mice within the South Australian reserve, free of cats and foxes. Maybe the baits laced with the indigenous toxin would enable stick-nest rats and bilbies to establish outside fenced sanctuaries. So a team of ecologists led by Katherine initiated a series of trials. Ironically for someone who had always loved and respected cats, Katherine was now actively trialling a novel technique designed to target cats. 'Although I still love cats as a species, my focus has changed from the challenge of befriending pet cats to the challenge of outsmarting feral cats,' Katherine mused.

I joined a squad of 10 intrigued spotlighters on the crest of a tall sand dune within the reserve for one of the strangest nights of fieldwork any of us had experienced. The rules had been set. We had to spread out evenly across the width of the dune and walk in a line, like the police do when searching for evidence at a crime scene. We had to search ahead and behind, on the ground, in trees and under bushes. For a few minutes we all moved along methodically, cracking jokes at the ridiculousness of our quest and wondering whether we were going to be successful.

'There's one,' yelled Bree Galbraith, with the excitement of a kid who has just found the first Easter egg in a hunt. 'And another!' Our line of torch-wielding marchers broke ranks and converged on the top of the sand dune where the young ecologist had hit the jackpot. With her folder and pen in hand, Galbraith bent over the little red cocktail sausage with a reflective tape girdle and scribed: 'on sand . . . 1 m in the open'. Meanwhile Katherine was scrabbling through a dead sandhill wattle towards the bright reflection I was 'holding' in the beam of my head-torch.

'I reckon this one is classified as inaccessible,' Katherine muttered through the scratchy twigs as she ticked the inaccessible box and wrote: 'on leaf litter . . . 1.7 m inside bush . . . foliage to ground . . . *Acacia ligulata*'. Ahead on the dune was a broken line of bright reflections, like drunken roadmarkers, scattered haphazardly throughout the grass and buckbush clumps.

A couple of hours earlier Galbraith had tipped 101 little reflective orange sausages out the window of a plane piloted by local Phil Goldsworthy. 'Goldy' loved the Arid Recovery flying jobs. Sometimes he swept over the stony plains scanning with his wing-mounted radio-tracking receiver for an errant tagged echidna or radio-collared feral cat that had wandered out of range of the ground-based radio-tracker. But never before had he conducted a smallgoods-bombing raid in the name of science.

The nocturnal wiener hunt had been planned to determine the proportion of Algar's special cat baits dropped from a plane or chopper that would actually be available to cats. If many of the baits were concealed inside bushes, or hung on trees above the reach of a cat, we would have to increase the density of baits dropped.

The following week Katherine and Galbraith tested the effectiveness of sausages placed in the open with those tucked under and into bushes. They followed cat tracks and were surprised to find more baits were taken under (but not in) bushes, possibly because cats avoided the more open areas. Katherine used the estimated percentage of accessible baits as the basis for determining likely bait uptake from the 25 of Algar's special cat sausages dropped per square kilometre.

A week later, staff and volunteers took turns in navigating the baiting chopper over the dunes while flicking out a toxic snag every 80 metres. The chopper could turn rapidly, allowing us to follow sandy creeks or hone in on a group of rabbit burrows where cats and foxes were likely to live. Even though the nearby town of Roxby Downs was in the process of enacting a registration and compulsory containment law for pet cats, we had to respect the licensing arrangements for use of cat baits, which stipulated a two-kilometre buffer zone around the town. Once all 45,000 baits had been laid covering a 10-kilometre radius around the reserve, Katherine and her team turned their attention to tracking radio-collared cats.

'Cats are so cryptic and difficult to detect in the desert,' Katherine explained, 'that in order to determine if the baits are effective we really need to follow the fate of individual cats. Radio collars enable us to compare their survival inside and outside the baited area.'

Modern radio collars can be fitted with a simple, yet amazingly useful feature that produces a more rapidly pulsing beep if the collared animal has not moved for an extended period. By scanning through the radio frequencies of all the collared cats, Katherine could quickly determine which ones had not moved and hence were likely dead. To confirm the cause of death, the Eradicat sausages had been infused with a red dye that showed up on the lips, whiskers or gut of poisoned cats.

Several collars indicated a mortality signal immediately after the baiting had finished. The scientists rushed out, expecting to find a still-warm corpse. But instead, seven of the nine cats had obviously been dead prior to the aerial baiting and subsequent tests confirmed 1080 poisoning was responsible. Conventional dried meat baits had been spread around a fortnight before the Eradicat trials to reduce fox numbers and hence maximise the potential of the fancy new baits to control cats. Paradoxically, given these special cat baits had been developed to redress inefficiencies of dry meat baits for cats, the collared cats had been desperate enough to eat the conventional baits. However, both cats still alive when the cat sausages were dropped succumbed to the red-dyed baits within a couple of days.

This dramatic knockdown in cats, along with foxes, provided the opportunity for the most eagerly anticipated project since the iconic bilbies had been reintroduced inside the Arid Recovery Reserve five years earlier. The newfangled cat baits were going to create a safe haven right outside the fence, so bilbies – and boodies – could be released. For the first time since rabbits, foxes and cats had overrun the desert, we were hoping these native animals could survive again beyond the expensive fences.

But the first trial release a year after our experimental trial was a dismal failure. No animals survived more than a few months despite an intensive cat-baiting campaign. To check the cat baiting remained effective, remotely triggered cameras were set up near cat baits and elsewhere in the release area. Alarmingly, and surprisingly given the success of the initial baiting, cats were photographed walking straight past baits time after time. Although baits had killed the collared cats, they were not effective against all cats all of the time.

Then the penny dropped. The year 2002, when we achieved good knockdown of baited cats, had been unusually dry, even by the vagaries of unpredictable desert climate. Rabbits had yet to recover from the calici virus that had decimated their populations five years earlier. Lizards, mice and ground birds, the other main prey of cats in the region, were also scarce because it was both dry and cool. The collared feral cats had been lured into baited cages because they were hungry enough to eat a meat lure – they were also most likely to take a poison bait. These desperate hungry cats were most likely to die of starvation during winter anyway. By contrast, most of the bilbies were killed by a few large expert hunters.

A subsequent larger release relied less on the baiting blitzkrieg and more on dedicated shooting and trapping of feral cats. Yet despite such anticipation and expectation, and in spite of a phenomenally dedicated team of ground staff working day and night to protect the released animals from the cats, this second release also ultimately failed. Within six months there was no trace of boodies outside the fence. The last of the bilbies was killed just over a year later.

Graduate student and volunteer Laura Cunningham's article in the local newsletter best expressed the young team's exasperation, anger and despair. Her epiphany was profound:

> The first time I found one of 'my' bilbies dead, I was devastated. This beautiful animal had been killed, and its body just left under a tree. It was heartbreaking and it did not get easier. In fact, each time I found another dead bilby it hit home ... and I got madder and madder at the feral cats.

It's one thing to 'know' something, but another to actually be confronted with it. Rationally I knew that feral cats kill native animals, but until I saw how effective they were at killing bilbies I didn't really understand the scope of the problem. Seeing bilby remains, a couple of hopping mice and several skinks all in the stomach of one cat really drove that message home. Now I can understand John Wamsley's 'cat hat' – and I want one too. I just want to get the mongrels before they do any more damage – and this from the 'animal loving vegetarian' . . .

Not to be deterred, Katherine and her team decided they needed to give their reintroduced animals a head start. The boodies were seemingly ill equipped to deal with exotic predators but the more wary and savvy bilbies offered hope. If the reintroduction biologists couldn't remove every cat they had to better prepare the bilbies to deal with their nemesis. Part of a bizarre wildlife experiment, I joined the team as a designated bilby chaser for three consecutive nights.

Jammed into the back of a 4WD ute with a large fishing net like the one we used to catch the stick-nest rats on Reevesby Island five years earlier, I scanned the sweeping spotlight beam. Arid Recovery ecologist Helen Crisp in the passenger seat had just noted a large male bilby she had seen in the area the previous week. Suddenly the Toyota screeched to a stop and Katherine, who was driving, yelled, 'There he is! A male on the road straight ahead in my headlights. Go, go, go!'

After tumbling out of the car with my net, the bilby had a 40-metre headstart. The spotlight was trained on the fleeing bilby, its white-tipped black tail held aloft like a flag as it bounded off the track and into the low shrubland. With their large ears, implausibly long nose and bizarre habit of holding their tail vertical like an alarmed warthog, bilbies are peculiar looking at the best of times. But in full flight, their knock-kneed bounding produces a most ungainly, almost humorous, gait. This chase was no laughing matter. The first two bilbies spotted that night had darted down their holes before we caught them and Katherine and Helen were frustrated.

As if feeling sorry for me, or perhaps volunteering to participate in a groundbreaking experiment, the next bilby jumped into a scraggly bush as I sprinted after it. By the time it had extricated itself, the panicked animal jumped straight into my net and I quickly knelt on the frame so it couldn't escape. I couldn't resist the urge to stroke the bilby's improbably soft silver and white fur, while covering its eyes to help calm it. Before I had caught my breath, the two scientists were racing up with a black cloth bag and a fisherman's tackle box. Within a couple of minutes the pair had expertly shaved the hair from the base of the bilby tail and fitted it with a tail transmitter that would enable them to follow it for several months. Like other bandicoots, bilbies could not wear conventional radio collars because they had a tendency to get their front feet caught in them while digging for food. With the bilby weighed and tracking device fitted to its freshly shaved tail, we were soon back spotlighting again for more.

The next time I caught a bilby, the two researchers were again close behind me with the bag and processing kit, but this time Katherine brandished a freshly defrosted cat carcass, growled angrily and almost pushed me off the net while rubbing the terrified bilby with her grotesque mummy. Crisp just had time to instruct me to move quickly before she sprayed the stricken bilby

An endangered marsupial bilby being trained to avoid cats with a cat carcass and spray of cat urine in an ultimately futile attempt to enable bilbies to withstand cat predation outside the Arid Recovery Reserve in Central Australia. (Photo: K. Moseby)

with repugnant cat urine. After attaching a tail transmitter, both bilbies were driven outside the reserve and released.

Before the traumatised bilby was released, the ecologists repeated their terrifying but harmless assault with the cat and spray bottle, while I quietly released the other bilby into the dark. The following nights this process was repeated, securing both quiet 'control' bilbies for comparison with those that had been terrified by the sight and smell of cats. The Arid Recovery scientists carefully monitored the survival of the different groups of bilbies to see if those trained to associate cats with a dangerous, unpleasant experience were safer.

Perhaps the most risky yet exciting reintroduction of Australian mammals is taking place in a 10,000-hectare area nestled between two conventional cat- and fox-free paddocks and the world's longest man-made structure, the semipermeable Dingo Fence, separating dingoes from sheep regions. Buoyed by promising responses from 'cat-trained' bilbies at Arid Recovery, the same researchers working at Wild Deserts in the far north-west corner of New South Wales are not eradicating feral cats from all paddocks of their new reserve but are deliberately exposing some bilbies, bettongs and quolls to cats. Novel cat control tools will be trialled to keep predation rates in check in the hope that these pioneering survivors will develop and pass on awareness and aversion skills to improve their survival outside fences.

Sure enough, as predicted, the trained bilbies were more vigilant, moving burrows more often, especially once the burrows were sprayed with cat urine. But ultimately, despite continued baiting and opportunistic shooting of cats, none of the bilbies, trained or otherwise, survived for more than 18 months.

While the desert reintroduction attempts were failing, the gravity of the cat predation issue in the northern savannahs of Australia was becoming more apparent. Until recently ecologists assumed that northern Australia had largely been spared the extinction crisis that has wiped out many desert and southern mammals. But when John Woinarski and a host of other scientists systematically surveyed mammals from a series of sites in Kakadu National Park in 2001 and 2009, their findings were alarming. Capture rates of 10 small mammal species had declined by an average of 75% within this period. These figures did not even take into account the brush-tailed rabbit-rat and northern brush-tailed phascogale, which once common had declined even before

> The pale field rat, one of the Kakadu mammals thought to be threatened by cats, was reintroduced into four large pens within their former range. Two of the pens built by Katherine Tuft and Sarah Legge from the Australian Wildlife Conservancy just kept the rats in; the other two matched the design of the Arid Recovery fence to prevent access to cats. Within two weeks, cats had discovered both the rat pens and wiped out all but one of the endangered mammals. By contrast the rats in the cat-free pens thrived. Legge and Tuft had no qualms about apportioning much of the blame of the mammal decline to cat predation and have both since moved on to research methods to control this major wildlife threat.

the intensive monitoring commenced. Woinarski and co-workers considered the most plausible reasons for this unfolding catastrophe to be too frequent fires and predation by feral cats.

I met with Pete McDonald in the home of arguably Australia's most critically endangered mammal, even rarer than the imperilled Kakadu rodents. For several years McDonald had been scaling rugged peaks searching for the enigmatic central rock-rat, which inhabited some of the most spectacular scenery in Central Australia. Feared extinct for most of the 20th century, rock-rats had been rediscovered a couple of hours west of Alice Springs in 1997 and had become the focus of concerted conservation action. As I caught my breath and wiped my brow from the strenuous climb, McDonald pointed out the few mountain tops that constituted the entire rock-rat range. We were standing in the epicentre of rock-rat habitat, a rocky ridge top vegetated by a dense knee-high legume that McDonald confirmed was, you guessed it, a *Gastrolobium*, or poison pea. The same species also grew at other sites inhabited by rock-rats but was scarce elsewhere in the MacDonnell Ranges, and hence may have played a role in protecting rats from foxes, although cats still penetrated the rock-rat habitat.

McDonald explained that analyses of feral cat scats collected from the mountains revealed that despite their rarity, the central rock-rat was found in one quarter of all cat scats, making it the dominant prey species for cats in the mountains. His data had shown a concerning crash in rock-rat numbers, most likely to cat predation. Continuously trapping cats to protect the rats in such inaccessible terrain was not sustainable and when rat numbers had dwindled to worrying levels, McDonald had arranged an emergency permit to aerially bait the critical habitat with Eradicat baits. Early signs were that this baiting had been successful, with fewer cats and more rats detected. However, McDonald was mindful that baiting should only be used when cats were at their hungriest.

Perhaps the most concerning and confounding conundrum of contemporary feral cat control was the response of brush-tailed bettongs, or woylies. Once inhabiting vast areas of southern Australia, by the 1990s these rabbit-sized kangaroos were restricted to the small patches of poison pea habitat where Harry Butler had collected his road-killed toxic pigeon. Subsequent 1080 baiting of foxes in and around these reserves saw woylies rebound so spectacularly that the species was removed from the national threatened species list. This recovery was heralded by conservationists around the country, indeed around the globe, as a rare but cherished example of the broad-scale recovery of a rare species outside of fenced reserves or islands.

But their recovery was short lived. Within a few years the woylie population had started to decline. Then it crashed, the little marsupials disappearing once more from areas they had recolonised. Authorities speedily reinstated them on the threatened list. At first scientists, including Adrian Wayne from the woylie recovery team, suspected a disease must be responsible for such a dramatic and widespread decline. But trials eventually revealed the culprit was most likely to be cats. The 1080 baiting had been so efficient at removing foxes, once the major threat to woylies, that cat numbers increased to fill the void left by the larger predator.

Sustainable control of feral cats had become so intractable, yet vital for the conservation of many species, that international conferences and workshops were held to brainstorm novel approaches to addressing the challenges. Established baiting, trapping and shooting strategies were suggested but most field ecologists recognised new tools were also needed.

One feral cat control proposal specifically targeted the super hunters, those problem cats causing problems for the boodies and bilbies at Arid Recovery, and presumably Wayne's woylies at Dryandra. Reliance upon toxic baits made the incorrect assumption that the most dangerous cats, the ace hunters, would abandon their predatory instincts and scavenge bait. But if prey animals themselves were toxic, the predatory instincts of the super hunters would eventually bring about their downfall. Inspired by a suggestion from *Gastrolobium* researcher and passionate quoll aficionado David Peacock, Katherine and I helped develop the concept of converting vulnerable wildlife into toxic Trojans. Toxic Trojan theory employs the low acidity of a cat's stomach to dissolve the casing of a tiny capsule harmlessly inserted in the neutral pH under the skin of wildlife. If the released quoll, bilby or boodie was not killed and eaten, its potentially lethal cargo would remain stable under its skin like a microchip for its entire life. However, a big cat hunting these toxic Trojans would be poisoned when eating its first kill and would not go on to inflict the multiple kills that have wiped out many populations of vulnerable species.

Another take on this philosophy was perhaps the most ingenious and simple solution to the feral cat problem, but also the most challenging to gain support from the policy makers. Adrian Wayne, from the woylie recovery team, proposed to restore the safety net once created by poison peas.

Wayne planned reinstating poison peas in the towering jarrah forests of Western Australia, only a couple of hours from the world famous breaks he surfed and the wineries of Margaret River. Fire management that encouraged cool fires to reduce fuel loads did not provide the heat necessary to germinate poison peas. On a visit to Wayne, dense groves of these three-metre-high shrubs with dazzling clusters of yellow and orange flowers were largely restricted to the bulldozed tracks marking closed forestry roads. Trapping wildlife in these patches afforded me one of my most memorable wildlife moments. Wayne was targeting woylies and chuditch (western quoll), some of which were destined for release in the far-away Flinders Ranges. But the standout capture for me was a squirrel-sized marsupial sporting an extravagant black brush on its tail and an endearing appearance. After measuring the black-tailed phascogale I had the pleasure of releasing it near an old hollow tree and thrilled as it weightlessly scampered up the tree and then launched itself, squirrel-like, into a neighbouring tree, brushy tail gliding behind. Several hours later, still high on the 10-second experience, I was struck by a photo pinned up in Wayne's office. Staring at the lens of a camera trap was a sooty cat, with one of my new favourite animals hanging limp and lifeless from its mouth.

A feral cat with the body of one of the author's favourite black-tailed phascogales on the margins of Western Australia's jarrah forests, which are, in part, protected from feral cats and foxes by poisonous Gastrolobium *peas. (Photo: Marika Maxwell)*

As the recruitment in the bulldozed patches attested, poison peas were favoured not only by hot fires but also by physical disturbance. Wayne hoped by spreading seeds and then ploughing around the margins of forests and national parks he could restore the biological safety net that had protected this vulnerable suite of marsupials from cat predation for a century or more. Wayne believed possums and pigeons would be attracted to, and gorge themselves upon, the flowers or seeds of his reinstated poison pea thickets. Although woylies might also ingest pea seeds and derive some protection from their toxins, Wayne envisaged a more strategic role for his little kangaroos in the reinstated ecosystem. Woylies are primarily mycophagus; they actively seek out, dig up and consume fungi buried beneath the forest floor. These fungi play a vital role in the ecology of the forest, both in assisting trees to take up nutrients and water but also enabling poison peas to sequester toxins from the soil. Without the fungi the poison peas lose their punch. Without the woylies to disperse fungal spores in their scats, the fungi dies out. Just as cats help spread toxoplasmosis that assists their hunting prowess, woylies help to spread the fungi that help protect them from cat predation. Cats and foxes immigrating into the forest refuges encounter toxin-laden birds and mammals and are poisoned. This natural process might replace the need for the expensive and ecologically flawed 1080-baiting program.

But unless local plants (like lilies particularly toxic to cats) could be used elsewhere, protection of wildlife from feral cats will need additional tools, such as the daunting but potentially powerful new technology offered by CRISPR. This developing gene-editing technology enables geneticists to alter genomes, potentially rendering species infertile, producing only males, or introducing other traits to reduce cats' ability to live or hunt in the wild. It is difficult to predict what this enormously powerful science will offer and how society will respond, let alone how pet and native cats could be protected from such genetic engineering.

Leaving technologies aside that have yet to progress from fiction to non-fiction, let's consider less radical and risky options for controlling feral cats.

Chapter 20

NO SILVER BULLET

A cat is a puzzle for which there is no solution. Hazel Nicholson

After spectacular successes on islands, the ability of cat-specific diseases to eradicate or limit cats has been touted as *the* silver bullet for the feral cat problem. It was the eradication of cats from Marion Island, due largely to the successful release of a cat virus, which convinced Gareth Morgan that cat control in New Zealand was both necessary and possible.

The rabbit-specific diseases myxomatosis and haemorrhagic disease (calicivirus) have conferred greater benefits to furred, feathered and leafy threatened species in Australia than all the poison baits and traps deployed for feral cats for over a century. Effects on tree regeneration and wildlife recovery were dramatic. I witnessed an unprecedented explosion in the range and distribution of four threatened mammal species following the spread of rabbit calicivirus in the mid 1990s. There are few more exciting discoveries for wildlife biologists than finding rare animals thriving well outside their known range. But that's exactly what a group of us found, repeatedly, when we headed off into the desert after the rabbit haemorrhagic disease had decimated cat and fox numbers previously bolstered by plagues of rabbits.

Despite initially low rainfall that typically limits desert mammals, Reece Pedler, who crunched the numbers from our surveys, found the extent of occurrence of two IUCN-listed native rodents (the dusky hopping-mouse and plains mouse) increased by well over 200%, whereas the even rarer crest-tailed mulgara increased 70-fold. These and other once-rare mammals were now common, sometimes even plaguing, as they did historically. After considering the effects of rain and other factors, we concluded this spectacular recovery was attributable mainly to the crash in cat and fox numbers in the wake of the rabbit biocontrol.

Buoyed by the remarkable success of these rabbit diseases and the Marion Island cat disease case study, ecologists have been keen to investigate the potential for cat diseases to directly limit populations. It sounds so easy. Release a virus and let it run its course. No more poisons, or traps, or countless hours of hunting. However, for the same reason so-called 'biological control' can be so effective and easy, it can also be highly risky. There have been instances where well-intentioned biological control has been spectacularly counterproductive.

The millions of cane toads poisoning wildlife across the Australian tropics is one of the most disastrous examples of not only failed, but devastatingly counterproductive, biological control. Imported to sugarcane fields from South America in 1935, in a largely unsuccessful attempt to control pest beetles, cane toads have spread well beyond agricultural areas to become one of Australia's most dangerous invasive pests. Many native animals, especially toad predators like marsupial quolls and large lizards and snakes, have been largely wiped out as the wave of toxic toads inundates their habitats.

As if the toad was not disastrous enough, the sugar industry also introduced mongoose and Indian mynas both to Australia and elsewhere. Like the misguided toad folly, introductions of mongoose to Hawaii and the West Indies to control rats overlooked the fact the primarily diurnal mongoose was inefficient at controlling nocturnal rats but remains an efficient predator of native wildlife on these islands. Stoats and weasels brought from Britain to New Zealand in the 19th century for rabbit control have become major pests of native wildlife in their own right, while the rabbit problem remains. After witnessing the initial success of the release of 300 cats to control feral rabbits near Geelong, in 1886 the New South Wales Government sent hundreds of cats to Bourke in the Australian outback to kill rabbits. The rabbits remain and those cats likely contributed to the wave of recent small mammal extinctions in western New South Wales. The harlequin ladybird introduced to the United States from Asia in the 1980s to control aphids and scale spread alarmingly to become a pest itself, threatening endemic North American ladybirds and other aphid predators.

But these catastrophic failures of biological control should not detract from the overwhelming success of other animals or diseases at restricting pest species. Matthew Cock is chief scientist for the science-based development and information organisation Centre for Agriculture and Biosciences International. He calculates of the 1300 biological releases against weeds over the last 110 years, only nine produced any collateral damage such as feeding on native species. Many, like *Cactoblastis*, achieved spectacular results. Prior to the introduction of a cactus-eating moth called *Cactoblastis cactorum* in 1920, hundreds of thousands of hectares of Australian forest and farming land were choked by the invasive prickly pear cacti. With no native cacti, authorities were confident a cactus-specific grub would be safe and effective, and they were right. Although pockets of prickly pear still persist, this little imported moth continues to keep the once invasive pest cactus under control, saving millions of dollars from lost production, thousands of litres of herbicide, and many plants from competition. By the same reckoning, because there are no native cats in much of the Pacific, cat-specific biological control should, in theory, provide ongoing safe management of feral cats. Encouraged by modelling suggesting a feline leukemia infection rate of only 4–12% could suppress cat populations by up to 20%, Hawaiian scientists investigated whether the retroviruses cat AIDs or feline leukemia could be used to regulate feral cats threatening endangered birds on Mauna Kea. They concluded that the low cat population density and inherited immunity to cat leukemia on Mauna Kea made effective feral cat control unlikely. Despite scientists' desire to find a solution to their feral cat problem, I imagine there was a degree of relief that they did not have to make an agonising decision about trading feral cat welfare for the welfare of endangered Hawaiian wildlife. Cat AIDs and feline leukemia, causing slow and often painful death, are the types of diseases you wouldn't wish on your worst enemy.

Unlike the two feline retroviruses, pet cats can be vaccinated against feline panleukopenia virus, also known as feline enteritis. Furthermore, feline enteritis can decimate cats on islands, such as Marion Island in the southern Indian Ocean, where generations of cats had been isolated from the virus. However, even without vaccination most mainland cats are immune. Therefore, rather than being a model for widespread use, Marion Island was an aberration.

Although not an issue on remote southern islands, like Marion or Hawaii where these diseases have been used or proposed, promoting feline diseases for feral cat control in habitats with native cats is risky. Cat AIDS has been recorded spreading from domestic cats to the rare Tsushima leopard cat in Japan, and even to lions and pumas. As we learnt in Spain, feline leukemia also spread from domestic cats to lynx, and to Florida panthers. Collateral damage to rare native felines rules out deliberately spreading cat diseases to feral cat populations where native cats are present.

However some scientists still feel cat AIDS, in particular, may offer a solution for feral cat control. Because it is highly specific to cats and readily transmitted between outdoor cats, but not indoor pets shielded from infected individuals, cat AIDS apparently offers potential for genetic engineering. One day, if funds are committed to the necessary research, the world might have an effective and humane biological agent for controlling unowned cats. Given the sensitivities around developing or promulgating a disease fatal for domestic cats, a more palatable and likely successful option would be to modify a benign cat-specific virus to transmit a neutering gene.

Genetically manipulated viruses may eventually become a silver bullet for feral cat control where no native felines exist. But in the absence of such developments and with threatened species facing extinction every year from cat predation and diseases like toxoplasmosis, other feral cat management tools are being urgently developed and trialled.

Steve Austin is one of the world's foremost authorities on dog training. For decades the Dog Whisperer's services have been valued for just about any conceivable dog training application by police, border security, conservationists and owners of problem dogs. Austin reveres his working line cocker spaniels and English springers; their devotion to him is also apparent whenever you

In the same way mouse cytomegalovirus has been used as a contraceptive vector to limit house mouse plagues, Michael Monks and co-authors from the National Jewish Health Center in Denver, Colorado, plan to genetically adapt cat herpes to render cats sterile. Feline herpesvirus establishes life-long latent infection in cats but generally does not affect their lifespan or health. Monks and his team plan to modify cat herpes to carry antibodies to the hormone that initiates oestrus, thus preventing pregnancy. If successful, their next challenge would be to spread the engineered virus to free-ranging cats without exposing wild native felines.

watch his dogs working. Before the National Parks authorities allowed his dogs onto Macquarie Island to help remove the last rabbits, Austin had to direct his dogs, off lead, to walk through crowded penguin colonies without so much as looking at the birds.

With their phenomenal sense of smell and ingrained dedication to the task, Austin's special 'feral cat' dogs will detect and follow cats through grassland or forest. One of his best cat dogs, an English springer named Maggie, works with Dotty, trained to detect the endangered smoky mouse. The New South Wales National Parks Service takes the two dogs out together, with Maggie instructed to focus her cat searches wherever Dotty detects evidence of the rare mice.

When I saw him operating on the west coast of South Australia's Eyre Peninsula, I was surprised Austin didn't allow his dogs to catch the cats endangering a precariously small population of bilbies and woylies. 'Have you seen what those cats can do to my dogs?' he asked. 'I have not spent months training a dog to have it sliced open by a feral cat.'

Austin deplores animal cruelty and therefore prefers to

dispatch the cats with a gun at close range after the dogs have scared it up a tree. If the cat seeks shelter in a burrow or rabbit warren, Steve calls his excited dogs away and fumigates the cornered cat. At a workshop I attended, run by Austin for farmers and wildlife managers interested in the use of working dogs, there was universal commendation for his ability to control and direct his dogs with well-rehearsed whistles and hand signals. However, the excitement of having so many onlookers might have got the better of Austin's crack cat-sniffer dog, which showed interest in nearly every tree in sight before finally honing in on the tree where Austin had hidden a scented cat tail. Subsequent local searches conducted by Austin's dogs on a large fenced peninsula with known feral cats failed to detect any. This mirrored the inability of trained dogs to detect any of the 23 known feral cats on Little Barrier Island during their eradication campaign, despite the dogs showing promise on the New Zealand mainland. Maybe the dogs' performance was compromised by unfamiliar coastal scents or other distractions.

Another crack team of cat hunters use an even more impressive technique. Nolia Yukultji Ward is a member of the Pintupi Nine, the last Indigenous Australians to make contact with Europeans. Until 1984 Nolia lived in the desert country around Lake Mackay in the remote Gibson Desert. Wearing only a hair-string belt adorned with 'pussycat' tails, Nolia and her family lived a traditional lifestyle: gathering seeds and hunting pythons, goannas and their favourite – the pussycat. When feral cats displaced the Pintupi's former key food animals like bandicoots and wallabies, they seamlessly filled the void in the diet of these nomadic hunters.

Kiwirrkurra, an incredibly isolated settlement of iron houses, sprang up in the Gibson Desert in the 1980s to accommodate the Pintubi tribe. Driving the 700 kilometres along corrugated dirt roads from the nearest town, Alice Springs, took a full day. The remoteness of the small community was reinforced at the lone diesel bowser that sold fuel for $3 a litre, more than double what I paid when I filled up in Alice. Despite the exorbitant price, few motorists drive past the bowser without refilling, the next fuel to the west is 360 kilometres away. Way out here, in one of the most remote deserts in the world, feral cats prosper.

Although she has now come in from the desert to live with her family at Kiwirrkurra, Nolia has retained her largely traditional diet. Although Nolia still regularly hunts cats using the techniques her family used when she was a child, she now wears second-hand skirts and baggy pullovers instead of her customary hair-string belt. While wandering around looking for witchetty grubs or seeds, or maybe lighting small fires to help locate goanna burrows, Nolia and her friends often encounter cat tracks in the red sand. Great excitement ensues; the goanna and grub hunt is immediately abandoned. These aren't pet cats, or even recent strays wandering from an owner's house. They are truly wildcats, living hundreds of kilometres and often hundreds of generations from their domestic forebears. Nolia doesn't hunt cats because she is concerned about their impact on wildlife, or because she is being paid to do so. Roasted cat meat is a cherished treat, much preferred to any frozen meat she could purchase on a polystyrene tray from the Kiwirrkurra store. '*Kuka wirru*,' Nolia said, excitement in her eyes, 'great meat.'

Nolia's nephew Patrick explained that cats are now prepared in a similar ceremonial way to the locally extinct mala and desert

Nolia Yukultji Ward with a feral cat she has tracked, hunted and is about to prepare for eating in the same way her Pintubi tribe in the Australian desert ate mala before they were forced to extinction by feral cats.
(Photo: Kate Crossing)

quoll once served by his tribe. The bladder is removed and the intestine squeezed out before being stuffed back inside the carcass to be cooked in coals. These soft clean intestines, along with the heart, liver and fat, are saved for the old people who often have no teeth. The hunter usually had the task of assigning who gets the head, with the prized brain being eaten as a health elixir. The Walpiri tribe to the north-east considered cats as bush medicine and Aboriginal rangers at Newhaven sanctuary, back toward Alice, had introduced white fellas to the medicinal meat as well. Finally the meaty legs are pulled from the charred carcass, the sweet moist white meat preferred to beef or even kangaroo.

With honed tracking skills, the crack Pintupi cat hunters relentlessly follow the tracks until they flush their quarry. Unlike

Steve Austin with his dogs, Nolia's team have no reservations about chasing the cat as they stride off after it brandishing their lightweight crowbars. For years I had harboured an ambition to spend time in the desert with the Pintubi and hopefully absorb some of their skills at tracking and reading the land. Nolia didn't disappoint me. I walked behind her, almost in her shadow, as I watched where she placed her feet and where she was looking. Almost as an aside she motioned towards a barely perceptible track of *ninu* (bilby) and quickly confirmed it was the 'crippled one', a bilby she recognised by its asymmetrical tracks. Nolia kept following the crippled *ninu*, pointing out where it had stopped to dig or feed. In 20 minutes with Nolia I learned more about bilbies than I had from years of naively looking at their tracks.

Nolia pointed out that her cousin John T must have found a fresh cat track because he had walked away from the group of trackers, across the sand plain. Earlier at the Kiwirrkurra store I had made a mental note to keep tabs on John T. Although Nolia was the celebrated leader of the feral cat tally displayed on the store wall (49 cats brought back to the community in the past 12 months), John T was second with 42. Leaving Nolia and her crippled bilby I raced over to follow her prodigy.

John T didn't seem to be intently searching for tracks as I was, rather he was reading the country, anticipating the cat's movements and motives, purposefully striding forwards while scanning the sand at his feet and the terrain ahead. He seemed unfazed we were walking over the baked clay roof of a subterranean termitaria that yielded no tracks; he just knew the cat would be headed for a small tree on the dune hundreds of metres ahead. Sure enough when we reached the tree John T found the tracks again and figured his quarry had been by the tree when we had driven up to start the hunt, because its pace had quickened. With at least half an hour's head start the cat was going to be difficult to run down, especially since the weather was cool and cloudy. Hot clear days were best for tracking and the cats tired more quickly, John T explained. Nevertheless, he was keen to close the gap on the cat hunter's board and net himself another $100 reward, offered per cat by the local threatened animal officer. Like experienced fishermen who anticipate the type of fish by the way it grabs the hook or pulls on the line, the Pintupi trackers excitedly predict the type of cat they will find by its tracks. 'This one is not too big, probably a female,' John T offered, as we doggedly followed its single line of clawless tracks.

Cats of course can sprint far faster than the pursuing Pintupi, but what they lack in speed the Aboriginal trackers make up for with persistence and stamina. If we were to catch up with the cat it would typically flush and sprint off, usually hiding under a bush or hummock of spikey spinifex grass. Next time when the cat takes off it does not run as far before it tires. Before long the exhausted cat will simply hide under a bush when the trackers approach to quickly dispatch it with a blow to the head. 'One hit,' Nolia emphasised, swinging her crowbar downwards, 'then we check they are dead by testing they don't blink.' Cloud and wind, along with a confusion of tracks, eventually saw the hunt abandoned for the day.

Now working with Nolia and her fellow Pintupi trackers at Kiwirrkurra is wildlife ecologist Rachel Paltridge. Breezy and patient, with the enviable ability to be productive without becoming stressed or frustrated, Paltridge has the ideal temperament to work with such an amazing woman. The two first met in 1999 when Paltridge was searching for rare bilbies in the remote desert country for her PhD dissertation. Nolia not only knows where to find bilbies but tracks them to their burrows, where Paltridge sometimes erects monitoring cameras. Paltridge quickly learned Pintupi hunting was instrumental in protecting the remnant bilby populations. The small burns carried out while hunting goannas stimulated growth of food plants for the bilbies. Bilbies and Pintupi share a close dietary overlap, especially for fire responsive seeds, fruits and grubs. Not surprisingly, areas where Aboriginal hunting and burning have maintained Pintupi bushtucker supplies are also prime feeding areas for bilbies.

Paltridge is convinced the hunting of cats has also been directly beneficial to threatened wildlife. Over more than two decades of studying bilbies in the Australian deserts, Paltridge has documented a continued and alarming contraction in their range. Sites where bilbies could be found during her doctorate studies are no longer inhabited. While changes in fire regimes have likely contributed, Paltridge has no doubt about the impacts of cats and foxes. She meticulously sorts scats of cats and foxes, and Nolia lets her inspect the stomachs of the cats she hunts. Bilbies, marsupial moles and other threatened wildlife are often easier to find in cat stomachs than alive in the desert.

Paltridge is also researching the value of Aboriginal cat hunting to survivorship of the increasingly rare and endangered great desert skink. Unfortunately for this mighty lizard it is both easy to catch and tasty, for Aboriginals and cats alike. Scat analysis has revealed great desert skink remains in more than half the cat scats she has analysed, much higher than the predation rate of foxes, dingoes or humans. Paltridge is testing whether these enigmatic lizards, that I had yet to observe in the wild, persist better at sites where traditional hunting also controls cats. Her hunch is although the Pintupi hunters occasionally find and eat the skinks, their control of cats is important for the survival of the last few skink populations. Other scientists had also showed that isolated remnant wildlife populations, including reintroduced bilbies like the ones from Arid Recovery, are often wiped out by feral cats if not intensively controlled.

So serious is feral cat predation in the central deserts that Paltridge has been able to find paid work for Indigenous cat hunting experts. Remote mine sites and wildlife sanctuaries employ Nolia and others to search and destroy cats from threatened species habitat. With so many problem sites, and such long distances to travel, Paltridge has spread the load by establishing a second expert Indigenous cat hunting team 300 kilometres away. As for Katherine and her reintroduced quolls at Wilpena Pound, Paltridge recognises it is most important to concentrate on the most likely killers, the large tomcats. Nolia doesn't mind, the bigger the cat the more meat to share with her family. Not only do they hunt cats, they use their innate understanding of fire and fire conditions to create mosaic burns at the same time, thus improving wildlife food resources and lessening the risk of devastating large fires.

Quietly spoken and sensitive, Paltridge is another of the unlikely animal-loving fraternity increasingly committed to controlling feral cats. Like her Aboriginal co-workers and many fellow wildlife ecologists she has no qualms about dispatching feral cats. But she has faced incredulous and accusational questioning from city-based cat advocates when she makes the mistake of elaborating on her seemingly idyllic work in the remote deserts.

'When I started protecting bilbies by controlling cats and foxes, neighbours and even some of my extended family found it impossible to differentiate between the cats I was targeting and their own pet moggie,' she explained. 'But thanks to the successes of cat-free sanctuaries, the advent of goPro cameras fitted to feral cats to film their hunting, and especially the photos and lists of prey items killed by feral cats, the public and our politicians have at long last recognised the seriousness of the issue.'

To reinforce this Paltridge pointed to the inaugural National Threatened Species Summit, hosted by the Federal Environment Minister in May 2015. It was here that cats were identified as the most serious threat to Australian wildlife. Nolia, her Pintupi offsider Monica Jurrah and Paltridge were flown by Gregory Andrews, Australia's Threatened Species Commissioner, to the summit in far-away Melbourne to explain the seriousness of the feral cat issue to senior politicians, business leaders and academics. Their invitation also served as an advertisement for the services they could provide to desert wildlife projects. Such exposure and opportunities were unheard of only a decade ago. At this summit, the Australian Government and other stakeholders announced a staggering AU$6.6 million of initiatives to address feral cats, including plans to exterminate them from many of the nation's largest islands and wildlife refuges. Although their expert cat hunting teams were not funded at the first summit, Paltridge and Nolia hope the political momentum is maintained and the Aboriginal cat hunting teams will be gainfully employed for decades to come.

Unfortunately, talented and persistent Aboriginal hunters, like laboriously trained cat detection dogs, are rare. In most cases less spectacular and less targeted techniques are required to protect our wildlife from cats. Despite confidence from trials in Arid Recovery's mini enclosure that our fence was largely cat proof, we wanted to further minimise the chance of cats invading the reserve. Occasionally, to be precise three times in the first 17 years, a particularly acrobatic and persistent cat breached the tall fence with its floppy overhang. Such an incursion precipitated an urgent coordinated plan to track down and remove the offender before it caused too much carnage. We frequently saw feral cats, or at least their tracks, skirting the outside of the fence. Like most other cat control projects, the Arid Recovery team turned to trapping to remove these cats.

To minimise the chances of kangaroos or other animals inadvertently stepping on our pairs of concealed leg-hold traps, we placed them inside corrals made from fallen branches. The aim was before the cat wised up to being deceived by a simple audio lure that crudely resembled a calling cat, the weight of its foot would trigger the trap, holding it in position until the cat was dispatched the following morning. Katherine and a research student found the audio lures worked even better than an evil-smelling concoction appropriately named pongo, which effectively combined cat urine and faeces in an eye-watering, throat-gagging brew. These traps accounted for 300 feral cats trapped immediately outside the Arid Recovery Reserve fence in the first decade. Foxes could not resist them either.

Despite attempting to discourage lizards, rabbits or other non-target animals from accessing the traps, it didn't take too many 6 am Sunday starts finding a trapped sleepy lizard sheepishly hiding in the corral to convince us a more targeted technique was desirable. We yearned for a trap that only exposed cats and foxes, leaving smaller or larger native wildlife unscathed. And even when we had caught a cat or fox, we pitied the animal that had been trapped for several hours. Shooting trapped animals appeals to few people, and definitely not me, and endlessly reconstructing and resetting traps also wears thin on the patience. Traps are not ideal for sustained feral cat control.

Despite her passion for providing meaningful and valuable work for skilled trackers, Paltridge concedes her cat hunting teams cannot hope to protect threatened species from more than a few select sites. Steve Austin also attests his sniffer dogs are not the silver bullet for cat control, especially in the dry desert or sea-misted coast when scents are rapidly lost. So innovative wildlife biologists continue striving for an effective control or deterrent for feral cats. One such alternative that has the bilby protector, the dog whisperer and sanctuary managers particularly excited is both automated and target specific.

Chapter 21

N = 1

*An inconclusive trial where only one example (sample size or 'n' = 1)
of a particular relationship or influence has been found.*

C2 looked every bit the archetypical cat lazing in a patch of
early winter sun. Rhythmic measured breaths were the only
signs of movement. Even the agitated white-plumed honeyeater
announcing C2's resting place to her fledglings in the nearby
eucalypt failed to rouse the sleepy cat, lying with his head resting
on his foreleg. His distinctive colouration made C2 appear like he
had been walking through leg-deep snow, with the white of his
legs, belly and throat contrasting vividly with his tabby back and
head. But there was no snow within walking distance.

A couple of hours earlier C2 had mooched past a box propped
up against the wall of his aviary-type enclosure and felt an
unexpected thwack on his flanks, at precisely the same time he
was startled by the flash of a hidden camera. After springing away
from the container, the surprised cat retreated to his shelter box
at the back of the pen where he scanned indignantly for who, or
what, had just photographed his shock. No one was visible, nothing
looked out of order. C2 was perplexed. Then he noticed the dollop
of gel on his fur, right where he had felt the slap. Instinctively he
licked at the blue-stained gel tasting of fish biscuits. Recognising
the distinctive taste, C2 no doubt worried he might have been
duped again. It was fish-flavoured cat biscuits that had lured the

feral cat into the trap at the rubbish dump yesterday and saw him transported to this strange pen. But his fastidiousness for cleanliness overcame any fear he felt about grooming the gel on his flank. Within minutes there was barely a trace left.

Sixteen minutes to be precise. Quietly concealed within a fitted-out shipping container about 20 metres away, Sue Darby was watching and timing C2's every move. He was the second cat she had studied in this pen at an animal research facility on the outskirts of Melbourne, Australia. Yesterday's cat, C1, had provided tantalising results but not exactly what Darby had anticipated. Her focus now was on the two screens that provided unfettered observation of C2. Fortunately for me, the paired images on the screens had already been timed and processed by Darby so she could fast forward the footage, pointing out the pertinent aspects.

'Watch this,' she instructed purposefully. 'That is the last time he groomed, sixteen minutes after the hit.' As she fast-forwarded the footage half an hour or so Darby explained what I was about to observe.

'This time when he jumps down you will notice he is a bit wobbly, not like the way he was striding confidently before being hit.' Sure enough, the brown-and-white cat now appeared more measured, maybe a little tipsy, as he moseyed around, yet still casting an inquisitive eye to the roof of his enclosure where the agitated honeyeater could be heard on the tape scolding him.

Darby fast-forwarded the tape again, tracking C2's wanderings to the patch of sunlight where he lay down. 'Watch this carefully,' Darby instructed. 'There is no sign at all of distress, or of convulsion. He just goes to sleep and this time he does not wake up.'

Even in fast forward, where his initial slow movements appeared jerky, C2 barely moved for the next two hours. An occasional flick of the tail and then he rolled on his side as the tape counter ticked past three hours. At the four-hour mark a man entered the enclosure, his movements feverishly quick on the accelerated tape. Within a few seconds C2 had been carried away and Darby turned to me beaming.

'He's the first one,' the passionate animal lover announced proudly, 'a 3.3 kg male officially pronounced dead after four hours from grooming PAPP. C1 was a 3.1 kg male and he started grooming eight minutes after being squirted. He showed the same symptoms and fell asleep just like C2, but after a few hours he woke up and fully recovered.'

Frank Gigliotti, Darby's partner, was the man who had collected C2's carcass and who had also pored over the video of C1 being sprayed and subsequently grooming. Gigliotti determined that C1 had received a glancing blow of gel when it walked straight towards the box that had automatically squirted the cat. As a result, much of the gel had deflected off its fur and the cat had ingested a sub-lethal dose of the toxin. Gigliotti, who had years of experience conducting pen trials on different toxins and delivery mechanisms for feral pests, concluded the sensor locations would have to be as far apart as a typical cat's rump and shoulder, to ensure cats walking side-on receive the full dose. The sensor array, housed in the unobtrusive box C1 had walked past, distinguished animals the size and shape of a cat from shorter, smaller or larger animals.

C1 and C2 were the first two cats involved in a trial of a stress-free technique for euthanasing feral cats. Trapped on nearby French Island where rangers were removing feral cats as part of their standard work protecting penguins, C1 and C2 were destined to be euthanased with a bullet to the head if they had not entered Gigliotti and Darby's trial. Like many cities around the world, Melbourne has a glut of stray cats taken in by shelters. For every four cats taken into an animal shelter in Melbourne, three are euthanased, amounting to more than 30,000 cats a year. If successful, the grooming trap trial could mean that rather than waiting in cage traps for their euthanasia, feral cats like C1 and C2 will die peacefully in their sleep without ever being contained, or necessarily even seeing a human. The penguins on French Island will also benefit from more efficient control of their most serious threat.

Para-aminopropiophenone, understandably abbreviated to PAPP, was originally used as an antidote to cyanide poisoning in humans. However early researchers discovered that although PAPP could help convert cyanide to less toxic compounds, unfortunately it interfered with our blood. Red blood cells contain iron-rich proteins called haemoglobin that transport oxygen throughout our bodies. PAPP oxidises this haemoglobin to form methemoglobin, a very different protein unable to carry oxygen. Without its vital oxygen fuel, the central nervous system and other bodily functions slow down. Cats, like humans, become drowsy. If methemoglobin levels increase further they cause the lethargy and eventual unconsciousness exhibited by the first of the two trial cats. If the dose is sufficient, as with C2, the unconscious cat dies in its sleep.

However, if the dose is insufficient, as with C1, the cat will gradually metabolise the PAPP, regain the oxygen-carrying capacity of its blood, and recuperate without side effects. What's more, unlike more common poisons that are irreversibly fatal if consumed, the effects of PAPP can be reversed. Methyl blue can convert the dangerous methemoblogin back to the useful haemoglobin. Administration of this reversal agent to a groggy or even unconscious pet cat that has consumed PAPP will, in theory, result in an immediate and total recovery – although some vets warn that treatment is not always so simple. Nevertheless, it's little wonder PAPP is now being researched by organisations like the Australian Invasive Animal Cooperative Research Centre as a potentially safe toxin for cat control in areas where goannas and other susceptible wildlife are not found.

Other common pharmaceuticals very toxic to cats, like the smallgoods preservative sodium nitrite and the human pain medication Tylenol, may also offer effective, targeted and, most importantly, humane control options for feral cats. Not surprisingly, given that most Australian wildlife have developed resistance, 1080 may be the toxin of choice in some cases. Unlike the oft-cited distressing response in dogs, cats poisoned by 1080 calmly succumb to the poisoning, arguably dying with far less stress and potential for pain and injury than a cat trapped and transported to a cat shelter hours later to be euthanased by lethal injection or gas.

Like the new poisons, automated 'grooming traps' are a novel technique being developed to reduce the effects of conventional feral cat control on wildlife or pets. Rather than distributing poison baits in the environment with the hope a cat may find and consume one, grooming traps only release the poison when a cat-sized animal activates the sensors. And even then, the grooming pathway provides additional protection for dogs and most other animals that typically don't groom as fastidiously as cats. This means that grooming traps can be used in places where

Large dogs chase and kill cats: it's as ingrained as cats chasing mice and birds. In an experiment just north of the Arid Recovery Reserve, two dingoes killed all seven radio-collared foxes and half of the cats in a paddock within three weeks. The last bastions of several threatened species have found refuge in remote locations where unbaited dingoes or 'camp dogs' restrict the predatory success of cats. The relic warru at Kalka, where Bronson and Jacob found the stick-nest rat tar, are largely restricted to a hill flanked by Aboriginal communities, complete with their camp dogs. Together with dingoes, these camp dogs create a hazardous environment for cats and foxes. Warru have, for centuries, avoided dingo predation by retreating to narrow crevices that keep the dogs out but present no such barrier to smaller introduced predators.

conventional baiting is not possible, or even counterproductive. Farmers can use these automated devices to control cats and maybe foxes in the knowledge that their working dogs are unlikely to activate the traps and even less likely to ingest the poison. Grooming traps also offer control of feral cats where maintenance of dingoes, coyotes or wolves is desirable.

Because grooming traps automatically reset themselves, the relentless task of driving around conservation reserves checking and resetting leg-hold and cage traps every morning of the year could one day be assigned to history. But it's not only at fenced reserves and council dumps where this targeted new technology is being welcomed. Feral cat-grooming traps provided the opportunity for me to realise one of my longest-held and elusive ambitions in the remote Queensland outback.

I can't remember concentrating so intently in my life. Both my hands were held just out from my ears with my spread fingers slowly waving back and forwards like a mighty shear, keeping flies out of my ears without disturbing the sweat-sucking swarm that had accumulated on my hat and shirt. An earlier swipe at an annoying fly had sent all its mates into a buzzing mass around my head, eliminating any chance of me hearing birdcalls. Half an hour earlier when I parked my 4WD on the isolated stony plain, the thermometer read 42°C, even as the sun was setting. My walk up the breakaway ridge had moistened my shirt with sweat that seemed to lure every fly for miles. With the flies mostly settled, I made myself comfortable for the most anticipated wildlife experience of my life. Once I managed to work the sharp rock from under my boot there was nothing else distracting me from a quest I had waited nearly 30 years for.

At times my eyes were shut so I could focus entirely on filtering birdcalls from the background noise of wind and recalcitrant flies. But occasionally I would open my eyes to observe the three other silent statues standing nearby. The place was right; the time just about perfect. The orange-smudged western sky still provided just enough light to convince me that I would be able to see a small green bird flying past. I scanned the others to see if they had seen something, or heard a plaintive call that I had missed?

Minutes later I heard what sounded like the start of a distant willie wagtail call, drifting up from a sparsely treed ephemeral creek line way down on the barren stony plains. Steve Murphy, one of the three adjacent statues, had mentioned earlier that one of the calls we were listening for resembled the start of a willie wagtail's song. Again I looked at Murphy, rhythmically nodding his head as though processing the calls he was hearing but not yet hitting the jackpot. A minute or so later, the same bird called again but this time it was Murphy who spun around, pointing in the direction of the barely audible song. 'Might be,' he whispered, 'let's move a bit closer.'

Retracing our steps through the dense spinifex clumps to a saddle in the ridge, we followed Murphy in the direction of the faint and intermittent call, watching every footfall to ensure we did not crack a twig or kick a stone. I was five steps behind Murphy. Katherine was behind me and Murphy's wife Rachel behind her. I was so focused on tracking the origin of the tantalising call that it took me a while to register the finger clicking behind me. When I finally turned I saw Rachel standing her ground, beaming and beckoning us back. When we reached her she whispered confidently, 'Two note call! Did any of you hear it?' When we all shook our heads Rachel declared, 'Well it must be over this side of the ridge because you were all over that side.'

We crept back over the dry rocky saddle and took up our positions, exactly where we had stood only minutes earlier. But it was darker now. The flies also thinned out in the enveloping darkness and the persistent south-westerly wind also seemed to abate. This time it felt like we were standing in a recording studio, shut off acoustically from the rest of the world, every sound amplified. '*Ding ding.*'

The call was as distinct and pure as if it had been heard through headphones, although the volume was turned down. Perhaps it was because I had dreamed for so long of this moment that the fragile chiming notes had an ethereal quality, like the sound of a slender stalactite being tapped by a spoon, or two droplets falling into a silent icy pool. A sense of euphoria enveloped me.

Neither Katherine nor I needed confirmation from the Murphys. Only hours before, we had first listened to a recording of the calls. Cautious to minimise the possibility that overenthusiastic birdwatchers may compromise initial research on this most elusive Australian bird, the hastily convened Night Parrot Recovery Team had quarantined release of the call until they had safeguarded this population. Had I not been privy to the recording, I may have assumed the faint peeping notes were the aberrant 'going to sleep' calls of a pied honeyeater or quail-thrush. Many birds make strange calls during their dawn chorus or at dusk that barely resemble their typical calls. But this diminutive call matched the recorded call now imprinted in my memory. For decades I had yearned to know and hear the elusive call of the night parrot. So many times while camped in the outback, drifting off to sleep or inexplicably waking in my swag in the darkness, I had heard unfamiliar calls and wondered if they were the night parrot. Four times I had driven to the remote outpost of Rocket Bore, four hours from Alice Springs, home of an old Aboriginal man who apparently knew the call, but my potential informant was never home when I visited.

Instinctively, perhaps inappropriately, I thumped Murphy on the shoulder. He just grinned, recognising and sharing the thrill of us joining a handful of other living birdos to finally hear the call of the night parrot. Katherine too was beaming and we gave each other a big sweaty but still silent hug, broken by Murphy's whisper. 'Three-note call.'

Neither of us heard it. Quickly we snapped back into listening mode, although this time I could hear my heart beating and the stressful anticipation had largely abated. '*Peee peee … Peee peee.*' Murphy held up four fingers signifying the 'four-note call', another of the night parrot calls he now recognised. This one reminded me of one of the calls of the western ground parrot. Being the closest cousin of the night parrot, I had joined researchers in the coastal heaths of southern Western Australia years earlier to help monitor this equally bizarre species in the evenings. Informed by a detailed compilation of their various calls, birdwatchers, or more correctly listeners, were assigned to different listening posts just before dusk. Although the methodical monitoring of one of the world's most endangered parrots was an enticement, my main motivation for joining the ground parrot survey was to learn more about that even more elusive quest, the search for the night parrot, which had not been recorded calling or confirmed seen alive for over half a century. While resembling the call of a ground parrot, to my desert bird attuned ears the 'nightie's' four-note call was a similar tone to a pied honeyeater *beep*, but with the almost telephone-ring structure of a red-capped robin call. We listened some more. Another four-note call; then a minute or so later, another.

Each time they called we each pointed to the direction we thought we heard the bird, often deceived by the ventriloqual nature of the calls. Were we listening to one bird or more? Was the bird, or birds, stationary or moving? We were also keen to hear the other call described by early naturalists when the night parrot had been widely distributed in Australian deserts. I desperately wanted to hear the intriguing 'frog-like croak'. But that final wish was not to be. After a couple of minutes of silence Murphy announced confidently and surprisingly loudly, 'They've gone.'

'How did you know to listen here?' I asked Murphy, not wanting to leave the site. Many times I had sat near waterholes or mound springs and spotlighted or camped out at localities where night parrots had been historically recorded. But I had never thought to wait silently on a rocky hill.

Murphy's brief story abbreviated a decades-long hunt by many of Australia's most eminent birdwatchers. Walter Boles, curator of birds at the Australian Museum placed the night parrot spotlight on western Queensland when he happened upon a road-killed specimen in October 1990, about 200 kilometres from the hill where we were standing. This bird was only the second confirmed record for the 20th century and discredited the widely held belief that the night parrot had followed 29 Australian mammals, mostly desert species, to extinction. It took 16 years for rangers from Diamantina National Park to find another dead specimen, this time on the ground adjacent to a barbed wire fence, only 20 or so kilometres from where we now stood.

Despite a meticulous follow-up search by talented and dedicated ornithologists, it was another seven years before scientists discovered a population. In 2013, naturalist John Young announced to the world he had photos, recordings and video footage of night parrots, the first ever taken. Even though the calls were kept a closely guarded secret, those breakthrough photographs of a live bird made headline news and reawakened my dreams. I'd pored over old drawings and less-than-convincing copies in modern bird field guides. I'd even been privy to observing, even briefly handling, the world's largest collection of night parrot specimens in the South Australian Museum. But neither revealed the intense lime green and gold colouration of Young's photo, nor the extraordinarily large eye of this enigmatic nocturnal bird.

Steve pointed to the darkening red sky. 'John Young's sighting was eight kilometres that way in a big patch of old spinifex. We only found this locality because a bird we radiotagged, still the only night parrot I have handled, flew here from his site one evening. Pretty much all we know about nighties is based on single observations and unreplicated records, which is tantalising but problematic for a scientist. I'm always being challenged by n=1!' conceded Murphy, referring to the difficulties in drawing conclusions about his iconic study species when the sample size (or 'n') for much of his research remained singular.

I had known Murphy well before he ever heard or saw a night parrot. Back then we both dreamed about how they could be found, and discussed where, how and when to search for this most elusive of birds. A decade earlier I convinced myself that I had pipped him to our quest when I was following distinctive parrot tracks along a spinifex dune about halfway between Sydney and Perth near the Indian Pacific railway line. Having nervously inspected several priceless museum specimens, I recognised that the night parrots' short claws would leave distinctive tracks. Unlike most other birds that have three forward pointing toes opposing one backwards claw, parrots have two toes in front and two behind, leaving distinctive chromosome-like elongated X tracks. I had located two sets of tracks that fitted my impression of night parrots in this remote area that supported few rabbits and cats but several threatened species. The further I followed the tracks the more convinced I had become. But after an hour of exhilarating tracking I eventually startled a pair of ringneck parrots at the end of the tracks and my excitement rapidly evaporated.

While other night parrot tragics desperately wanted to collect a $50,000 reward for definitive photographic proof that night parrots were not extinct, my quest had always been to hear them call to inform more searches. Steve later revealed only a handful of people had ever heard the call in real life, and few more had been privy to the recording. That single second of plaintive call rated right up at the pinnacle of my wildlife experiences, along with my first experience of a nesting leatherback turtle on a jet black sand beach on a remote Pacific island, or the mesmerising wail of an indri in a Madagascan forest remnant, or even my first sighting of a wild bilby comically running away, tail aloft, in the Australian desert.

Ironically, given the lengths I had already taken to hear a night parrot, this was not my main motivation for the visit. The location was shrouded in secrecy in order to safeguard the parrots from overenthusiastic birdos from around the world. All I had been told a day earlier was that I was to drive five hours from Longreach in western Queensland. A large section of the remote pastoral station where we now sat was in the process of being transferred to one of Australia's largest conservation organisations. Bush Heritage Australia had lobbied and fundraised to protect the site, and Murphy wanted my help to safeguard this precious population.

Murphy, who had been intensively studying this vulnerable group of night parrots for nearly two years, considered fire the main risk. 'All the evidence suggests nighties avoid predators, seek shade, and nest within hummocks of razor-sharp spinifex. And fire destroys this invaluable cover for maybe ten or more years, depending on rainfall,' Murphy told me. 'And after fire, the threat is feral cats.'

After more than 15,000 nights of camera trapping in the area nighties had been found, Murphy had never photographed a parrot but had seen five different cats, predominantly large striped tabbies or lanky ginger toms. Like those Nolia and John T hunted at Kiwirrkurra, these cats lived independently, often hundreds of kilometres from houses or towns. Significantly, introduced foxes were strangely absent from the region although dingoes remained abundant. It was no coincidence the last remaining relict bilbies in Queensland were found not far from where we were sitting.

In his *Journey to Central Australia in search of the Night Parrot*, published in 1924, F. Lawson Whitlock stated emphatically: 'Whatever may be said to the contrary, domestic cats gone wild are accountable for the disappearance of this species.' J.N. McGilp, in a similar odyssey seven years later, consulted several locals familiar with night parrots who concluded: 'If you ask me what happened to much of our former day bird and animal life I'd say that the domestic cat gone wild was the reason.' Notes of the Horn Biological Expedition to Central Australia in 1894 noted in one of the operator rooms of the Alice Spring telegraph station 'several picture frames were covered with wings and tails of the porcupine parrot', which had been caught last summer by the telegraph station cat. Night (or porcupine) parrots then disappeared after an 'invasion' of cats.

National Park rangers had shot an incredible 3000 cats around this isolated and dwindling bilby population in the couple of years following a long-haired rat plague, which boosted cat numbers. On his laptop Murphy carried an alarming photo of a local shooters' vehicle, piled with the carcasses of about 40 cats shot in a single night.

To address the cat problem Murphy had first tried the shooters who had proven effective in the bilby habitat. But unlike the open plains where the bilbies lived, the spotlighters could not even glimpse cats in the tall spinifex country that was home to the night parrots. Cage trapping caught only goannas and crows. Trained sniffer dogs struggled to follow scent in the dry environment and work in the intense heat of the desert. And the Night Parrot Recovery Team, comprised of bird and wildlife management experts from around the country, had dismissed the use of cat baits at the site. 'No one wanted to trial poison baits because we are all so concerned about exacerbating the cat problem if dingoes take the baits. Although they are potentially night parrot predators, we were unanimous in considering the dingo to be an ally of the nighties by helping control cats and maybe foxes, which are a greater threat, and also 'roos,' Murphy explained. Where dingoes were baited by pastoralists, kangaroo populations had exploded to unnatural and sometimes devastating numbers. Driving out of Longreach on the way to meet Murphy I was astounded by the number of dead kangaroos that had fallen victim to vehicles at night. For stretches of several kilometres you could literally hopscotch from one carcass to the next. After nightfall I couldn't drive at more than 80 km/hr due on an erratic slalom course, created by the live kangaroos along the road. These kangaroos competed with less common herbivores, like the nighties, who probably relied on small succulent plants for both food and moisture.

'Grooming traps are our best hope,' Murphy continued, 'that's why I'm so excited you're here.' Murphy had been instrumental in encouraging Bush Heritage Australia to contribute to the development of the novel technology and funding the construction of the fancy new prototype I had brought to the site.

Two years after C2 had died peacefully in the original pen trial, grooming traps, now known as Felixers, had evolved considerably. An initial investment by the conservation group Foundation for Australia's Most Endangered Species encouraged other donors and government grants to develop the technology. Now boasting carefully positioned arrays of range-finding sensors, and individual toxic doses fired at a staggering 60 metres a second, the new generation grooming traps were designed to spray a feral cat walking past up to four metres away. They also played recordings of cats on heat and distressed prey on an audiolure program and photographed any animal that walked within range. The green dollhouse-shaped devices sprayed cats with toxin and recorded the type of audiolure playing at the time.

The morning after we heard that plaintive call on the hill, Murphy was eager to test the new Felixer at the station homestead where we were staying. First Rachel apprehensively walked in front of the beams to test they were performing as planned. She held her breath but wasn't squirted; the trap didn't fire. The display indicated she had triggered a 60-second shutdown mode, as planned whenever an animal taller than a cat walked past. This would prevent activation by people, kangaroos or even vehicles. While we were listening to the programmed audiolures a pet labrador bounded past the Felixer. Again, as programmed, the trap shut down after taking a photograph labelled as 'non-target'.

'I want to see how it fires,' said Murphy. So he folded a towel over a long-handled shovel to imitate a cat. Squatting about three metres away he pushed it quickly past the sensors at cat height. *Bang!* Before any of us could react, the towel was sporting a green blob of non-toxic gel and Murphy, a little shocked, was laughing. 'Wow, that was quick. They won't stand a chance. I'll take you to the creek line where my cameras have detected a large tabby and now a ginger tom patrolling.'

Carefully blocking the dry narrow creek beds with branches to divert the cats along a cleared path on the bank, we meticulously levelled the ground using the Felixer's built-in laser. Five metres away and out of site, a solar panel would provide the power to keep the Felixer operating for months. The five-second yowl of a cat on heat signified the Felixer was activated and ready for action.

That evening I shared with Murphy two photos taken at Venus

*A Felixer monitored by two additional cameras set along a small creek.
A feral cat had been photographed here approaching the recently
rediscovered, incredibly rare, night parrot population on an undisclosed
outback Australian location that has now become the Bush Heritage
Pullen Pullen Reserve. (Photo: J. Read)*

Bay Conservation Park in South Australia, where another of the
brand-new Felixers had been installed weeks earlier. A perilously
small population of critically endangered woylies and bilbies were
threatened by a dozen or more cats that had breached the exclosure

fence on the Venus Bay peninsula and avoided conventional trapping, shooting and even Steve Austin's cat dogs. The first photo showed a large tabby patrolling the fence line within centimetres of the infrared activation beams, visible on the photo but not to the oblivious cat. The next photo, taken two seconds later, showed the cat in mid air, with a pale patch of toxic gel clearly visible on its rump. Talya Bowden, who had been monitoring the cats, bilbies and Felixers, informed me this distinctive cat, one of her nemeses, had not been recorded on any of her camera traps since being sprayed and she assumed it had groomed and died.

> The first large field trial of Felixers in and around the Arid Recovery Reserve squirted 72 feral cats in 10 weeks and only one 'non-target' kangaroo out of the hundreds of wildlife also photographed by the Felixer. Two of the cats were wearing radio collars and were found dead within hours of being sprayed. Unlikely to thoroughly groom and tolerant of 1080 toxin, the single squirted kangaroo was not at risk. None of the lizards, bilbies, boodies, rabbits or quolls that approached the Felixers were fired upon.

Murphy had responded enthusiastically to the evidence but I reminded him that the presumed dead cat at Venus Bay essentially equated to n=1. We were a long way from demonstrating that Felixers would provide a reliable and efficient control tool for feral cats in a range of hostile environments. But these early trials had convinced a host of organisations to contribute to optimising and developing Felixers, and we were steadily improving reliability and reducing costs.

Not only do Felixers offer another tool for targeting problem cats in conservation settings, they may ironically represent a lifeline to some TNR advocates. Clowder feeders rarely restrict their feeding to just neutered and vaccinated cats. Wily stray cats that refuse to be trapped move in and perpetuate the cycle of kittens, fighting, transmission of disease, and other animal welfare issues that TNR sets out to manage. However, rapidly evolving Felixers fitted with wireless identification (WID) blockers would allow registered and tagged cats to be identified and protected from grooming traps; only non-registered cats would be sprayed. Where human disease, wildlife predation or animal cruelty issues are not considered extreme, programmed Felixers might convince authorities to allow managed clowder cats to gradually die out, hoping that immigrants or unsolicited dumped cats will be automatically and humanely euthanased.

Many suburbs and cities have now enacted laws to reduce both the impact of, and danger from, free-roaming cats. Just like dogs, these cats are now required to be registered and contained. But unlike wandering dogs that will generally approach a warden or be readily cornered, it is nearly impossible to apprehend wandering cats. Have you ever tried to 'puss, puss, puss' an unfamiliar roaming cat from its home so you can pat or hold it, let alone check its registration details? Cats are inherently wary and elusive when outside their homes. Even if they can be cage-trapped once, for their obligatory warning, most free-ranging cats are highly unlikely to be trapped again. Cat containment laws are benign, lacking any real means of enforcement. However, automated detection and recording of the registration status of a cat, without having to catch it, would open a range of opportunities. Any time a registered cat fitted with a simple radio-frequency tag approaches a Felixer the machine would automatically shut down, ensuring pets were not sprayed. WID blockers would, for the first time, allow the control of unowned and feral cats, without affecting pets.

Cat owners controlling their pet cats will help prevent the devastating impact of domestic cats on native wildlife. From Haida Gwaii to Rome, it is still free-ranging pet cats, and deliberately fed strays or their progeny, which present the greatest risk to the public, pets and wildlife alike. We know bells and bibs are only partially useful in reducing wildlife predation. There must be other ways caring cat lovers can help.

Chapter 22

LAP CATS, THE PURR-FECT DOMESTIC CATS

One small cat changes coming into an empty house to coming home.
Pam Brown

Chopper is a challenging Russian Blue. Like many of the other rehomed cats featured in this book – Amelia Bedelia, Bubbles, Max, Bella and Michael – Chopper was granted a reprieve from death row by a devoted cat lover. Emma Coates, from the South Australian fishing town of Port Lincoln, is a biologist-cum-behaviourist. Her day jobs include managing conservation projects, advising on living with wildlife and working as a veterinary nurse. After hours, her passion is dog training with an emphasis on applied animal behaviour. Coates' accredited behavioural dog training business Train Humane employs evidence-based positive reinforcement methods. In short, Coates loves animals. She understands pets and wildlife, their roles, their benefits *and* their risks. It is difficult to picture anyone more qualified to appreciate the value of responsible pet ownership, or better equipped to succeed.

I'd met Coates through a conservation project she was involved with, aiming to protect rare wildlife from feral cats. Unlike many in conservation circles who follow established guidebooks for cat control, Coates advocated trialling novel, ethical and sustainable methods and her project was one of the first to trial Felixers. I soon learned that Coates's patience and skills were sorely tested by Chopper's misdemeanours. Early in the genesis of this book

I decided to profile her experiences and triumphs with her recalcitrant adopted cat.

Chopper is affectionately nicknamed 'Chop-chop' for his disarming mood swings. One minute he seeks out cuddles and then, for no apparent reason, he growls at Coates like a tiger.

Vet nurse and animal trainer Emma Coates with her cat Asha who shares Coate's house with Alfonz, the bronzewing pigeon (pictured here), Podge the brushtail possum and several other rescued wildlife. (Photo: Samantha Cordell)

Chopper was of course kept indoors along with Coates's other pet cat Asha, a female chocolate tortoiseshell, and her menagerie of other rescued animals, including a tawny frogmouth, bronzewing pigeon, pygmy possum, and two dogs. Coates loves the birds in her garden, especially the New Holland honeyeaters attracted to her native grevillia and callistemon flowers. She could tell from his intent watching through the windows that her hyperactive Russian blue would like to get among these birds too.

To distract him from the birds outside, Chop Chop had daily play sessions with laser pointers and toys, especially feathers on a string that flicked around in the air like a circling bird. He was also taken for regular outdoor walks on a lead. But Coates worried that despite all the attention and exercise, Chopper appeared stressed. He groomed and meowed incessantly, paced the house, cried at the windows, and attempted to dash out the door as soon as the opportunity presented. Despite being desexed, Chopper also started attacking good-natured Asha.

Outdoor cat enclosures were not allowed in Coates's rental agreement. The deal breaker came when Chopper developed bladder crystals and began spraying urine inside. Under anaesthetic, a veterinarian passed a catheter into Chopper's bladder and removed the crystals. The pampered pet was then placed on a strict diet that promoted urinary tract health. But much to Coates's self-described 'disgust', the indoor spraying had taken a toll on her resolve and Chopper became an outside cat. Working three jobs between them, Coates and her partner simply did not have time to stimulate their adored rogue cat indoors. Rehoming was considered, as was euthanasia, but Coates felt strongly that, as his owner, she owed Chopper a duty of care.

One of the more unique risks he faced outdoors was exposure

to neighbours' 'crappy cheap cat food' that exacerbated his bladder crystals. As part of his transition to an outdoor life, Coates the dog trainer ensured Chopper was 'trained' to ignore birds and other cats, not cross roads and avoid neighbours' cat food, using rewards of his favourite food, squid. Coates also rewarded Chopper, as dog trainers do, when he eliminated in her yard and discouraged him from doing so in other yards using a high-powered water sprayer. She letter dropped notes with photos to all her neighbours letting them know who Chopper was, where he lived and how to contact her if he became a nuisance. A neighbour responded after Chopper urinated in their car after they left the window open. Luckily the neighbour was a forgiving friend who accepted the heartfelt apology and professional car cleaning that followed.

Despite having access outside, Chopper was brought in before sunset and let out after sunrise to avoid the critical hunting periods at dawn and dusk when local wildlife are most vulnerable. Coates is scathing of the 'owners' of four other roaming toms in her street that don't appear to be managed at all. At her vet surgery, she sees numerous tomcats presenting with feline AIDS and worries that Chopper, too, will be inflicted with the debilitating disease after fighting with local males.

Although it's possibly an oxymoron to even suggest an outdoor cat can be well managed, Chopper comes as close as possible. He is desexed, microchipped, tattooed and wears a collar with at least one bell and ID tag. But after watching Chopper expertly hunting, Coates concedes bells have had little effect on whether he kills or not.

Chopper's favourite doorstep presents are mice, at least one a month, but he also displays honeyeaters, black birds and sparrows. But, of course, he only drops off a fraction of his kills. Although not represented on the doorstep with the mice and birds, Coates assumes he also hunts the skinks and geckoes in her garden. Victims are proudly announced with a characteristic growling meow, despite her repeated reinforcing that she doesn't condone hunting. If Chopper's prey is still alive he tries to keep it away from Coates who promptly dispatches the maimed animal if necessary.

Coates' anguish and frustration were palpable. 'I am totally conflicted,' she explained, 'between my duties to provide the pet I adopted with the best possible life and my conviction that cats should be kept inside. Asha is easy,' Coates acknowledged, stroking the short-haired tortoiseshell on her lap. 'Like all the other cats I've owned she is an indoor cat and loves flopping on my lap for a cuddle whenever I sit down for the evening. But Chopper looks miserable or paces up and down and I feel that I need to let him out, even though he has largely got over his bladder problem.'

I told Coates the stories of Michael, convicted booby killer turned content indoor pet, and of once-feral Bubbles and Brandy that now enjoy contented lives in a Virginia office. I challenged the animal trainer and wildlife enthusiast. 'If these cats can make the transition, why can't Chopper?' Surely she could try, once again, to provide him with a stimulating and safe indoor life?

A few months later I checked in with Coates. After 30 days wearing a pheromone collar that was supposed to reduce anxiety, Chopper's behaviour had not changed. His obsessive crying at the door continued, as did his persistent swiping and lunging at the good-natured Asha. Coates's trial of the halfway house in the form of a modified outdoor aviary with shelves, ladders and scratch poles was even less successful. Despite using all her animal psychology guile, Chopper sulked and whined, ignored his treats of chicken and squid and glared at Coates when she repeatedly petted and talked with him. Sometimes she left him to settle down alone, other times she heaped affection on him. Coates tried acclimatising Chopper through short aviary stints in the morning or afternoon, or longer periods at other times. But for weeks on end she could not appease her stubborn pet. Chopper has been so physically, mentally and morally draining for Coates that she has decided to stick to dogs and rescued birds and marsupials as pets.

Being an informed, committed and obsessive pet owner, Coates's epiphany struck me as surprising and remarkable. But she was far from alone in abandoning her intention to keep cats. Other former passionate cat owners who have now sworn off owning another cat include Peter Budd from RSPCA's West Hatch Wildlife Hospital, who we met in Chapter 3. Initially ambivalent about the tattered offerings his adopted and free-spirited cat brought home, *New York Times* columnist Richard Conniff also declared he would never have another outdoor cat after reading the conservative projections of 15 billion animals falling victim to free-ranging cats in the US.

Despite all Coates has been through I'm not convinced prohibition is necessary for the lion-hearted animal lover, or for others who derive so much affection from owning good-natured cats. Despite their shortcomings outside the house, cats can be invaluable companion animals. Animal behaviourist Desmond Harris wrote: 'To the sensitive human being it becomes a privilege to share a room with a cat, exchange its glance, feel its greeting rub, or watch it gently luxuriate itself into a snoozing ball on a soft cushion.'

During my lifetime there has been a profound change in the way society views outdoor cats. Outdoor cats were once considered entirely natural and appropriate, now we understand the benefits for cats, owners, neighbours and wildlife of desexing cats and keeping them indoors. Recent surveys show consistent increases in the percentage of cat owners who contain their pets, at least at night. Grant Sizemore's current cat Amelia Bedeila was desexed and vaccinated as a kitten, so, unlike Snowball, she will not have a litter that needs to be rehoused, in all likelihood to families that adore kittens but are not prepared or aware of the attention a cat deserves. Richard Conniff defined this trend as 'beginning to make outdoor cats as socially unacceptable as smoking cigarettes in the office, or leaving dog droppings on the sidewalk'.

'Owning a cat should not be an impulsive decision, it's not a choice to be made lightly,' said Sizemore, who graduated from his ornithological studies to become the Cats Indoors officer for the American Bird Conservancy. The ABC's views on cats are less radical than Morgan's in New Zealand, but also advocate for the humane removal of all unowned cats and that cat owners keep their pets indoors. This pragmatic attitude is driven not only by the negligible risk posed by indoor cats but also by the reality that cats are important and loved companion animals that are here to stay. The challenge should not be how to eliminate them but how to manage our feline friends.

Proactive and informed cat breeders are increasingly promoting characteristics and personality traits in house cats to increase their chances of breeding cuddly Ashas rather than troublesome Choppers. A common confession when cats are handed in to refuges is that the temporary owners adored their kitten but became less attached, or able to manage, their pet when it matured into a cat. Kittens are cute and vulnerable and savvy cat fanciers are now selecting breeding adults that more closely resemble kittens. Neoteny favours cats that, like cartoon characters, mimic juveniles by displaying disproportionately large faces and eyes.

Anthropologist Peter McAllister has even suggested that since domestication, cats have evolved characteristics that trigger instinctive parent-like behaviours, or fixed action patterns, in humans. Examples of fixed action patterns include the instinctive feeding response of an adult bird when a squawking nestling opens its brightly coloured gape, or the overwhelming urge of a mother to cradle or suckle a crying baby. So powerful are these patterns they have become targets for parasites, like the cuckoo chick that takes advantage of their host parents' automated feeding response. But with a cat's meow, it is we humans who are the target of this parasitism. Our bonding hormone oxytocin surges when we play with cute cats. McAllister cites a survey where 83% of the population confessed they view their pets as children.

Just as lapdogs are becoming increasingly popular pets, specially bred homebody lapcats with friendly temperaments and baby eyes are perfect indoor companions. From an ecological perspective these pale lapcats are conspicuous to prey if they do escape the house. Another advantage of breeding pale pet cats is they photograph well. The Blue Cross reported a 65% rise in the number of black cats taken into their shelters each year between 2007 and 2013, speculating the increase was because black cats don't show up as well in 'selfies'.

British and American shorthairs, Burmese and ragdolls are among the more common pedigrees recommended for indoors. Cat fanciers desiring more unusual lapcats could opt for bizarre Sphinx cats, which look bald and wrinkled, yet feel like suede. Devon and Cornish Rex breeds are ideal house cats, craving heat and reluctant to venture outside, they prefer to sit on laps when it is cool – ideal traits for a cold climate pet. Ironically, given the dramas Coates has experienced with Chopper, one of the breeds most recommended for indoors, even apartments, is Russian blues. Chopper the rescue cat exemplifies that content indoor cats reflect their upbringing as much as their genetics. The likelihood of sharing your home with a content indoor cat is far higher with a bred-for-purpose pedigree acclimatised to living indoors than a stray brought in from the street.

Dr Truda Straede has been ahead of her times. Like many other devoted cat advocates featured in this book, the registered cat breeder and practising ecologist is also concerned about the impacts of stray and feral cats on wildlife. In the 1970s, Straede predicted the advent of sensible restrictions on keeping outdoor cats and pragmatically developed the Australian Mist breed from carefully selected Burmese, Abyssinian and domestic stock. Straede confided that although as a cat-show aficionado she appreciates the more bizarre lapcats, she prefers Australian Mists as elegant 'proper-looking' cats with temperaments for living indoors where they will not threaten wildlife. Desexed, microchipped and vaccinated, Australian Mists are only sold to pet owners who keep their cats indoors, perfect for pedigree cats bred and raised for indoor life.

The very antithesis of a lapcat was very nearly introduced into Australia in 2008. Savannah cats are derived from the African serval that can grow much larger and jump far higher than domestic cats. Their stately appearance and apparently excellent temperaments had some cat fanciers lining up to purchase the long-legged breed. But despite being the focus of a determined campaign by devoted supporters of the exotic breed, Federal Environment Minister Peter Garrett banned the Savannah cat from being brought into the country, citing its 'extreme risk to Australia's environment and biodiversity'.

As the tragic stories of the mala, stick-nest rat, chuditch and bilby have already exemplified, Australian wildlife is both highly susceptible and perilously threatened by cats. Virtually all predation-caused extinctions have occurred to native mammals weighing less than five kilograms. Scientists and wildlife enthusiasts alike were concerned that introduction of the large Savannah cats would raise the ceiling of this critical weight range, exposing even more animals to cat predation. Larger wallabies and even koalas might be threatened, not to mention bulky goannas and waterbirds that would be vulnerable to these water-loving cats.

Informed and rational public policy and legislation are not only preventing introduction of dangerous or inappropriate cat breeds, they are also driving responsible cat ownership. Responsible cat owners typically support laws that decree cats are contained in houses or cat runs like dogs and other pets and minimise the disease and animal welfare risks of free-ranging cats. Truda Straede is one of many cat breeders who support initiatives that are not only good for cats but also assist in maintaining bloodlines of carefully bred indoor cats. Despite devoting her life to breeding, showing and advocating for cats, Straede is also adamant that control of stray and feral cats is imperative. 'It's pretty straightforward,' Straede conceded, 'we need to acknowledge that there are way too many unowned cats for good homes, and the most compassionate welfare option for those extra cats, not to mention to reduce disease and the impacts on wildlife, is euthanasia.'

But it's not for responsible cat owners and breeders (and, yes, that probably includes anyone who is still reading this book!) that these new containment and management laws are being

After years of grappling with how to encourage responsible pet ownership, and to differentiate wandering pet cats from feral cats that were controlled to protect rare wildlife, the Roxby Downs Council in northern South Australia passed a bylaw, drafted by cat owners and vets. It was paraphrased as 'treat pet cats exactly the same as pet dogs'. Over 90% of respondents to a much-discussed public survey agreed cats should be contained within yards or on leashes and that registration fees for desexed cats would be substantially discounted, just like dogs.

introduced. Rather it's for the backyard breeders and pseudo-'owners' of wandering cats that continue to live 'in the past', as Straede describes them.

Until recently, enforcement agencies had little power, or indeed motivation, to enforce containment laws. Owners of wandering cats and clowder feeders who perpetuate the disease and welfare risks of free-ranging cats had little to fear. Alerted by residents' concerns, the Brisbane City Council feared unowned cats inhabiting Brisbane's parks and water reserves were causing the localised extinction of stone curlews, bandicoots and my favourite brush-tailed phascogales (which were also being killed by cats in the *Gastrolobium* belt of Western Australia). Equally of concern to the council was residents' and health professionals' fears of toxoplasmosis spread from free-ranging cats toileting in gardens and children's playgrounds. But by only responding to domestic complaints about unowned and feral cats, the problem was growing.

Enter Bill Manners, Principal Officer Natural Environment for the Brisbane City Council, who is leading the way in proactive urban feral cat management. Manners explained to me that a pivotal council decision made in 2012 was to transfer management of unowned and feral cats to the same pest department that dealt with the city's feral foxes. The Brisbane City Council was determined to prosecute feeders of illegal cat clowders. Like councilman Pop Barnes rallying against the flawed TNT program that is placing public health at risk from stray cats in Georgia, Manners is also being proactive. With an annual budget of $200,000, Manners set his staff a target of removing at least a thousand feral cats a year, which they achieved from 2015 to 2017. Any cats captured in traps that were microchipped or thought to be pet cats were taken to the council's Animal Rehoming Centre. Unmarked stray and feral cats were immediately euthanased to minimise animal welfare issues. Despite initial protest from some feral cat lobbyists, Manners is now buoyed by widespread community support for his program of reducing the numbers and stamping out feeding of feral cats. Five prosecutions for feeding, keeping or 'supplying' feral cats have attracted penalties of $1000 to $5000. The judges, observe Manners, have a straightforward task of enforcing laws designed to protect both public health and cat welfare. Already the haunting calls of stone curlews are increasing in city parks and Manners is fielding enquiries from other councils keen to replicate his success.

CONCLUSION

The cat domesticated itself – if with some imagined assistance from man. Paul Leyhausen

During the 20th and early 21st centuries, global domestic cat numbers exploded past 200 million. As a result, the postwar period also led to a spike in feral cat numbers and cat diseases and an overwhelming increase in sick, injured and malnourished cats. The immense environmental impacts of cats are now well known with hundreds of billions of wild animals killed each year. In striking parallel to the repercussions of human-induced climate change, warnings issued by forward thinkers were largely denied or overlooked. But we ignore these issues at our peril. In every country, in nearly every town, increasing numbers of sick or starving cats are suffering from injury and disease. Cat shelters are overflowing. Hundreds of thousands of cats are euthanased every year by despondent animal welfare workers but the problem keeps growing. Misplaced sentimentality, sometimes promoted by corporate greed of cat food companies, has exacerbated this situation through promoting feeding of unowned strays.

The cat boom has of course not happened in isolation as we career through these dynamic early decades of the third millennium. Although less intimately connected with the natural world than we have been at any other time in history, an increasing number of people in wealthy countries are embracing nature as a hobby or,

In New York in 1906, one year after similar sentiments were expressed in Australia, the following resolution was made at the annual meeting of the pre-eminent US bird society: 'In the interests of humanity and bird protection the National Society of Audubon Societies endorses the movement to make the owners of cats responsible for their acts and welfare.' More than a century later, with vastly higher pet and unowned cat populations and despite the impact of cats on global wildlife now clearly demonstrated, it is public health and animal welfare that are now the main drivers of appeals for cats to be kept indoors. History shows us when issues like smoking and asbestos are demonstrated to affect the public good, sentiment and legislation rapidly follow.

for some, a passion. Membership and donations to environmental charities continue to rise. In the US, birders contribute over US$100 billion to the economy annually. Markets for free-range livestock and their produce are surging and opposition on welfare grounds to formerly mainstream sports that were unconscionable only decades ago is becoming the norm. Around the globe, at different rates, our societies are coming to terms with balancing our desire to interact with animals with the ideals of animal welfare and protection of the environment and our health. Responsible cat ownership is increasingly becoming one of the most important, if not contentious, exemplar of this broader trend.

For the past century, the debate against outdoor cats has mainly been prosecuted by bird enthusiasts but their arguments failed to gain traction with most cat owners who either didn't care about birds or the welfare of their pet, or were just too lazy to provide a stimulating indoor environment for their cat. However in the past decade the discussion has broadened considerably. Free-ranging

REASONS TO KEEP CATS INDOORS

1. Safety from road accidents that kill or injure roaming pets

2. Prevention of cat fights that injure pets and disturb neighbours

3. Protection from diseases spread by roaming cats to pets and humans

4. Biodiversity benefits from reduction in wildlife toxoplasmosis infections

5. Animal welfare benefits of less wildlife maimed and killed

6. Conservation benefits to wildlife species threatened by cat predation

7. Economic benefits from reduced agricultural losses and improved tourism

8. Safeguarding rare felines from genetic swamping

9. Reduced carbon, protein and fisheries impact from feeding unowned cats

10. More accessible and cared for companion animals

cats now also draw the ire of those concerned with other wildlife, from bandicoots to bats, harp seals to native cats. As we have learned in this book, many of the most passionate and informed advocates for cat management reform are now cat breeders, keepers and animal welfare campaigners. With new evidence of disease risks, outdoor cats are now also widely denounced by animal welfare and public health advocates. Allowing cats to roam is uncompassionate, unhealthy and unethical – and unfair for the cat, wildlife and society.

It is my hope that the 'cat among the pigeons' will revert to being an expression of mayhem rather than a description of reality. But first we must fully embrace the most contentious part of the stray cat conundrum. Compassionate and effective control of unowned cats will reduce disease, wildlife suffering and feline genocide and help us to cherish the uniqueness of the natural world. The era of the indoor lapcat is rapidly approaching and I, for one, am ready to embrace it.

ACKNOWLEDGEMENTS

I was introduced to the complex and intriguing world of cat management through my ecological interests. Scientists who informed, inspired and broadened my interest and understanding and were instrumental in steering a research course that led to the writing of this book include Chris Dickman, Chris Lepczyk, Katherine Moseby, Rachel Paltridge and David Paton.

As anyone involved in the cat debate will attest, ecological science alone can neither fully explain nor resolve the complex of cat management issues and I have benefited greatly from the patient instruction of veterinarians, geneticists, animal welfare professionals, toxicologists, parasitologists and human health professionals. Dick Balharry, Carlos Driscoll and Jeremy Usher-Smith explained the extent of genetic swamping of wildcats by their domestic cousins. Cristian Bonacic, Peter Budd, Don Richardson and Antonio Rivas patiently informed me of the veterinarian issues. Peter Bird, Charles Eason, Frank Gigliotti, Dave Peacock and Laurie Twigg introduced me to the fascinating world of toxicology. Thank you Jaroslav Flegr for enthusiastically sharing your comprehensive research on the latent effects of toxoplasmosis and Amanda Kristancic, for your parasitology advice and for challenging trendy perceptions about toxoplasmosis.

Possibly my greatest thanks are reserved for cat welfare professionals who took the risk in sharing their stories and views with me. Every last one of these dedicated individuals I interviewed had received abuse from the public and media who were either ill informed or harboured contradictory views on appropriate and sensitive cat management. Teresa Chagrin, Yasushi Komatsu, Mary-Rose Krijgsman, Elizabeth Oliver and Jenny Woods are thanked for not only helping their furred friends but also opening up to me with their experiences and opinions.

High-profile anti-cat protagonists Gregory Andrews, Gareth Morgan and John Wamsley are acknowledged for the professional and social courage they too have shown to raise the profile of cat management. Behind the scenes, the tireless research and advocacy of Linda Cherkassky, Paul Martinson, Sarah Rowe and Johanna van de Woestijne were invaluable in enlightening me on the extent of 'fake news' perpetrated by organisations and individuals who don't share our priorities of ethical and compassionate cat and wildlife welfare.

Thank you to the many cat owners and cat welfare volunteers for sharing your stories and checking my interpretations. Emma Coates, Dorothy Garrett, Julie Okamoto, Conny Salden, Grant Sizemore, Truda Straede and Julia Wilson in particular, for their significant role in the preparation of this book including revision of several drafts of 'their' sections. And thank you for the frankness and patience of the scientists whose research is profiled here, including Dave Algar, Peter Copley, Kazuo Horikoshi, Masako Izawa, Chris Lepczyk, Hugh McGregor, Katherine Moseby, Steve Murphy, Rachel Paltridge, Dave Paton, Laurie Twigg, Adrian Wayne and Laurie Wein. You might have noted that each of these lists of contributors is ordered alphabetically so that

I don't need to justify relative importance of their contributions.

Field practitioners, including Steve Austin, Tayla Bowden, Sue Darby, Dan Franks, José Galán, Frank Gigliotti, Pat Hodgens, John T and Nolia Yukultji Ward shared observations about cats that I could never have learned from books or journal articles. A host of other helpful souls, including Karl Adamson, Dave Argument, Mike Bell, Ed Clark, Nigel Clark, Peter Forward, Katie Haman, Shekhar Kolipaka, Paul Martinson, Penny Paton, Steve Trutwin, Rudi van Aarde and Chris West assisted with invaluable contacts and advice.

Julia Beaven, editor at Wakefield Press, is thanked for her outstanding job of improving and streamlining the text, fact checking and ensuring that explanations of scientific concepts were simple and interesting. Thank you to Johanna van de Woestijne's at Coriolis Films LLC for her tireless encouragement invaluable in finalising this book. And heartfelt thanks to Katherine who advised, challenged, endured and supported the research process that began 20 years ago on our atypical honeymoon.

Despite all these contributions, I take full responsibility for any inaccuracies or misrepresentations that may have inadvertently infiltrated the text.

FURTHER READING

Sources are cited only once within their most relevant chapter.
See also website www.johnlread.com/cat-related-research-references.html for
further resources

The tale of two cats

American Bird Conservancy. *American Bird Conservancy Resolution on Free-roaming Cats*. Available from http://www.abcbirds.org/cats

McAllister, P. (2014) *The pet keeping species* www.cosmosmagazine.com/cosmos_ online 31 March 2014

Newby, J. (1999) *The Animal Attraction. Humans and their animal companions*. ABC Books, Sydney

Survival of the fittest or subliminal genocide?

Concannon, P., Hodgson, B. and Lein, D. (1980) Reflex LH release in estrous cats following single and multiple copulations. *Biol. Reprod.* 23: 111–117

Low, T. (2001) *Feral future. The untold story of Australia's exotic invaders*. Penguin, Ringwood, Australia

Kilshaw, K., Johnson, P.J., Kitchener, A.C and Macdonald, D.W. (2014) Detecting the elusive Scottish wildcat *Felis silvestris silvestris* using camera trapping. *Oryx* 49 doi:10.1017/S0030605313001154

Say, L. and Pontier, D. (2004) Spacing pattern in a social group of stray cats: effects on male reproductive success. *Anim. Behav.* 68: 175–180

Skinner, J.D. and Smithers, R.H.N. (1990) *The Mammals of the Southern African Subregion*. University of Pretoria, South Africa

Smithers, R.H.N. (1983) *The mammals of the southern African subregion Pretoria, decline in pure wild populations of the African wildcat and black-footed cat following hybridisation with domestic cats*. University of Pretoria, South Africa

Feeding cats birdseed

Barratt, D.G. (1997) Predation by house cats, *Felis catus* (L.), in Canberra, Australia. I. Prey composition and preference. *Wildl. Res.* 24: 263–277

Barratt, D.G. (1998) Predation by house cats, *Felis catus* (L.), in Canberra, Australia. II. Factors affecting the amount of prey caught and estimates of the impact on wildlife. *Wildl. Res.* 25: 475–487

Blancher, P. (2013) Estimated number of birds killed by house cats (*Felis catus*) in Canada. *Avian Cons, & Ecol.* 8: 3 http://dx.doi.org/10.5751/ACE-00557-080203

Campbell, A.J. (1905) Domestic wild cats v native birds. *Emu* 5: 201–202

Carss, D.N. (1995) Prey brought home by two domestic cats (*Felis catus*) in northern Scotland. *J. Zool.* 237: 678–686

Churcher, P.B. and Lawton, J.H. (1987) Predation by domestic cats in an English Village. *J. Zool.* 212: 439–455

Crooks, K.R. and Soule M.E. (1999) Mesopredator release and avifaunal extinctions in a fragmented system. *Nature* 400: 563–566

Dowling, B., Seebeck, J.H. and Lowe, K.W. (1994) *Cats and wildlife; results of a survey of wildlife admitted for care to shelters and animal welfare agencies in Victoria.* Arthur Rylah Institute for Environmental Research Technical Report Series No. 134. Department of Conservation and Natural Resources: Heidelberg

Lepczyk, C.A., Mertig, A.G. and Liua, J. (2004) Landowners and cat predation across rural-to-urban landscapes. *Biol. Cons.* 115: 191–201

Loss, S.R., Will, T. and Marra, P.P. (2013) The impact of free-ranging domestic cats on wildlife of the United States. *Nat. Comms* 4: 1396

Loyd, K.T., Hernandez, S.M., Carroll, J.P., Abernathy, K.J. and Marshall, G.J. (2013) Quantifying free-roaming domestic cat predation using animal-borne video cameras *Biol. Cons.*160: 183–189

McDonald, J.L., Maclean, M., Evans, M.R. and Hodgson, D.J. (2015) Reconciling actual and perceived rates of predation by domestic cats. *Ecol. & Evol.* 5: 2745–2753

McGregor, H., Legge, S., Jones, M.E. and Johnson, C.N. (2015) Feral Cats Are Better Killers in Open Habitats, Revealed by Animal-Borne Video. *PLoS ONE* 10(8): e0133915

McRuer, D.L., Gray, L.C., Horne, L. and Clark, E.E. Jr (2016) Free-roaming cat interactions with wildlife admitted to a wildlife hospital. *J. Wildl. Manage.* DOI: 10.1002/jwmg.21181

Paton, D.C. (1990) Domestic cats and wildlife. *Bird Observer* 696: 34–35

Paton, D. (1991) Loss of wildlife to domestic cats, in Potter, C. (ed), *The Impact of Cats on Native Wildlife: Proceedings of a Workshop held on May 8-9 1991*, ANPWS, Canberra

Paton, D.C. (2001) Death of Treecreeper and we only celebrate. *Xanthopus* 19: 8–12

Woods, M., McDonald, R.A. and Harris, S. (2003) Predation of wildlife by domestic cats *Felis catus* in Great Britain. *Mamm. Rev.* 33: 174–188

Bells and whistles

Adamec, R.E. (1976) The interaction of hunger and preying in the domestic cat (*Felis catus*): An adaptive hierarchy? *Behav. Biol.* 18: 263–272

Calver, M.C. and Thomas, S. (2006) *Effectiveness of the CatBib in reducing predation on wildlife by pet cats.* Murdoch University, Perth, Western Australia

Calver, M., Thomas, S., Bradley, S., McCutcheon, H. (2007) Reducing the rate of predation on wildlife by pet cats: The efficacy and practicability of collar-mounted pounce protectors. *Biol. Cons.* 137: 341–348

Clark, N.A. (1999) *Progress report on the effectiveness of the MarkII CatAlert TM Collar at reducing predation by domestic cats.* British Trust for Ornithology, Thetford, England

Gordon, J.K., Matthaei, C. and van Heezik, Y. (2010) Belled collars reduce catch of domestic cats in New Zealand by half. *Wildl. Res.* 37: 372–378

Nelson, S.H., Evans, A.D. and Bradbury, R.B. (2005) The efficacy of collar-mounted devices in reducing the rate of predation of wildlife by domestic cats. *Appl. Anim. Behav. Sci.* 94: 273–285

Ruxton, G.D., Thomas, S. and Wright, J.W. (2002) Bells reduce predation of wildlife by domestic cats. *J. Zool.* 256: 81–83

Willson, S.K., Okunlola, I.A. and Novak, J.A (2015) Birds be safe: Can a novel cat collar reduce avian mortality by domestic cats (*Felis catus*)? *Global Ecol. & Cons.* 3: 359–66

Stealth and subterfuge

Bowie, W.R., King, A.S., Werker, D.H., Isaac-Renton, J.L., Bell, A., Eng, S.B. and Marion, S.A. (1997) Outbreak of toxoplasmosis associated with municipal drinking. *Lancet* 350: 173–177

Dabritz, H.A., Miller, M.A. Atwill, E.R., Gardner, I.A., Leutenegger, C.M., Melli, A.C. and Conrad, P.A. (2007) Detection of *Toxoplasma gondii*-like oocysts in cat feces and estimates of the environmental burden. *J. Am. Vet. Med. Assoc.* 231: 1676 –1684

Darwin, C.R. (1877) *The various contrivances by which orchids are fertilised by insects.* John Murray, London

Ferreira, E.C., Marchioro A.A., Guedes T.A., Mota D.C., Guilherme A.L. and de Araújo S.M. (2013) Association between seropositivity for *Toxoplasma gondii*, scholastic development of children and risk factors for *T. gondii* infection. *Trans. R. Soc. Trop. Med. Hyg.* 107: 390–396

Fischer, S., Agmon-Levin, N., Shapira, Y., Porat Katz, B., Graell, E., Cervera, R., Stojanovich, L., Gómez Puerta, J.A., Sanmartí, R. and Shoenfeld, Y. (2013) *Toxoplasma gondii:* bystander or cofactor in rheumatoid arthritis. *Immun. Res.* 56: 287–292

Flegr, J. (2016) *Watch out for Toxo! The Secret Guide to Practical Science.* Faculty of Science, Charles University, Prague

Flegr, J. and Escudero, D.Q. (2016) Impaired health status and increased incidence of diseases in Toxoplasma-seropositive subjects – an explorative cross-sectional study. *Parasitology* 143: 1974–1989

Frenkel, J.K., Ruiz, A. and Chinchilla, M. (1975) Soil Survival of Toxoplasma Oocysts in Kansas and Costa Rica *Am. J. Trop. Med. Hyg.* 24: 439–443

Fuller, T.E. and Yolken, R.H. (2013) Toxoplasma oocysts as a public health problem. *Trends in Parasit.* 29: 380–384

Gajewski, P.D., Falkenstein, M., Hengstler, J.G. and Golka, K. (2014) *Toxoplasma gondii* impairs memory in infected seniors. *Brain Behav. & Immun.* http://dx.doi.org/10.1016/j.bbi.2013.11.019

Guerina N.G., Hsu H-W., Meissner H., et al. (1994) Neonatal serologic screening and early treatment for congenital *Toxoplasma gondii* infection. *N. Engl. J. Med.* 330: 1858–1863

Kliks, M.M. (2003) *Feral cats can transmit diseases to humans.* Honolulu Star Bulletin

Kocazeybek, B. Oner, Y.A., Turksoy, R., Babur, C., Cakan, H., Sahip, N. et al. (2009) Higher prevalence of toxoplasmosis in victims of traffic accidents suggests increased risk of traffic accidents in Toxoplasma-infected inhabitants of Istanbul and its suburbs. *Forensic Sci. International* 187: 103–108

Miman, O., Mutlu E.A., Ozcan, O., Atambay, M., Karlidag, R. and Unal, S. (2010) Is there any role of *Toxoplasma gondii* in the etiology of obsessive-compulsive disorder? *Psychiatry Res.* 177: 263–265

Poirotte, C., Kappeler, P.M., Ngoubangoye, B., Bourgeois, S., Moussodji, M. and Charpentier, M.J.E. (2016) Morbid attraction to leopard urine in Toxoplasma-infected chimpanzees. *Current Volume* 26: 98–99

Seebeck, J., Greenwood, L. and Ward, D. (1991) Cats in Victoria. pp. 18–29 in: Potter, C. (ed.) *The impact of Cats on native wildlife.* Australian National Parks and Wildlife Service: Canberra

Torrey, E.F. and Yolken, R.H. (2013) *Toxoplasma* oocysts as a public health problem. *Trends in Parasitology* 29: 380–384

Torrey, E.F., Bartko, J.J. and Yolken, R.H. (2012) *Toxoplasma gondii* and other risk factors for Schizophrenia: An update. *Schizophrenia Bulletin* 38: 642–647

Vyas, A., Kim, S.K., Giacomini, N., Boothroyd, J.C. and Sapolsky, R.M. (2007) Behavioural changes induced by Toxoplasma infection of rodents are highly specific to aversion of cat odors. *Proc Nat. Acad. Sci.USA* 104: 6442–6447

Webster, J.P., Lamberton, P.H.L., Donnelly, C.A. and Torrey E.F. (2006) Parasites as causative agents of human affective disorders? The impact of anti-psychotic, mood-stabilizer and anti-parasite medication on *Toxoplasma gondii's* ability to alter host behaviour. *Proc. R. Soc.* B 273: 1023–1030

Wong, W.K., Upton, A. and Thomas, M.G. (2013) Neuropsychiatric symptoms are common in immunocompetent adult patients with *Toxoplasma gondii* acute lymphadenitis. *Scand. J. Infect. Dis.* 45: 357–361

Worth, A.R., Lymbery, A.J. and Thompson, R.C.A. (2013) Adaptive host manipulation by *Toxoplasma gondii*: fact or fiction? *Trends in Parasitology* 29: 150–155

Yazar, S., Arman, F., Yalcin, S.A. and Demirtas, F. (2003) Investigation of probable relationship between Toxoplasma gondii and cryptogenic epilepsy. *Seizure* 12: 107–109

Zhou et al. (2011) *Toxoplasma gondii* infection in humans in China. *Parasites & Vectors* 4: 165

More than meets the eye

Artois, M. and Redmond, M. (1994) Viral diseases as a threat to free-living wild cats (*Felis silvestris*) in Continental Europe. *Veterinary Record* 134: 651–652

Ballash, G.A., Dubey, J.P., Kwok, O.C., Shoben, A.B., Robison, T.L., Kraft, T.J. and Dennis, P.M. (2005) Seroprevalence of *Toxoplasma gondii* in White-Tailed Deer (*Odocoileus virginianus*) and Free-Roaming Cats (*Felis catus*) Across a Suburban to Urban Gradient in Northeastern Ohio. *Ecohealth* 12: 359–367

Birkenheuer, A.J., Marr, H.S., Warren, C., Acton, A.E., Mucker, E.M., Humphreys, J.G. and Tucker M.D. (2008) *Cytauxzoon felis* infections are present in bobcats (*Lynx rufus*) in a region where cytauxzoonosis is not recognized in domestic cats. *Vet. Parasitol.* 153: 126–130

Brown, P.R. (1989) *Management plan for the conservation of the Eastern Barred Bandicoot* Perameles gunnii *in Victoria*. Arthur Rylah Institute for Environmental Studies Technical Report Series No. 63. Department of Conservation, East Melbourne

Chadwick, E.A., Cable, J., Chinchen, A., Francis, J., Guy, E., Kean, E.F., Paul, S.C., Perkins, S.E., Sherrard-Smith, E., Wilkinson, C. and Forman, D.W. (2013) Seroprevalence of *Toxoplasma gondii* in the Eurasian otter (*Lutra lutra*) in England and Wales. *Parasites & Vectors* 6: 75

Courchamp, F., Say, L. and Pontier, D. (2000) Transmission of Feline Immunodeficiency Virus in a population of cats (*Felis catus*). *Wildl. Res.* 27: 603–611

Cunningham, M.W., Brown, M.A., Shindle, D.B., Terrell, S.P., Hayes, K.A., Ferree, B.C., McBride, R.T., Blankenship, E.L., Jansen, D., Citino, S.B., Roelke, M.E., Kiltie, R.A., Troyer, J.L. and O'Brien, S.J. (2008) Epizootiology and management of feline leukemia virus in the Florida puma. *J. Wildl Dis.* 44: 537–552

Fancourt, B.A. Nicol, S.C., Hawkins, C.E., Jones, M.E. and Johnson, C.N. (2014) Beyond the disease: Is *Toxoplasma gondii* infection causing population declines in the eastern quoll (*Dasyurus viverrinus*)? *International Journal for Parasitology* 3: 102–112

Gage K.L., Dennis D.T., Orloski K.A., Ettestad P.J., Brown T.L., et al. (2000) Cases of cat-associated human plague in the Western US, 1977–1998. *Clin. Infect. Dis.* 30: 893–900

Miller, M.A., Gardner, L.A., Kreuder, C., Paradies, D.M., Worcester, K.R., Jessup, D.A., Dodd, E., Harris, M.D., Ames, J.A., Packham, A.E. and Conrad, P.A. (2002) Coastal freshwater runoff is a risk factor for *Toxoplasma gondii* infection of southern sea otters (*Enhydra lutris nereis*) *Int. J. Parasitol.* 32: 997–1006

Izawa, M., Doi, T., Nakanishi, N. and Teranishi, A. (2009) Ecology and conservation of two endangered subspecies of the leopard cat (*Prionailurus bengalensis*) on Japanese islands *Biol. Cons.* 142: 1884–1890

Jessup D.A., Pettan K.C., Lowenstine L.J., et al. (1993) Feline leukemia virus infection and secondary spirochetemia in a free-ranging cougar (*Felis concolor*). *J. Zoo. Wildl. Med.* 24: 73–79

Kreuder, C., Miller, M.A., Jessup, D.A., Lowenstine, L.J., Harris, M.D., Ames, J.A., Carpenter, T.E., Conrad, P.A. and Mazet, J.A. (2003) Patterns of mortality in southern sea otters (*Enhydra lutris nereis*) from 1998-2001. *J. Wildl. Dis.* 39: 495–509

Kuiken T., Rimmelzwaan G., van Riel D., van Amerongen G., Baars M., Fouchier R. and Osterhaus A. (2004) Avian H5N1 influenza in cats. *Science* 306: 241

Meli, M.L., Cattori, V. et al. (2009) Threats to the Iberian lynx (*Lynx pardinus*) by feline pathogens pp 223–233 in *Iberian Lynx Ex situ Conservation: An Interdisciplinary Approach* ed. A. Vargas. Foundacion Biodiversidad, Madrid

Meli, M. L., Cattori, V., Fernando, M. et al. (2010) Feline leukemia virus infection: A threat for the survival of the critically endangered Iberian lynx (*Lynx pardinus*) *Vet. Imm. & Immunopathology* 134: 61–67

Obendorf, D.L. and Munday, B.L. (1990) Toxoplasmosis in wild eastern barred bandicoots, *Perameles gunnii*. pp.193–197 in: *Bandicoots and Bilbies*, Seebeck,

J.H., Brown, P.R., Wallis R.L. and Kemper, C.M. (eds), Surrey Beatty & Sons

Riley, S.P.D., Foley, F. and Chomel, B. (2004) Exposure to feline and canine pathogens in bobcats and gray foxes in urban and rural zones of a national park in California. *J.Wildl. Dis.* 40: 11–22

Pratt, T.K., Atkinson C.T., Banko P.C., Jacobi, J.D. and Woodworth, B.L. (2009) *Conservation Biology of Hawaiian Forest Birds.* New Haven: Yale University Press

Ting, H.R., XiuPing, S.; XiuHuan, Y., et al. (2015) Investigation of infection with Bartonella in domestic and feral cats in Beijing, China. *Chinese J. Vector Biol. & Control* 26: 19–22

Work, T.M., Dagenais, J., Rameyer, R. and Breeden, R. (2015) Mortality patterns in endangered hawaiian geese (Nene; *Branta sandvicensis*). *J. Wildl. Dis.* 5: 688–695

Yamaguchi, N., Macdonald, D.W., Passanisi, W.C., Harbour, D.A. and Hopper, C.D. (1996) Parasite prevalence in free-ranging farm cats, *Felis silvestris catus*. *Epidemiol. Infect.* 116: 217–223

Catastrophic cats

Cooper, J. (1977) Food breeding and coat colour of feral cats on Dassen Island. *Zoologica Africana* 12: 250–252

Legge, S., Murphy, B., McGregor, H., Woinarski, J., Augusteyn, J., Ballard, G., Baseler, M., Buckmaster, T., Dickman, C., Doherty, T., Edwards, G., Eyre, T., Fancourt, B.A., Ferguson, D., Maxwell, M., McDonald, P.J., Morris, K., Moseby, K., Newsome, T., Nimmo, D., Paltridge, R., Ramsey, D., Read, J., Rendall, A., Rich, M., Ritchie, E., Rowland, J., Short, J., Stokeld, D., Sutherland, D.R., Wayne, A.F., Woodford, L., and Zewe, F. (2017) Enumerating a continental-scale threat: How many feral cats are in Australia? *Biol. Cons.* 206: 293–303

Middlemiss, A. (1995) *Predation of Giant* (Leiolopisma otagense, Leiolopisma grande*) and Common Skinks by Feral House Cats* (Felis catus*) and Ferrets* (Mustela furo*) in the Tussock Grasslands of Otago, New Zealand.* M.Sc. Thesis, University of Otago, Dunedin

Moseby, K.E., Peacock D.E. and Read, J.L. (2015) Catastrophic cat predation: A call for predator profiling in wildlife protection programs. *Biol. Cons.* 191: 331–340

Read, J. and Bowen, Z. (2001) Population dynamics, diet and aspects of the biology of feral cats and foxes in arid South Australia. *Wildl. Res.* 28: 195–203

Peck, D.R., Faulquier, L., Pinet, P., Jaquemet, S. and Le Corre, M. (2008) Feral cat diet and impact on sooty terns at Juan de Nova Island, Mozambique Channel. *Anim. Cons.* 11: 65–74

Weatherby W.J. (1976) *Conversations with Marilyn.* Mason Charter, New York

Woinarski, J.C.Z., Murphy, B.P., Palmer, R., Legge, S.M., Dickman, C.R., Doherty, T.S., Edwards, G., Nankivell, A., Read, J.L. and Stokeld, D. (2019) How many reptiles are killed by cats in Australia? *Wildl. Res.* doi.org/10.1071/WR17160

Woinarski, J.C.Z., Murphy, B.P., Legge S.M., Garnett S.T., Lawes M.J., Comer S., Dickman, C.R., Doherty, T.S. Edwards, G., Nankivell, A., Paton, D., Palmer, R. and Woolley, L.A. (2017) How many birds are killed by cats in Australia? *Biol. Cons.* 214: 76–87

Someone else needs to solve my problem

Borroto-Paez, R. and Reyes Perez, D. (2018) Predation impacts by a single feral cat in a Cuban rural farm. *Revista Cubana de Zoologia* 506: 53–55

Collinson, C.W. (1926) *Life & laughter 'midst the Cannibals.* Hurst and Blackett Ltd. London

Read, J.L. (2013) The birds of Tetepare Island, Solomon Islands *Aust. Field Orn.* 30: 67–78

Wallace, G.D., Zigas, V. and Gajdusek, D.C. (1974) Toxoplasmosis and Cats in New Guinea. *Am. J. Trop. Med. Hyg.* 23: 8–14

Trap, Neuter, Then?

www.popsbarnes.com, January 2017

Castillo, D. (2001) *Population estimates and behavioural analyses of managed cat (Felis catus) colonies located in Miami-Dade County, Florida.* MS thesis, Department of Environmental Studies, Florida International University, Miami

Chandler, J. (2016) *The Best Australian Science Writing* (2016), NewSouth Publishing, Sydney

Fu, G., Lees, R.S., Nimmo, D., Aw, D., Jin, L., Gray, P., Berendonk, T.U., White-Cooper, H., Scaife, S, Phuc, H.K., Marinotti, O., Jasinskiene, N., James, A.A. and Alphey, L. (2010) Female-specific flightless phenotype for mosquito control *PNAS* 107: 45504554

Johnson, K.L. and Cicirelli, J. (2014) Study of the effect on shelter cat intakes and euthanasia from a shelter neuter return project of 10,080 cats from March 2010 to June 2014. *Peer J.* 2014: 2: e646

Jones, A.L. and Downs, C.T. (2011) Managing feral cats on a University's campuses: How many are there and is sterilization having an effect? *J. Appl. Anim. Welf. Sci.* 14: 304–320

Kellert, S.R. and Berry, J. (1981) *Knowledge, affection and basic attitudes towards animals in American society* DOC# 024-010-00-625-1 Washington DC Govt Printing Office

Leyhausen, P. (1973) Social organization and density tolerance in mammals (1965) In: *Motivation and Animal Behaviour: An Ethological View.* K. Lorenz and P. Leyhousen (Eds) New York: D. Van Nostrand, pp 120–143

Lepczyk, C.A., Conant, S., Duffy, D., Bird, D.M., Calver, M., Duval, F.P., Hutchins M., Lohr, C.A., Loyd, K.A., Marra, P.P., Pitt, W.C., Sizemore, G., Sprague, R., Temple, S.A., Van Heezik, Y. and Wallace, G. (2013) Feral cat management (Letter). *J. Am. Vet. Med. Assoc.* 243: 1391–1392

Lepczyk, C.A., Dauphin'e, N., Bird, D.M., Conant, S., Cooper, R.J., Duffy, D.C., Hatley, P., Marra, P.P., Stone, E. and Temple, S.A. (2010) What Conservation Biologists Can Do to Counter Trap-Neuter-Return: Response to Longcore et al. *Cons Biol.* 24: 627–629

Levy, J.K., Gale, D.W. and Gale, L.A. (2003) Evaluation of the effect of a long-term trap-neuter-return and adoption program on a free-roaming cat population. *J. Am. Vet. Med. Assoc.* 222: 42–46

Lohr, C.A. and Lepczyk, C.A. (2014) Desires and Management Preferences of Stakeholders Regarding Feral Cats in the Hawaiian Islands. *Cons. Biol.* 28: 392–403

Loss S. and Marra, P. (2018) Merchants of doubt in the free-ranging cat conflict. *Biol. Cons.* 2: 265–266

McCarthy, R.J., Levine, S.H. and Reed, J.M. (2013) Estimation of effectiveness of three methods of feral cat population control by use of a simulation model. *J. Am. Vet. Med. Assoc.* 243: 502–511

Mendes-de-Almeida, F., Faria, M.C.F., Landau-Remy, G., Branco, A.L., Serricella, A., Barata, P., Chame, M., Pereira, M.J.S. and Labarthe, N. (2006) The impact of hysterectomy in an urban colony of domestic cats (*Felis catus* Linnaeus, 1758). *Int. J. Appl. Res. Vet. Med.* 4: 134–141

Natoli, E. and De Vito, E. (1991) Agonistic behaviour, dominance rank and copulatory success in a large multi-male feral cat *Felis catus* L. colony in central Rome. *Anim. Behav.* 42: 227–241

Natoli, E., et al. (2006) Management of Feral Domestic Cats in the Urban Environment of Rome (Italy). *Prev. Vet. Med.* 77: 180–185

Roberts, M. and Clements, J. (2015) Using early neutering to control unwanted litters *Vet. Rec.* 176: 570–571

Say, L., Pontier, D. and Natoli, E. (2001) Influence of oestrus synchronization on male reproductive success in the domestic cat (*Felis catus* L.) *Proc. Roy. Soc. Lond.* 268B: 1049–1053

Segna, D.L. and Schumacher, R. (2002) The success of the California feral cat altering program, in Proceedings. *139th Ann. Conv. Am. Vet. Med. Assoc.* 2002: 690

Sparkes, A.H., Bessant, C., Cope, K. Ellis, S.L.H., Finka, L., Halls, V., Hiestand, K., Horsford, K., Laurence, C., MacFarlaine, I., Neville, P.F., Stavisky, J. and Yeates, J. (2013) Guidelines on Population Management and Welfare of Unowned Domestic Cats (*Felis catus*). *J. Feline Med. Surg.*15: 811–817

Spotte, S. (2014) *Free-ranging cats: behaviour, ecology, management.* Wiley Blackwell, West Sussex, UK

Zaunbrecher, K.I. and Smith, R.E. (1993) Neutering of feral cats as an alternative to eradication programs. *J. Am. Vet. Med. Assoc.* 203: 449–452

When giving is taking

Nogales, M., Vidal, E., Medina, F.M., Bonnaud, E., Tershy, B.R., Campbell, K.J. and Zavaleta, E.S. (2013) Feral Cats and Biodiversity Conservation: The Urgent Prioritization of Island Management. *Bioscience* 63: 804–810

Oppel, S., Burns, F., Vickery, J., George, K., Ellick, G., Leo, D. and Hillman, J.C. (2014) Habitat-specific effectiveness of feral cat control for the conservation of an endemic ground-nesting bird species. *J. Appl. Ecol.* 51: 1246–1254

Peterson, M.N., Hartis, B., Rodriguez, S., Green, M. and Lepczyk, C.A. (2012) Opinions from the Front Lines of Cat Colony Management Conflict. *PLoS* ONE 7: 1–7

Shermer, M. (2015) *The moral arc: how science and reason lead humanity toward truth, justice, and freedom.* St Martin's Press, New York

Protecting cats or duping cat lovers?

Dunn, E.H. and Tessaglia, D.L. (1994) Predation of birds at feeders in winter. *J. Field Orn.* 65: 8–16

Hawkins C.C., Grant W.E. and Longnecker M.T. (1999) Effects of subsidized house cats on California birds and rodents. *Trans. West Sect. Wildl. Soc.* 35: 29–33

Weidensaul, S. (2000) *Living on the Wind: Across the Hemisphere with Migratory Birds.* Northpoint Press, New York

'Misplaced sentimentality'

Judge, S., Lippert, J. S., Misajon, K., Hu, D., and Hess, S. C. (2012) Videographic evidence of endangered species depredation by feral cat. *Pac. Cons. Biol.* 18: 293–296

Loyd, K.T. and DeVore, J. L. (2010) An evaluation of feral cat management options using a decision analysis network. *Ecol. & Soc.* 15: 10

Okin G.S. (2017) Environmental impacts of food consumption by dogs and cats. PLoS ONE 12(8): e0181301.

Pet Food Market (2018)*Wet Food, Dry Food, Nutrition, Snacks and Other for Cats,*

Dogs, and Other Animals: U.S Industry Perspective, Comprehensive Analysis, and Forecast, 2016-2022, report at https://www.zionmarketresearch.com/report/pet-food-market

Roberts, C. (2013) *The Ocean of Life: The Fate of Man and the Sea*. Penguin, New York

Compassionate Conservation

Bekoff, M. (2013) *Ignoring Nature No More: The Case for Compassionate Conservation*, University of Chicago Press

Jessup, D.A. (2004) The welfare of feral cats and wildlife. Animal Welfare Forum: Management of Abandoned and Feral cats *J. Am. Vet. Med. Assoc.* 225: 1378-1381

Robertson, S.A. (2009) A review of feral cat control. *J. Feline Med. & Surg.* 10: 366-375

Russell, J.C., Jones, H.P., Armstrong, D.P., Courchamp, F., Kappes, P.J., Seddon, P.J., Oppel, S., Rauzon, M.J., Cowan, P.E., Rocamora, G., Genovesi, P., Bonnaud, E., Keitt, B.S., Holmes, N.D. and Tershy, B.R. (2016). Importance of lethal control of invasive predators for island conservation. *Cons. Biol.* 30: 670-672

Sagoff, M. (1984) Animal Liberation and Environmental Ethics: Bad Marriage, Quick Divorce. *Osgoode Hall Law Journal* 22: 297-307

Goodnight kitty

Rollin, B.E. (2006) Euthanasia and quality of life. *J. Am. Vet. Med. Assoc.* 228: 1014-1016

RSPCA Australian National Statistics 2016-2017 https://www.rspca.org.au/.../RSPCA%20Australia%20Annual%20Statistics%20final%2

Michael the wonder cat

Algar D., Angus G.J., Brazell R.I., Gilbert, C., and Withnell, G.B. (2010)

Eradication of feral cats on Faure Island, Western Australia. *J. R. Soc. West Aust.* 93: 133-140

Campbell, K.J., Harper, G., Hanson, C.C., Algar, D., Keitt, B.S. and Robinson, S. (2011) Review of feral cat eradications onislands. In: Veitch, C.R., Clout, M.N., Towns, D.R. (eds) *Island invasives: eradication and management*. International Union for Conservation of Nature, Gland pp. 37-46

Courchamp, F. and Sugihara, G. (1999) Modelling the biological control of an alien predator to protect island species from extinction. *Ecol. Appl.* 9: 112-123

DeVillard, S., Santin-Janin, H., Say, L. and Pontier, D. (2011) Linking genetic diversity and temporal fluctuations in population abundance of the introduced feral cat (*Felis silvestris catus*) on the Kerguelen archipelago. *Mol. Ecol.* 20: 5141-5153

Hanson, C.C., Jolley, W.J., Smith, G., Garcelon, D.K., Keitt, B.S., Little, A.E. and Campbell, K.J. (2015) Feral cat eradication in the presence of endemic San Nicolas Island foxes. *Biol. Invasions* 17: 977–986

Jones, E. (1977) Ecology of the feral cat, Felis catus (L), (Carnivora: Felidae) on Macquarie Island. *Aust. Wildl. Res.* 4: 249–262

Jones, H.P., Holmes, N.D., Butchart, S.H.M., Tershy, B.R., Kappes, P.J., Corkery, I., Aguirre-Muñoz, A., Armstrong, D.P., Bonnaud, E., Burbidge, A.A., Campbell, K., Courchamp, F., Cowan, P.E., Cuthbert, R.J., Ebbert, S., Genovesi, P., Howald, G.R., Keitt, B.S., Kress, S.W., Miskelly, C.M., Oppel, S., Poncet, S., Rauzon, M.J., Rocamora, G., Russell, J.C., Samaniego-Herrera, A., Seddona, P.J., Spatz, D.R., Towns, D.R. and. Croll, D.A. (2016) Invasive mammal eradication on islands results in substantial conservation gains. *PNAS* 113: 4033–4038

Keitt, B.S., and Tershy, B.R. (2003) Cat eradication significantly decreases shearwater mortality. *Anim. Cons.* 6: 307–308

Ratcliffe, N., Bell, M., Pelembe, T., Boyle, D., Benjamin, R., White, R., Godley, B., Stevenson, J. and Sanders, S. (2009) The eradication of feral cats from Ascension Island and its subsequent recolonization by seabirds. *Oryx* 44: 20–29

Richards, J. (2007) Return to Faure Island. *Landscope* 22: 10–17

Robinson S.A. and Copson, G.R. (2014) Eradication of cats (*Felis catus*) from subantarctic Macquarie Island. *Ecol Manage. Rest.* 15:1–7

Rodríguez, C., Torres, R. and Drummond, H. (2006) Eradicating introduced mammals from a forested tropical island. *Biol. Cons.* 130: 98–105

Russell, J.C., Jones, H.P., Armstrong, D.P., Courchamp, F., Kappes, P.J., Seddon, P.J., Oppel, S., Rauzon, M.J., Cowan, P.E., Rocamora, G., Genovesi, P., Bonnaud, E., Keitt, B.S., Holmes, N.D. and Tershy, B.R. (2016) Importance of lethal control of invasive predators for island conservation. *Cons. Biol.* 30: 670–672

Twyford, K.L., Humphrey, P.G., Nunn, R.P. and Willoughby, L. (2000) Eradication of feral cats (*Felis catus*) from Gabo Island, south-east Victoria. *Ecol. Manage. & Rest.* 1: 42–49

Van Rensburg, P.J.J., Skinner, J.D. and van Aarde, R.J. (1987) Effect of feline panleucopenia on the population characteristics of feral cats on Marion Island. *J. Appl. Ecol.* 24: 63–73

Veitch, C.R. (1985) Methods of eradicating feral cats from off-shore islands in New Zealand. In: *Conservation of Island Birds.* P.J. Moors (ed.) International Council for Bird Protection Technical Publication 3:125–141

While the cat's away . . .

Legge, S., Woinarski, J.C.Z., Burbidge, A.A., Palmer, R., Ringma, J., Radford, J.Q., Mitchell, N., Bode, M., Wintle, B., Baseler, M. Bentley, J., Copley, P., Dexter, N., Dickman, C.R. Gillespie, G.R., Hill, B., Johnson, C.N., Latch, P., Letnic, M., Manning, A., McCreless, E.E., Menkhorst, P., Morris, K., Moseby, K., Page, M., Pannell, D and Tuft, K. (2018) Havens for threatened Australian mammals: the contributions of fenced areas and offshore islands to the protection of mammal species susceptible to introduced predators. *Wildl. Res. https://doi.org/10.1071/WR17172*

Moseby, K.E. and Read, J.L. (2006) The efficacy of feral cat, fox and rabbit exclusion fence designs for threatened species protection. *Biol. Cons.* 127: 429–437

Moseby, K.E., Read, J.L., Paton, D.C., Copley, P., Hill, B.M. and Crisp, H.A. (2011) Predation determines the outcome of 10 reintroduction attempts in arid South Australia. *Biol. Cons.* 144: 2863–2872

Read, J.L., Dagg, E. and Moseby, K.E. (2018) Prey selectivity by feral cats at central Australian rock-wallaby colonies. *Aust. Mamm.* https://doi.org/10.1071/AM17055

Read, J., Copley, P., Ward, M., Dagg, E., Olds, L., Taggart, D. and West, R. (2018) Bringing back warru: return of the black-footed rock-wallaby to the APY Lands. pp. 237–248 in: *Recovering Australia's threatened species: a book of hope*. Garnett, S., Woinarski, J., Lindenmeyer, D. and Latch, P. (eds) CSIRO Publishing, Clayton South, Victoria

The Sounds of Silence

Cemmick, D. and Veitch, D. (1987) *Kakapo Country. The story of the world's most unusual bird*. Hodder and Stoughton, Auckland

Clout, M.N. and Craig, J.L. (1995) The conservation of critically endangered flightless birds in New Zealand. *Ibis* 137: S181-S190

Farnworth, M.J., Campbell, J. and Adams, N.J. (2011) What's in a Name? Perceptions of Stray and Feral Cat Welfare and Control in Aotearoa. *N. Z. J. Appl. Anim. Welf. Sci.* 14:59–74

Flux, J.E.C. (2007) Seventeen years of predation by one suburban cat in New Zealand. *N. Z. J. Zool.* 34:289–296

Karl, B.J. and Best, H.A. (1982) Feral cats on Stewart Island; their foods, and their effects on kākāpō. *N.Z.J. Zool.* 9:287–294

van Heezik, Y., Smyth, A., Adams, A. and Gordon, J. (2010) Do domestic cats impose an unsustainable harvest on urban bird populations? *Biol. Cons.* 143: 121–130

Walker, J.K., Bruce, S.J. and Dale, A.R. (2017) Survey of Public Opinion on Cat (*Felis catus*) Predation and the Future Direction of Cat Management in New Zealand. *Animals* 7: 49

On a hot tin roof

Burbidge, A.A. and George, A.S. (1978) The flora and fauna of Dirk Hartog Island, Western Australia. *J. Roy. Soc. W. Aust.* 60: 71–90

Christensen, P.E.S., Ward, B.G. and Sims, C. (2013) Predicting bait uptake by feral cats, *Felis catus*, in semi-arid environments. *Ecol. Manage. & Rest.* 14: 47–53

Dickman, C.R. (1993) Raiders of the last ark: Cats in inland Australia. *Aust. Nat. Hist.* 24: 44–52

Eason, C.T. and Frampton, C.M. (1991) Acute toxicity of sodium monofuoroacetate (1080) baits to feral cats. *Wildl. Res.* 18: 445–449

King, D.R., Oliver, A.J. and Mead, R.J. (1981) Bettongia and fluoroacetate: a role for 1080 in fauna management. *Aust. Wildl. Res.* 8: 529–536

Marra, P.P. and Santella, C. (2016) *Cat Wars: The devastating consequences of a cuddly killer.* Princeton University Press

Moseby, K.E. and Hill, B.M. (2011) The use of poison baits to control feral cats and red foxes in arid South Australia I. Aerial baiting trials. *Wildl. Res.* 38: 338–349

Peacock, D. (2003) *The search for a novel toxicant in* Gastrolobium *(Fabaceae: Mirbelieae) seed historically associated with toxic native fauna.* PhD thesis, The University of Adelaide

Peacock, D.E., Christensen, P.E. and Williams, B.D. (2011) Historical accounts of toxicity to introduced carnivores consuming bronzewing pigeons (*Phapschalcoptera* and *P. elegans*) and other vertebrate fauna in south-west Western Australia. *Aust. Zool.* 35: 826–842

Read, J.L., Peacock, D., Wayne, A.F. and Moseby, K.E. (2015) Toxic Trojans: Can feral cat predation be mitigated by making their prey poisonous? *Wildl. Res.* 42: 689–696

Sherley, M. (2007) Is sodium fluoroacetate (1080) a humane poison? *Anim. Welf.* 16: 449–458

Silva-Rodriguez, E.A. and Sieving, K.E. (2011) Influence of care of domestic carnivores on their predation on vertebrates. *Cons. Biol.* 25: 808–815

Tuft, K., May, T., Page, E. and Legge, S. (2014) *Translocation of the Pale Field Rat to Wongalara, NT from Mornington, WA.* Australian Wildlife Conservancy, Perth, WA

Twigg, L. and Parker R. (2010) Is sodium fluoroacetate (1080) a humane poison? The influence of mode of action, physiological effects, and target specificity. *Anim. Welf.* 19: 249–263

Wayne, A.F., Maxwell, M., Ward, C.G., Vellios, C.V., Wilson, I. and Wayne, J.C. (2013) Sudden, rapid and catastrophic decline of an abundant marsupial, *Bettongia penicillata*: characterising the decline and identifying the potential causes. *Oryx*. doi:10.1017/S0030605313000677: 1–11

Woinarski, J.C.Z., Armstrong, M., Brennan, A. K., Fisher, A., Griffiths, A. D., Hill, B.M., Milne, D. J., Palmer, C., Ward, S., Watson, M., Winderlich, S. and Young, S. (2010) Monitoring indicates rapid and severe decline of native small mammals in Kakadu National Park, northern Australia. *Wildl. Res.* 37: 116–126

No silver bullet

Christensen, P. and Burrows, N. (1994) Project desert dreaming: experimental reintroduction of mammals to the Gibson Desert, Western Australia. pp. 199–207 In *Reintroduction Biology of Australian and New Zealand Fauna.* M. Serena (ed.) Surrey Beatty & Sons: Sydney

Danner, R.M., Goltz, D.M., Hess, S.C. and Banko, P.C. (2007) Evidence of Feline Immunodeficiency Virus, Feline Leukemia Virus, and *Toxoplasma gondii* in Feral Cats on Mauna Kea, *Hawaii J. Wildl. Dis.* 43: 315–318

Gong, W., Sinden, J., Braysher, M. and Jones, R. (2009) *The Economic Impacts of Vertebrate Pests in Australia.* Invasive Animals Cooperative Research Centre, Canberra

Pedler, R.D., Brandle, R., Read, J.L., Southgate, R., Bird, P. and Moseby, K.E. (2016) Bio-control triggers landscape-scale recovery of threatened desert mammals. *Cons. Biol.* 30: 774–782

Vantassel, S.M. (2013) The practical guide to the control of feral cats. http://wildlifecontrolconsultant.com

n = 1

Commonwealth of Australia (2015) Threat abatement plan for predation by feral cats. Dept for Environment, Canberra

McGilp J. N. (1931) Night Parrot (*Gepsittacus occidentalis*) *S.A. Ornithologist* 31: 68–71

Moseby, K.E., Neilly, H., Read, J.L. and Crisp, H.A. (2011) Interactions between a Top Order Predator and Exotic Mesopredators in the Australian Rangelands. *Int. J. Ecol.* 2012: 1–15

Murphy, S.A., Paltridge, R., Silcock, J., Murphy, R., Kutt., A.S and Read, J. (2017) Understanding and managing the threats to Night Parrots in southwestern Queensland. *Austral Orn.* doi.org/10.1080/01584197.2017.1388744

Read, J.L., Bowden, T., Hodgens, P., Hess, M., McGregor, H. and Moseby, K. (2019). Target Specificity of Felixer Grooming 'Traps'. *Wildl. Soc. Bul.* doi: 10.1002/wsb.942

Read, J.L, Gigliotti, F., Darby, S. and Lapidge, S. (2014) Dying to be clean: Pen trials of novel cat and fox control devices. *Int. J. Pest Manage.* 60: 166–172

Whitlock, F.W. (1924) Journey to Central Australia in search of the Night Parrot. *Emu* 23: 248–281

Lap cats, the purr-fect domestic cats

McLeod, L.J., Hine, D.W. and Bengsen, A.J. (2015) Born to roam? Surveying cat owners in Tasmania, Australia, to identify the drivers and barriers to cat containment *PREVET* doi.org/10.1016/j.prevetmed.2015.11.007

Slater, M.R. (2004) Understanding issues and solutions for unowned, free-roaming cat populations. *J. Am. Vet. Med. Assoc.* 225: 1350–1354

Stewart, R. (1997) *Enviro Cat: A new approach to caring for your cat.* Hyland House, Melbourne

INDEX

Wakefield Press is an independent publishing and
distribution company based in Adelaide, South Australia.
We love good stories and publish beautiful books.
To see our full range of books, please visit our website at
www.wakefieldpress.com.au
where all titles are available for purchase.
To keep up with our latest releases, news and events,
subscribe to our monthly newsletter.

Find us!

Facebook: www.facebook.com/wakefield.press
Twitter: www.twitter.com/wakefieldpress
Instagram: www.instagram.com/wakefieldpress